DATE DUE

INSTABILITY AND CONFLICT IN THE MIDDLE EAST

Instability and Conflict in the Middle East

People, Petroleum and Security Threats

Naji Abi-Aad

and

Michel Grenon

Foreword by Robert Mabro
Director, Oxford Institute for Energy Studies
and Fellow of St Antony's College, Oxford

First published in Great Britain 1997 by
MACMILLAN PRESS LTD
Houndmills, Basingstoke, Hampshire RG21 6XS and London
Companies and representatives throughout the world

A catalogue record for this book is available from the British Library.

ISBN 0–333–68936–4

First published in the United States of America 1997 by
ST. MARTIN'S PRESS, INC.,
Scholarly and Reference Division,
175 Fifth Avenue, New York, N.Y. 10010

ISBN 0–312–17254–0

Library of Congress Cataloging-in-Publication Data
Abi-Aad, Naji, 1959–
Instability and conflict in the Middle East : people, petroleum,
and security threats / Naji Abi-Aad, Michel Grenon ; foreword by
Robert Mabro.
p. cm.
Includes bibliographical references and index.
ISBN 0–312–17254–0
1. Middle East—Politics and government—1979– 2. Middle East–
–Strategic aspects. I. Grenon, Michel. II. Title.
DS63.1.A246 1997
956.05—dc20   96–46169
                                                                  CIP

This book is printed on paper suitable for recycling and made from fully managed and
sustained forest sources.

10 9   8   7   6   5   4   3   2
06 05 04 03 02 01 99 98

Printed and bound in Great Britain by Antony Rowe Ltd, Chippenham, Wiltshire

To my parents
N.A.

To my wife
M.G.

Contents

List of Figures and Maps

List of Tables

List of Boxes

Foreword

The Middle East has always been, and will remain for decades ahead, a fascinating and critically important region of the world. It was the birth place of religions which gave Western and some Eastern civilisations their values, much of their culture and many traits of their physiognomy. The Middle East lies in the small area where Europe, Africa and Asia come into contact. It belongs to neither continent but it owes something to all of them and, in turn, has contributed to their cultural and historical development. If it is true to say that the history of the world is essentially the history of religions, the Middle East should then be seen as a fountainhead.

The Middle East is strategically located. Hence, throughout the centuries, starting long before our era, it frequently became coveted by whoever happened to wield power. In the old days those who sought to dominate came from within the region or from nearby places; in modern times distant powers also fixed their ambitions and brought their rivalries to the Middle East.

Finally, the Middle East is endowed with considerable oil and gas resources. The modern world is a big and ever-growing consumer of energy. The degree of its dependence on the hydrocarbon reserves of the Middle East may vary from time to time but even in those periods when this dependence is at its lowest the feeling that it may suddenly increase tends to prevail.

The political stability of the Middle East worries powers with either strategic or economic interests in the region. It worries Europe which fears the social, economic and cultural impact from migration waves originating in the southern shores of the Mediterranean. It worries the USA because of its commitments to regimes which may be threatened by neighbours or by domestic unrest, and because of its commitment to the security of an Israel unwilling to buy peace at even its minimum price. It worries all those who do not understand the connections between underdevelopment, peoples frustration with the politics of their governments and of the foreign powers, and the emergence of a militant Islam.

A large part of the Middle East problem is one of lack of empathy and understanding.

Naji Abi-Aad and Michel Grenon seek in their book to improve understanding. They are well equipped for the task. Michel Grenon is an energy expert of international reputation and Naji Abi-Aad is a son of the region and a keen analyst of its problems. They diagnose and analyse the causes of potential instability in the Middle East from politics to ethnicity, colonial history to old and valuable cultural and religious heritages, population pressures to frustrated economic development, abundance of oil reserves which elicits greed to paucity of water resources which threatens livelihoods. There is also the intractable problem of security for the states which make up the region and for the peoples which inhabit it, a security which cannot be achieved as an outcome of wars, only by mutual recognition through a permanent peace that nobody seems able to achieve.

The authors link the issues of political conflict to that of stable petroleum supplies to the world. Middle Eastern oil is of interest to the world and the book rightly focuses on this problem. But the importance of the Middle East, as Abi-Aad and Grenon clearly recognise, goes well beyond oil. Stability which can be only achieved through the resolution of internal and external conflicts is of vital significance to the many millions who live in the area, and to all those who live outside it but remain inevitably related by the multiple links of an interdependent world.

ROBERT MABRO
Director
Oxford Institute
for Energy Studies

Preface

The present book is about instability and conflict in the Middle East at a time when many people still believe that peace between the Arabs and Israel will bring an end to all problems in the region. Maybe that is due to the fact that the Arab–Israeli conflict has dominated much of the general discussion about the area over the past fifty years. Insufficient attention has therefore been devoted to other important issues that may not be quite as eye-catching or newsworthy or even maybe about which there is lack of information. This is exactly what the book is aiming to offer.

This book is one of the fruits of a collaborative enterprise between us since 1987. The foundation of the present work was provided by a project undertaken by the Observatoire Méditerranéen de l'Energie in the early 1990s about the security of petroleum supplies from the Middle East. We then thought that it would be interesting to carry out further reflections on the broader subjects treated thereby. Needless to say, writing this book presented us with an exciting challenge due to the sensitivity of the issues analysed that we have tried to assess in a very objective way.

The actual book is not designed exclusively for specialists. It should be of use to everybody interested in the problems of the region and the countries discussed. We hope that those who wish to learn more about the Middle East, for political and economic reasons, or for purely personal interest, will find the information they need adequately presented within the framework we have chosen, and that our interpretation of data, events and policies will contribute to greater understanding of the region.

We wish here to illustrate a debt of gratitude to so many institutions and persons whose efforts have been of particular help to us in preparing this book. We would like to express our warmest thanks to Dr Robert Mabro, the founder and Director of the Oxford Institute for Energy Studies (OIES), for his encouragement and his contribution to this work by writing its foreword.

August 1996
NAJI ABI-AAD
MICHEL GRENON

List of Abbreviations

Aramco	Arabian American Oil Company
BCCI	Bank of Credit and Commerce International
b/d	barrels per day
CDLR	Committee for the Defence of Legitimate Rights
CIA	Central Intelligence Agency
CID	current international dollar
CPE	centrally planned economies
cu m	cubic metre
dwt	dead weight tonnage
ECB	Economic Commisioning Board (OPEC)
EEZ	Exclusive Economic Zone
EII	expansion investment intensity
EU	European Union
FFG	Fund for Future Generations
FSU	former Soviet Union
GAP	Great Anatolian Project
GCC	Gulf Co-operation Council
GDP	gross domestic product
GNP	gross national product
ICJ	International Court of Justice
IFLB	Islamic Front for the Liberation of Bahrain
IGAT	Iranian Gas Trunkline
IISS	International Institute for Strategic Studies
ILC	International Law Commission (UN)
IMF	International Monetary Fund
in	inch
IPSA	Iraqi Pipeline across Saudi Arabia
IT	Iraq–Turkey pipeline
km	kilometre
km^2	square kilometre
LNG	liquefied natural gas
m	metre
mm	millimetre
MMC	Ministerial Monitoring Commitee (OPEC)
na	not available
NATO	North Atlantic Treaty Organisation
ns	not specified

OAPEC	Organisation of Arab Petroleum Exporting Countries
OECD	Organisation for Economic Co-operation and Development
OIES	Oxford Institute for Energy Studies
OPEC	Organisation of Petroleum Exporting Countries
PKK	Kurdish Labour Party
PLO	Palestine Liberation Organisation
PPP	Peace Pipeline Project
SCU	Supreme Council of Ulema
Sumed	Suez-Mediterranean Pipeline
Tapline	Trans-Arabian Pipeline
Tipline	Eilat–Ashkelon pipeline
UAE	United Arab Emirates
UK	United Kingdom
UN	United Nations
UNRWA	UN Relief and Works Agency
USA or US	United States of America
USGS	US Geological Survey
USSR	Union of Soviet Socialist Republics
$	dollar (US)
– (used in tables)	non existent

Introduction

The term 'Middle East' is now widely used throughout the world although it is derived from an Eurocentric view of the map. There is no standard definition of the term, which seems first to have been used by the British in the late nineteenth century with reference to a region around the Gulf, the Arabian or the Persian, somewhere between the 'Near East' and the 'Far East'. During and after the Second World War, term 'Middle East' has expanded to take in all the Arab states of southwest Asia, together with Turkey, Iran, Israel, and Cyprus. Afghanistan is sometimes included, and in many definitions Morocco through Egypt and Sudan are also regarded as 'Middle Eastern' states.

In the present book, the Middle East is defined as stretching from Egypt to Iran and from Turkey to Yemen. Specifically, this means, in addition to these four border countries, Bahrain, Iraq, Israel, Jordan, Kuwait, Lebanon, Oman, the Palestinian territories (West Bank and Gaza Strip), Qatar, Saudi Arabia, Syria, and the United Arab Emirates (UAE).[1] The work has a special focus on the Gulf region as a result of the abundant petroleum resources in this sub-area, without neglecting the other states in the region that are politically and economically interrelated, and some of which play the important and growing role of petroleum transit countries.

The Middle East witnessed the nativity of the three main monotheistic religions and has seen the birth of most historic and contemporary civilisations. It is here that expression in writing through the alphabet was first conceived, and the use of land for agricultural purposes was originally established. In addition, the region commands considerable geopolitical importance by virtue of its global location and territorial shape. Fringed by five seas (the Mediterranean, the Red Sea, the Black Sea, the Gulf, and the Arabian Sea), the Middle East is easily accessible by sea and provides many important transit maritime waterways such as the Suez Canal, the Strait of Hormuz and the Turkish straits (see Box I.1). It constitutes a land bridge between Africa and Asia and a short sea crossing between Europe, Asia and Africa (see Figure I.1). The area is located on the most convenient routes linking the populous regions of Europe and North America with the Far East. It was seen as a vital cross-roads by the Europeans long before modern transport came on the scene, and wars were fought over control of its routes. The proximity of Europe needs to be stressed: this geographical fact above all explains the long history of European

1

Box I.1   Maritime Waterways in the Middle East

The Suez Canal

The Egypt-controlled Suez Canal was opened in 1869, providing a short cut between the Mediterranean and the Red Sea, and between the Atlantic and Indian oceans beyond. Using the Canal can save vessels from 10 to 50 per cent in distance and 50 to 70 per cent in fuel consumption, depending on ship speed, size and destination. The Canal's overall length is 193.5 km with a maximum width of 350 m; with the depth of the navigable channel varying between 15 and 18 m only, the Canal can be easily blocked.

Following an eight-year closure (1967–75), a two-phase development project was decided, the first phase of which was completed in 1980, increasing the width of the Canal from around 200 m on average to 286–350 m and deepening the draught to around 16.2 m (150 000 dwt laden). Phase two, that would have deepened the draught to 20.5 m (250 000 dwt laden), has been shelved, however, largely because of world recession. As an interim solution, the Canal Authority increased the permissible draft to 17.1 m (160 000 dwt laden) in October 1994, and decided to deepen the draught to 18 m by October 1996, enabling carriers of up to 200 000 dwt (laden) to transit the Canal.

The Canal's importance for world trade remains considerable. Around 6 per cent of world seaborne trade currently transits the Canal, or around 360 million tons in 1994, of which about 42 million is of crude oil and petroleum products. Between 40 and 50 ships transit the Canal daily.

The Strait of Hormuz

The Strait of Hormuz consists of a 60–100 km-wide channel linking the Gulf and the Gulf of Oman, and separating the two riparian states of Iran and Oman. The narrowest part of the Strait lies between the Iranian Larak Island and Quoin Islands of Oman, a distance of 39 km.

Until 1979, ships were permitted to use the passage that lies in Omani internal waters between the Quoins and the mainland. The current main navigation channels lie close to the Omani Musandam peninsula; they are 70–90 m deep, and thus difficult to physically block, although potentially exposed to shore-based attacks. Around 75 vessels transits the Strait per day.

The Strait of Bab Al Mandeb

The Strait of Bab Al Mandeb (in Arabic, Gate of lamentation) between the Red Sea and the Gulf of Aden lies in the territorial waters of Yemen, Djibouti, and Ethiopia (including Eritrea). Of these, Yemen is best placed to exercise direct control over shipping lanes through its possession of the 8-km^2 Perim Island.

The main shipping routes in Bab Al Mandeb are west of Perim Island, where the channel is 16 km wide and 100–200 m deep. There is no restriction on ship size, and it would be difficult to block such a wide waterway. The number of ships using the Strait is not recorded, but must be similar to Suez Canal transits. This, allowing for Red Sea destinations, is probably about 40 ships per day.

Box I.1   Maritime Waterways in the Middle East   (*continued*)

The Strait of Tiran

The Strait of Tiran is the narrow waterway connecting the Red Sea with the Gulf of Aqaba. It is between 19 and 32 km wide, reaching 1.1 km at its narrowest point with a minimum depth of 50 m. The Strait touches the southern tip of Egypt's Sinai peninsula on the one side and the far northwestern tip of Saudi Arabia on the other, and belongs to the territorial waters of the two countries. The Sinai fortress at Sharm Al Sheikh dominates the Strait, which is vital to ships using either the Israeli port of Eilat or the Jordanian port of Aqaba.

The Turkish Straits

The Turkish Straits which give the Black Sea countries access to the Mediterranean and beyond comprise the Bosporus and Dardanelles. The Bosporus is about 27 km long and only 640 m wide at its narrowest point. Its main channel is 70 m deep. The Dardanelles are 58 km long, narrowing to 868 m. Depths vary from 50 to 90 m. The two straits are separated by the Sea of Marmara, whose length of over 200 km represents several hours of navigation in Turkish waters for ships in transit. Both shores of the Turkish Straits are in the hands of a single state, and control is easily exercised because of their length and narrowness. Around 70 ships transit the Straits per day.

---

intervention in the Middle East especially during the nineteenth and the twentieth centuries.

Nevertheless, the present geopolitical and strategic importance of the Middle East is especially the result of its petroleum resources.[2] As holder of the world's most abundant proved reserves of crude oil (about 65 per cent of the total in 1995), or around 664 000 million barrels, as well as the world's highest reserve-to-production ratio (87 years compared to around 43 years world-wide), the paramount importance of the region within the international system is self-evident. Middle Eastern oil production amounted to around 31 per cent of the world's total in 1995 when around 50 per cent of the world's oil trade originated from the region which is expected to retain the role of major source of incremental supplies that has had since the 1940s.

The Middle East also includes large actual and potential natural gas producers that can significantly alter the international supply picture. A helping factor is the quite huge gas resource base in the area in relation to its current and expected level of demand. At the beginning of 1996, natural gas reserves in the region accounted for about 30.5 per cent of the world total, or around 45 900 billion (thousand million) cubic metres (cu m) that alone are sufficient to satisfy current world-wide consumption

4

Figure I.1   The Middle East

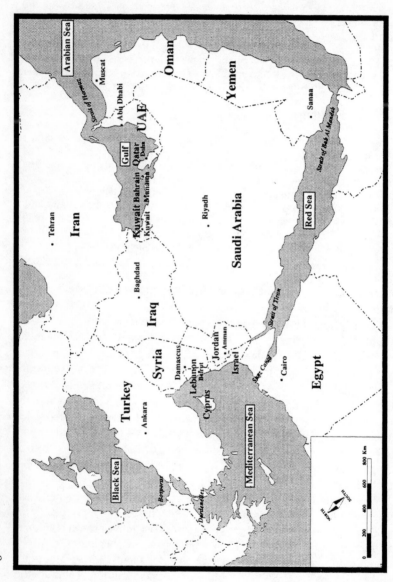

Source: Observatoire Méditerranén de l'Energie (Sophia Antipolis, June 1996).

for more than twenty years. However, considering the enormous potential of the Middle East, little has been done so far to exploit its natural gas reserves. The 1995 gas reserves-to-production ratio was relatively very high, covering 221 years compared to only 62 years world-wide.

While petroleum confers on the Middle East its geopolitical and strategic weight, it is the region's Achilles' heel: any dispute or conflict there could be tempted to materialise first by striking at the petroleum industry which remains the backbone of many states in the area. Some of the recent crises in the Middle East were associated with either a threat to or an actual disruption of oil supplies. Oil was even used as a political weapon by Arabs in the aftermath of the 1967 and 1973 conflicts with Israel.

The Middle East has been a long-standing source of immense human vitality, a complex of people, religious sects, ethnic groupings, styles of government, and external interests and loyalties, applied not only to each state in the area, but to each province and town. Even the most cursory survey of the developments in the area reveals a veritable mosaic of domestically- and regionally-based security threats. Underscored by the turbulent events of the last fifty years, this highlights the ominously fragile bases of stability in the region as a complex geopolitical fault line in the earth's crust.

Although it has recently seen some serious reconciliatory attempts and moves towards peace (with many ups and downs...), the Arab–Israeli confrontation has been the longest-running and most serious regional conflict that has dominated the geopolitics of the Middle East since at least 1948. Apart from the continuing saga of minor incidents, cold struggle has turned to hot regional war on three occasions, in 1948, 1967, and 1973. Additionally, there were Israeli military actions against neighbouring Arab states in 1956 (Egypt), 1978, 1982, 1993, and 1996 (Lebanon). The significance of this issue is that it directly interests all Arabs and provides them with their most obvious focal point. Add to that the deep political frustrations which cause extremism and terrorism on both sides of the conflict, in the Arab world and in Israel.

The existence of Israel has provided further excuses for the establishment of dictatorships and coercions – the argument being that strong regimes are needed to stand up to the outside enemy. This enemy has frustrated every Arab very deeply because of the failure of the Arab nation and all its governments to solve the main related Palestinian problem and as a result of repeated military defeats in the confrontation with Israel. The conflict has helped to polarise the states of the region and to further increase foreign intervention in the area's internal affairs.

In fact, by using the pretext of the Arab–Israeli confrontation, the foreign powers became more entangled in the concerns of the Middle East, a region used to seeing many powers getting involved in its affairs. Even before the collapse in the First World War of the Ottoman Empire which had ruled the region for around four centuries, British and other Entente powers entered into a series of engagements which were to have a profound impact on the post-war political map. In 1916, British and French representatives negotiated the so-called Sykes–Picot agreement which envisaged the establishment of direct French rule in what is now Lebanon, Syria, and southern Turkey, British rule in Iraq, and an international regime in Palestine.

Meanwhile, the British, who were attempting to foster an anti-Turkish rebellion in the Arab lands, entered into vaguely worded commitments to the Hashemite family who were the hereditary governors of Mecca and Medina, and nominal vassals of the Sultan. The Hashemites began their revolt also in 1916, after receiving British promises of support for an independent kingdom in the Arab territories, with the disputed exclusion of Lebanon and western Syria. To add to the confusion, a declaration was issued to the Zionist movement in 1917 by the British Foreign Secretary Arthur Balfour, pledging support for the establishment of a 'national home for the Jewish people in Palestine'. Britain and France were then forced to reconcile these conflicting commitments with US President Woodrow Wilson's anxiety to secure independence for small nations (self-determination).

The pattern established after 1918 attempted to square the circle. Wilson's contribution was the establishment of the League of Nations, which in 1920 awarded supposedly temporary mandates for the governments of Syria and Lebanon to France. Having separated Lebanon from the rest of Syria, the French further muddied the political water by including in the Lebanese boundaries a number of Muslim areas, as a counterbalance to the Maronite Christian Lebanese and to give more economic viability to that political structure. Britain was awarded mandates for Iraq and Palestine. As a consolation prize for the loss of the pan-Arab kingdom, the Hashemite Emir Faisal Bin Hussein was made King of Iraq. The region east of the Jordan river was meanwhile separated from the rest of Palestine as the Kingdom of Transjordan, under Faisal's brother Abdallah. In Palestine, the British established a direct colonial authority. A trickle of Jewish immigration began and gathered pace during the 1930s. In 1932, Iraq legally became an independent state, though thereafter remained under substantial British influence. The mandate regimes meanwhile continued in Syria, Lebanon, Palestine, and Transjordan until the mid-1940s when these countries acquired their independence, with the exception of Palestine where the Jewish state of Israel was declared in May 1948.

Equally dramatic changes were taking place in the Anatolian peninsula, the Turkish heartland of the old Ottoman Empire. Wartime agreements among the allies, later confirmed in the Sèvres Treaty in 1920, had envisaged the establishment of a Greek state in western Anatolia, another in the east, and French- and Italian-ruled zones in the south. Greek troops landed in Izmir in 1919, but they triggered off a Turkish nationalist movement led by Mustafa Kemal Ataturk who established his base in Ankara. By early 1922, the Greeks had suffered a devastating defeat, while the French and the Italians abandoned their claims to Anatolian territory. The verdict of the battlefield was formalised by the Treaty of Lausanne of 1923 that established the Turkish state within its present frontiers (the sole subsequent territorial change was the transfer of Alexandretta (Hatay) province from Syria to Turkey in 1939, still disputed by Damascus).

With the discovery of petroleum in the Middle East, the USA placed its first step on the region in Saudi Arabia in the 1930s and the 1940s, then started expanding through Iran after the overthrow in 1953 of the regime led by Mussadiq, and through the Gulf Arab dynasties following the retreat of Britain from the east of Suez at the end of 1971 after almost two centuries of direct and formal involvement. Although the Islamic revolution in Iran caused a major blow to the American hegemony over most of the Middle East, the two Gulf wars in 1980–8 and 1990–1 and the collapse of the USSR have both helped the USA to put a strong hand on the region again.

The foreign powers became trapped in the affairs of the Middle East mainly to defend the multiple threats to their large interests that included oil. In addition to oil, a combination of factors, including global communications and geographical proximity to the Soviet Union and Western Europe, ensured that the two superpowers, the USA and the USSR, gave the area high priority.

The USSR was naturally interested in what happened along its southern flanks, and was much preoccupied with minimising US predominance there. Soviet interests in the Middle East had had one overriding strategic goal from which the Russian Empire/Soviet Union never deviated. This consisted of preventing hostile power from having paramount influence in or from occupying Turkey, Iran and Afghanistan. These three countries constituted a 'zone of denial', flanking the southern borderlands of the USSR. Other countries, peripheral to that zone, such as Syria, Iraq, and Pakistan had subordinate roles, which from time to time gained special importance. In these terms, Soviet policies in the Middle East were essentially defensive.

In implementing its strategic goals, the USSR had been supported by military facilities and assistance in Egypt (at the time of Nasser), Syria, and South Yemen, based on classical 'co-operation' defence alliances. In addition, Moscow had gained considerable political influence in the area by supporting communist/socialist dictatorships as well as non-communist strongmen who happened to be allies.

Although the USSR had theoretically no need for Middle Eastern petroleum, Soviet interests in the area's hydrocarbons lay in the possibility of preserving its own reserves by exploiting the low-cost resources of the region, in denying them to the members of the North Atlantic Treaty Organisation (NATO) and to Japan in a prelude to or during a general conventional war, and in contriving interruptions in supply that could be turned to the Soviet advantage by splitting allies from the USA in a divisive tactic to create oil shortages as a means of weakening allied commitments to US-led security arrangements.

The USSR was faced by a USA determined to prevent the spread of pro-Soviet parties and regimes in the Middle East, and favoured therefore military dictatorships or right-wing traditional governments. For more than half century, the USA has had important interests in the region, variously defined as the protection of the zone from Soviet encroachment, unimpeded access to Gulf oil, and the security of Israel. More recently, the protection of Gulf Arab states first from Iran and then from Iraq has been added to the list, bringing to four the number of generally agreed US interests in the area. None of these interests is truly vital to the very existence of the USA, though each in its own particular way contributes to its security. But the Middle East cannot be considered without awareness of the links between the region, Europe, and the rimlands of Asia.

To implement the policy goal of limiting Soviet (and probably now Russian) encroachment in the Middle East and confronting its control and influence, the USA has been creating strong political, economic, and military positions in the region. The USA has consequently had military facilities in strategically favourable locations, notably in Egypt (since the time of Sadat), Turkey, Oman, Kuwait, Qatar, Saudi Arabia, and lately Jordan, based on the NATO pact in case of Turkey, and on defence pact alliances signed with the others.

The second US interest, an unimpeded access to Gulf oil, can be closely defined. Gulf oil for the USA is currently such a minor share of total consumption (around 20 per cent in 1995) that a supply cut-off would be altogether manageable, with the US Strategic Petroleum Reserve always ready be employed to diminish its impact. However, the USA must also be concerned about the expected increasing dependence in the future on the region's oil and gas, about its allies – NATO and Japan – that are far more dependent on Gulf oil, and about the economic interests of American major oil companies working in the region (such as Aramco's four founders, namely Standard Oil of California, Texaco, Exxon (Standard Oil of New Jersey), and Mobil).

The third US interest, the protection and well-being of Israel, is an unchanged commitment that has been a very large factor in US policies and actions in the region. Until recently, the relationship with Israel had alternately baffled and frustrated Arabs and made progress in the peace process far more difficult, since the USA, although being the main impetus behind the process, has been widely regarded as a prejudicial participant.

In terms of the fourth related interest – the role of protecting Gulf Arab states – the USA may be relatively ready to apply military force and to be the 'policeman of the Gulf' in the post-Cold War era, assuming that potential target countries are willing to provide the USA with the bases and related facilities required for defensive military action. A far more complicated and difficult policy problem is how the USA might help Gulf Arab regimes to withstand internal pressures and challenges.

Indeed, there are still those who believe that since the USA appears prepared to act as the policeman in the region, future conflicts in the Middle East can effectively be localised and threats to stability quickly eliminated. But such a complacent approach towards potential regional instability implies a serious misunderstanding of the dynamics of conflict in the area, which could ultimately result in reverse impacts.

Likewise, there are still those who believe that a final peace between Arabs and Israel will bring an end to all problems in the Middle East. Maybe that is due to the fact that the Arab–Israeli conflict has dominated much of the general discussion about the region's developments over the past fifty years. Insufficient attention has consequently been devoted to other important issues which may not be quite as eye-catching or newsworthy or even maybe about which there is lack of information. We believe that while a peace environment in the Middle East will surely shift the perception of political risk of the area, it will not be able to eliminate many of the tremendous factors of conflicts and instability militating in favour of the region's continuous political volatility.

Some of the potential sources of instability and conflicts in the Middle East are imminent, while others are inherent and historic, incipient, latent and potential, and internal or interstate. Most attention in the following chapters is given to long-term problems although the scarcity of reliable sources of information makes such judgements difficult. The different factors of instability and sources of conflict faced by the states of the Middle East are broadly comparable, and include the autocratic nature of the regimes and the struggle for power, interstate ideological cleavages, military antagonisms and race, ambition and structure of armed forces, sectarian minorities and religious rivalry, ethnic heterogeneity and minorities, border disputes, disparity in economic development, social impacts of economic constraints, divergence in petroleum policies, struggles over water, demographic explosion, disparity in population growth, and troubles caused by foreign labour migration, internal flight and flows of refugees. These factors are most of the time interrelated and interdependent.

The approach followed in the present book is to evaluate the nature, and tentatively the magnitude, of each potential factor of conflict and dispute in the Middle East, together with an analysis of their background, present status, and future possible evolution, and to attempt a comparative perspective of every factor through an overview of the region, rather than to deal individually with each Middle Eastern state in assessing its elements of instability.

Indeed, listing the region's states according to their potential strengths or weaknesses so as to forecast the likelihood of their regimes' survival could prove to be a futile exercise. Although comparing Saudi Arabia, for example, with the tiny island of Bahrain could be regarded as inappropriate because the collapse of the Bahraini dynasty would not have the same catalytic impact on the entire region as a collapse of the Saudi regime, it is nevertheless worth looking at the existing patterns and trends in all states of the region because they are intimately linked. A chain reaction in the area might indeed be triggered off by a change in one country. Moreover, the fact that there are many in one state who would like to see change does not make change imminent. Similarly the fact that people in a country in the region might conclude that they would be worse off under a different regime does not preclude the possibility of an internal flare-up.

It is also extremely difficult, and it may even be pointless, to try to devise a scale that will quantify how potent are the various sources of conflict and instability in each of the region's states. With the different issues interwoven and mutually reinforcing, any attempts to point to the saliency of certain factors to attempt to create a hierarchy of threats could be misleading: to say that the Kurdish question in Iraq is more acute than that in Syria and Iran, or that the Shia problem in Bahrain is more persistent than the question of the immigrants in the UAE, would be pointless. Perhaps the possibility of a coup in Iraq and Syria may indeed be more likely than elsewhere owing to the army's past record but that does not mean that, because the Kuwaiti and Omani armies have proved passive until now, the two dynasties are immune from military take-over. This, and other potential sources of unrest, could erupt any time and anywhere in the region regardless of what has happened in the past. The book thus starts with the assumption that no conflict factor is inherently more important than any other.

Given the non-legalistic tradition of the area, disputes in the Middle East are rarely settled *per se*. Rather owing to the perceived interest of the parties involved, they remain dormant or deferred, yet always bearing the potential to re-emerge as a catalyst of conflict under the appropriate conditions. Thus, rather than identifiable threats to peace, factors of instability and conflicts are grounds for uncertainty about the future, their unpredictable and varied nature rendering the job of countering them more difficult.

Moreover, it is widely accepted as almost axiomatic that the factors governing the activation of interstate conflicts are largely reflections of internal weaknesses. Indeed, regimes are prone to use external threats as means of distracting public attention from the more immediate problems of national integration and development. This opinion is rejected by almost all the regimes in the Middle East, which argue that the danger to their survival is only external. However, this cannot obviate the fact that in addition to its fears of external threats, each of the region's regimes is troubled by persisting challenges from within, although it cannot foresee exactly how such challenges will manifest themselves, especially since internal tensions tend to persist and re-emerge after some time in a more violent way.

1 Autocratic Regimes and Struggles for Power

POLITICAL AUTOCRACY

The autocratic nature of governments throughout the Middle East points at least to long-term insecurity. The pressure for more representative regimes in the region is likely to grow and threatens to become a major source of instability.

Only four countries in the region have indulged in liberal electoral politics for sustained periods of time, namely Israel, Lebanon, Turkey, and Jordan, while Egypt has pursued a highly controlled liberal experiment since 1976. Israel is a limited and guided democracy with some restrictions on voting rights, whereas Lebanon's experience of liberal/multi-confessional regime has lost most of its shine with the civil war (1975–90). Turkey has oscillated between freewheeling electoral politics in the 1950s and 1970s and military rule in the 1960s and early 1980s. Since 1983 another attempt has been made to revive civilian electoral politics. Jordan is described as a constitutional monarchy ruled by the Hashemite dynasty, but the king actually dominates policy-making, legislation, armed forces and all significant decisions.

Of all the regime types that have characterised the Middle East since the Second World War, the most prevalent has been the socialist republic. Egypt, Iraq, Syria, and North and South Yemen have all replicated to some extent the socialist model. They all have seen changes of government, although none has enjoyed real democracy with multiple political parties. Generally speaking, the socialist Middle Eastern regimes are governed by rulers supported by single parties, like Hafez Assad (born in 1930) and Saddam Hussein (born in 1937) and their respective Baath parties in Syria and Iraq, Hosni Mubarak (born in 1928) and the National Democratic Party in Egypt, which succeeded to the Arab Socialist Union, still in power in the unified Yemen with its chief Ali Abdallah Saleh (born in 1942). These technocratic ruling parties all allow 'brother parties' to operate, but only under their auspices. The ruling parties, which always retain the majority of seats in the parliaments or the so-called 'people councils', nominate the candidates for presidency, who used always to be the persons already in the office. In these regimes, the president has absolute and uncontrolled power, and is the pivot of a small circle of people, mainly the chiefs of state security and the military who uphold the regime, ensuring its stability and its very existence.

Iran underwent a different experience, moving from a totalitarian dynastic rule to an authoritarian theocratic republic where the clergy has the final word although parliamentary elections in early 1996 showed that the monolith had some cracks. The Islamic constitution of 1979 created a parliament (*Majlis*), an elected body controlled by a speaker who is a leading member of the Shia clergy. Both the president of the state (actually Rafsanjani, born in 1934) and the prime minister are subordinate to the *Wali Faqih*, the Ruling Theologian, a post created by Ayatollah Khomeini and now occupied by Ayatollah Khamenei (born in 1939). Political and legal legitimacy resides in the *Wali Faqih*, and his power to intervene in state affairs is unlimited. He is assisted by the fifteen-man Revolutionary Council he heads which controls thousands of local revolutionary committees commanded by the *Mullahs* (those learned in holy scripture) that have come to overshadow the government, which reigns but does not rule.

The kings, princes and sheikhs of the Middle East (see Box 1.1) have fostered different economic systems from those of the socialist republics but have built similar autocratic regimes. As autarchies, each is ruled by tiny hereditary elites that are absolute monarchs and govern by decree. They may have an advisory council of ministers, but in most cases these are members of the monarch's immediate or extended family. In fact, the different members of the ruler's family in these countries usually take over the key ministries of finance, security, defence, sometimes oil, sometimes foreign affairs, and almost always inter-Arab relations. In some less sensitive and more technical ministries and state agencies, so-called commoners, or people who do not belong to the ruling families, are used as ministers. The power of commoners, however, remains under close royal control.

These states are alike in prohibiting political parties, labour unions and syndicates, a fact leading to two interrelated levels of political life in the region: an open government or a sanctioned democratic process, and a rich underground and clandestine political activity. As means of communication between the ruler and his subjects in these countries, informal institutions exist, serving to keep subordinates in contact with the regime through open audience with the leader. Providing subjects with direct access to the palace – where they can air their grievances, present their petitions and be rewarded if the 'giver of gifts' deems it necessary – is a long-held tradition that enables the ruler to exert influence. As formal

---

Box 1.1   Ruling Dynasties in the Middle East

Al Bu Said Dynasty

The Al Bu Said dynasty has ruled Oman from 1749 to the present. Sultan Qaboos Bu Said has been reigning since 1970 when he overthrew his father Sultan Said Bin Taimur in a British-supported coup. Identified with the vital port of Muscat, the centre of its realm, the Al Bu Said family, with British assistance, has spread its authority along the southern coast of the Arabian peninsula as far as Dhofar and the Yemeni border, and inland to Nizwa where its historic rivals for long held sway. Identified with Ibadi Islam, the Al Bu Said family has traditionally been less theocratic in outlook than their hinterland subjects. Al Bu Said's cosmopolitanism, although narrow by most definitions, has been influenced by Oman's geographic position astride vital international sea lanes. Indeed, Al Bu Said rule was extended to Zanzibar and the coast of East Africa in the nineteenth century. They were also active in southern Persia and the southern coast of Arabia during this period. European imperialism reduced the Al Bu Said empire, but it buttressed the monarchy against local adversaries.

Hashemite Dynasty

The Hashemites originate from the Bani Hashem clan of Quraysh of Mecca, the tribe of the Prophet Mohammed. The family had ruled Mecca and the Hijaz section of the Arabian peninsula from the tenth century to the second decade of the twentieth century. As protectors of the holy cities of Mecca and Medina, the Hashemite leaders bore the title 'Sherif', an aristocratic rank. It was they to whom the British turned for support during the First World War, and they responded by providing troops for the war against the Turks, their ambition stimulated by the acknowledgement that the Ottomans would be forced from the Arabian peninsula and possibly from the Arab world. The Sherif of Mecca, Hussein Bin Ali, observing the opportunity to establish his claim to broader Arab leadership, amassed a large army somewhat in concert with British forces. Moreover, the Sherif's religious credentials were sound. His alliance with Europeans against the Turks nullified the Ottoman Sultan-Caliph's declaration of a *Jihad* (holy war) against Britain. The Sherif of Mecca called upon his sons to lead his army, and after the war was over Britain rewarded their performance by installing one son, Faisal, in Damascus and the other, Abdallah, in the Transjordanian sector of Palestine. The French forced Faisal to leave Syria in 1920, but the British re-established his throne in Baghdad. Hussein meanwhile continued to rule in Mecca and the Hijaz. In 1924, he claimed the Caliphate after an order abolishing it was made by the leader of the new Turkish republic. But, except for his sons in Iraq and Transjordan, no other Arab or Islamic authority recognised the claim. In that same year, Hussein was attacked by an army led by Abd Al Aziz Bin Abd Al Rahman Bin Faisal Al Saud (Ibn Saud) and was defeated. Hussein was forced to abdicate in favour of his third son, Ali, but the Sauds defeated the latter in 1925 and incorporated the Hijaz into their realm. The Hashemites lost the seat of their power to Ibn Saud, but with the

Box 1.1   **Ruling Dynasties in the Middle East**   (*continued*)

assistance provided by the British, their rule over Iraq and Transjordan was pre-served. The Hashemites of Iraq were eventually overthrown by disaffected army officers in 1958, King Faisal and his family were murdered, and the dynastic line was terminated. The only remaining Hashemite authority resides in the territory east of the Jordan river. At its creation Transjordan was a desert hinterland with a population made up of several hundred thousand Bedouin tribesmen. The state lacked economic resources and was almost completely dependent on a British subsidy and the Arab Legion, organised and officered by the British. The British granted autonomy to Abdallah, but full sovereignty was not conferred until 1946, at which time the country became the Kingdom of Transjordan. The character of Jordan was altered by the Arab–Israeli War of 1948. The Arab Legion seized the West Bank territories and the eastern part of Jerusalem, including the holy shrines. In December 1948, Abdallah was pro-claimed King of Palestine by a conference of prominent West Bank Arabs. In 1950, the king annexed the West Bank (a decision annulled late in 1988 by King Hussein), and the country was renamed the Kingdom of Jordan. When King Abdallah was assassinated in July 1950 by disgruntled Palestinians, his son Talal succeeded to the throne but was deposed in 1952 because of a debili-tating mental disorder. Talal's son, Hussein, assumed the throne in 1953, upon his eighteenth birthday. The Hashemite dynasty has clung to a precarious perch in the intervening years. Martial law was imposed over the country in 1957–63, 1966–7, and 1970–3. King Hussein has survived numerous assassination at-tempts, although his ministers and close associates have not been as fortunate.

Al Khalifa Dynasty

The Al Khalifa family has ruled the Gulf island of Bahrain since 1783. At that time, the Arab Utaibi rulers of Zubarah on the Qatari coast, related to the Al Khalifa family, wrested Bahrain from Persian control. After a series of tribal wars, the Al Khalifa family emerged as the dominant force, and has sustained its authority to the present day, helped by the British. The Al Khalifa family, and especially the current ruler Sheikh Issa Bin Salman Al Khalifa, has not stressed Islamic tradition as much as the mainland sheikhs, no doubt due to their long-term association with international merchants. The ruling family does emphasise its Arab character, however, and it gives vocal support to Arab nationalism.

Al Sabah Dynasty

The Al Sabah family traces its origin to the same Utaibi tribe that gave rise to Al Saud of Arabia and Al Khalifa in Bahrain. The dynasty has dominated the politi-cal life of Kuwait since 1756, and is now represented by Emir Jabir Al Ahmad Al Sabah. The monarchy is a traditional hereditary emirate, and succession is made by selection of a sheikh from the descendants of the seventh ruler of Kuwait,

Box 1.1   Ruling Dynasties in the Middle East   (*continued*)

Sheikh Mubarak Al Sabah Al Sabah. The Al Sabah dynasty rests upon a network of interrelationships that link the royal family, the pre-eminent tribal leaders, the *Ulemas* (learned theologians), the military establishment, and the commercial families like the Al Khalil, Al Ghanim, and Al Salih. Earlier, the rule of the Al Sabah was dependent on its nobility and the capacity to mediate conflict between competing Kuwaiti tribes.

Al Saud Dynasty

The Al Saud dynasty had developed during the eighteenth century in the Nejd highland of the Arabian interior. Mohammed Ibn Saud, the son-in-law and disciple of Mohammed Bin Abd Al Wahhab (an austere Muslim theologian and jurist), led his tribal army in a triumphal campaign that conquered a good portion of the Arabian peninsula. The death of Mohammed Ibn Saud in 1765 did not terminate the Saudi action. His son and successor, Abd Al Aziz, pressed the Sauds to more extensive conquests, and in 1787 he established the hereditary succession of the Saudi house by having his own son confirmed as his successor by Al Wahhab before a great popular assembly of tribal leaders. In the years that followed, the Saudi Wahhabis continued their advance into Iraq undeterred by the Pasha of Baghdad. The Sauds also spread their authority into the Hijaz of Arabia, seizing the Sunni Muslim holy places of Mecca and Medina. But the Ottoman Sultan recognised that a threat to his own rule and ordered his army to crush the Wahhabis and the House of Saud. The Sauds were forced to give up their gains and retreat into the Arabian interior. They settled in Riyadh, received the loyalty of the powerful Shamar tribe, and proceeded to reconstitute their forces. Wahhabism and the Sauds remained somewhat in the shadows of Arabian history in the latter half of the nineteenth century. During the First World War, however, their association with the British and their total opposition to the Ottomans, propelled them back onto the Arabian stage. But after a halting involvement in the war, the leader of the House of Saud, Abd Al Aziz Bin Abd Al Rahman Bin Faisal Al Saud (Ibn Saud), decided to hold his forces in reserve as the British Colonial Office in London seemed more inclined toward mobilising the forces of the Sherif of Mecca, the then keeper of the holy places in Mecca and Medina and the dominant force in the Hijaz. When the Sherif of Mecca attempted to establish himself as the Caliph of Islam following the collapse of the Ottoman Empire, Ibn Saud who had already defeated his old rival Sheikh Rashid of Hail in 1921, had his *casus belli*. By identifying the Sherif of Mecca as a heretic and usurper, Ibn Saud was able to rally a large and determined following, and in the name of a revived Wahhabism, they assaulted and defeated the Sherif and his forces. Hijaz as well as Nejd now came under the rule of the House of Saud. By 1926 the Sauds were recognised as the new protectors of Islam's holiest places. In 1930 Ibn Saud was crowned King of Nejd and Hijaz, and the modern dynasty was established. The Kingdom of Saudi Arabia was formally proclaimed in 1932, and assumed a place in the family

Box 1.1   Ruling Dynasties in the Middle East   (*continued*)

of nations. Assisted by the British, the new king attempted to consolidate his power and bring the other reigning Arabian monarchs and chieftains under his influence. Family alliances were pursued with the dominant sheikhs, and links were forged through intermarriage to stabilise Saudi authority throughout the peninsula. When Ibn Saud died in 1953, he left his heirs a monarchy with strong ties to both Britain and the USA. Abd Al Aziz' successor, Saud, did not have his father's talents or strength, however, and the new king was neither able to manage the traditional system nor cope with the challenges presented by a changing world. The Saudi family thus took matters into their own hands, and in a bloodless coup in 1964 they retired King Saud and placed his brother Faisal on the throne. The assassination of Faisal in 1975 by an estranged member of the extended family was a blow to the Sauds, but their system prevailed. Faisal was succeeded by his brother, Khalid, who was quickly recognised to be a figurehead king. Khalid did not interfere with the administration of the country or the fashioning of its policies in the years of his reign (1975–82), leaving them to Crown Prince Fahd. The latter assumed the throne after Khalid's death, and still another brother, Abdallah was named crown prince.

Al Thani Dynasty

The Al Thani family has ruled Qatar since the latter half of the nineteenth century. They were among those Arabian sheikhs with whom the British had intimate relations. They are also devotees of Wahhabism, and are traditional in their tastes and performance. Like the Sauds, the Al Thanis have practised intermarriage with the tribes of the Arabian peninsula. After a century of such activity, the family has spread its branches throughout the country, and represents today the largest network of filial relationships of all the Gulf sheikhdoms. This broad family structure has solidified the monarchy and contributed to a diffuse stability. But while Qatar has enjoyed relative tranquillity, the Al Thani family has not been without conflict. In 1960, the ruling emir was deposed by his son, Sheikh Ahmad, with assistance from the British. In 1972, Ahmad was forcibly removed by his cousin Sheikh Khalifa Bin Hamad Al Thani. Then, in June 1995, Crown Prince and Minister of Defence Sheikh Hamad Bin Khalifa Al Thani overthrew his father in a bloodless coup.

institutions, consultative nominated councils exist in Qatar, the UAE, Oman, and Saudi Arabia, while elected national assemblies have existed only in Kuwait and for some time in Bahrain.

Qatar, now ruled by Sheikh Hamad Bin Khalifa Al Thani (born in 1949) under the order of Wahhabism, has had an Advisory Council of thirty appointed members since 1970. The Council has the power to debate legislation drafted by the government before ratification and promulgation. It also has the power to request ministerial statements on matters of general and specific policy, including the draft budget.

In contrast, the Federal National Council in the UAE has limited power. The forty-member council was established by the provisional constitution of 1971, which has been renewed every five years. The Council, nominated by the rulers of individual emirates, reviews legislation and oversees the workings of federal ministries. The chief power in the UAE federal government is held by the Supreme Council of Rulers, where the presidents of Abu Dhabi and Dubai have more votes than the rest. Sheikh Zayed Bin Sultan Al Nahyan (born in 1918) has been UAE president since the federation was formed in 1971, and has also been the ruler of Abu Dhabi since 1966, when the British agreed that he should replace his conservative brother, Shakhbut (who died in 1989). Sheikh Zayed's presidency has been renewed every five years, most recently in 1996. The federal cabinet, led by Crown Prince Maktum Bin Rashid Al Maktum from Dubai, does not exercise authority as a whole, but some ministers and ministries have considerable power and influence. On the other hand, ministers who assume more power than they should are quietly dropped from the government in favour of traditionalists.

In Oman, Qaboos Bu Said (born in 1940), who has been the reigning sultan since 1970, took a daring step in 1990 when he permitted the establishment of an advisory assembly (*Majlis Al Shura*) consisting of fifty-nine members. Local leaders and men of high standing from each province nominate three candidates, one of whom is elected by the citizens to represent the province in the *Majlis*; the *Majlis* has a dual role: it is a channel for citizens to express their points of view, and it is a forum in which solutions to problems can be suggested. The members have the right to request government statements on economic and social issues, while the ministers of public services have to give a brief account of the policies and accomplishments of their ministries. Actually, however, the *Majlis* is an extension of the idea of the consultative council founded in 1981; the citizen right to elections is the only new development. Rights to debate the annual budget and to discuss foreign policy issues are still restricted.

In Saudi Arabia, and after many years of resistance and procrastination, King Fahd (born in 1921) from the family Al Saud that has ruled the country since the early 1930s, announced in November 1990 that a *Majlis Al Shura* was to be established, restricted to a purely advisory role. According to its statute, which was originally issued in March 1992, the *Majlis'* function was to 'express its views on state policies referred to it by the prime minister (the king himself!)', and in particular to debate the general strategy for economic and social development and express its views on it; to study laws, regulations, treaties, international agreements and concessions and propose what it saw fit regarding them; to comment on regulations; and to discuss the annual reports presented by the ministries and other government organisations. In August 1993, the sixty members of the *Majlis* were nominated, drawn from many walks of Saudi life, including businessmen, religious leaders, tribal chieftains and intellectuals. The members would be elected at a later stage. The *Majlis* held its inaugural session at the beginning of 1994.

While the composition of the Saudi *Majlis* may have fallen short of the expectations of both the Islamist and liberal constituencies, it represents an important milestone in the kingdom's political development, particularly should the king decide to accord it some functional responsibilities. At this nascent stage, it is unclear whether the *Majlis'* deliberative and advisory functions will be fully utilised by the monarch in the formulation and legitimation of his decisions and policies. Should it be permitted to emerge as a sounding board or as a channel for public sentiments to the king, it could act as a counterweight to all opposition groups in the kingdom, including the fundamentalists.

The Saudi king heads the government as prime minister. He must govern under Islamic law according to the Wahhabi rule, with the help of the council of ministers, many of whom belong to the royal family. The king consults weekly with the *Ulemas*, notably those who are descended from the founder of Wahhabism and allied to the royal family by marriage. The *Ulemas*, conservative in outlook, are an integral part of the governing establishment, but their basic concern is the purity of faith.

Bahrain, currently ruled by Sheikh Issa Bin Salman Al Khalifa (born in 1933), knew an elected national assembly for two years only, between 1973 and 1975. Twenty-two of the forty-two-member council were elected by direct male suffrage. The assembly was dissolved twenty months after its inception when the ruling family found that the elected members challenged the family's political legitimacy. Violent unrest erupted in 1994–6, partly demanding a return to the parliamentary regime. Consequently, in early 1996 the nominated assembly was given the right to 'initiate debate' on social, cultural, educational, and health matters, after being limited to studying and commenting on government policy.

The political experience of Kuwait that is governed by Emir Jabir Al Ahmad Al Sabah (born in 1928) differs from the rest of the Gulf states. It has had elected parliaments, although from a very narrow (literate adult Kuwaiti male-only) electorate. Political parties are not allowed, and press freedom is constrained. The concept is simply that, although national issues can be debated by the parliament and thus permit a venting of ideas, the assembly will ultimately rubber-stamp the decisions of the ruling family.

Following major differences between the government and parliament, the Kuwaiti assembly was dissolved and the constitution suspended in the summer of 1976. The government permitted new elections at the end of a four-year suspension period, in February 1981. The new parliament proved to be as difficult to control, and the government again dissolved it and suspended the constitution in July 1986, following a period of political unrest. The ruling dynasty used the hiatus between the different assemblies to restore the emirate's traditional dependence on 'Bedouin democracy' (decision by tribal consensus) to offset the influence of non-Kuwaitis. After the occupation and then the liberation of the emirate in 1990–1, Emir Al Sabah was constrained to reintroduce the parliamentary system. Elections were held in October 1992, and then in October 1996.

Needless to say, for the rest of the Gulf regimes, especially that in Riyadh, the consequences of Kuwaiti 'democracy' could be quite severe. Disenchanted with the nature and the content of the political debate and liberalisation of the political system in the emirate, and assuming that it would have some impact on its own intelligentsia, Saudi Arabia has always exerted pressure to do away with the parliamentary system which, in the opinion of the Saudi rulers, will ultimately result in dislocation and collapse of the existing central authority. The Sauds fear that the reintroduction of a Kuwaiti parliament (even if it remains limited in power and co-opted in its membership) would present the Saudi dynasty in an unfavourable light and might result in increased demands within and outside the kingdom to follow the same path, something Riyadh has never desired to do.

Nevertheless, the countries not only in the Gulf but in the larger Middle East are no longer as isolated as they were in the past and their populations are bound to be influenced by events elsewhere in the region. Though they differ in some respects, all regimes face unpalatable choices. They fear that introducing any kind of participatory democracy would hasten their demise and that any change would ultimately mean polarisation and use of more repression which could result in political decay and collapse. At the same time, regimes have been alerted to the possibility that things could get out of control if they do not introduce new measures (despite the fact that these would be risky) so as to gain time in the hope that they will somehow succeed in maintaining stability and cementing their position while avoiding introducing sweeping changes that might threaten their very existence. Rather than accommodating the new realities, the governments have opted for limited social reforms so as to try and gain the loyalty of the population by creating vested interests for them in the well-being of the regime.

But the process of decision-making in all these states remains exclusively in the hands of small groups – whether senior technocrats in Egypt, Iraq and Syria, the ruling families in the Gulf or the clergy in Iran – all of whom take account to some degree of public opinion in the hope that this will bolster their own position while granting only a minor sense of participation to those excluded from power. This limited action is unlikely to prevent opposition from the rapidly growing intelligentsia, but the fact that educated classes remain disorganised, divided and have demonstrated little readiness for sacrifice has made it easier for the regimes.

The reluctance of the autocratic rulers in the Middle East to make real changes stems from their fear that nothing they can grant can satisfy the expectations of those outside the present system. The latter will insist on far-reaching changes and will view any minor modifications as simply a step on the way to full participation. But while the rulers remain hesitant to put the resilience and flexibility of their own political systems to the test, the pressures for something more than cosmetic measures are likely to grow.

Due to the absence of representative political institutions, totalitarism increases the vulnerability of Middle Eastern regimes and lays them open to extremist movements which in turn can lead to volatility or even instability. That is aggravated by the impact of modernisation.

IMPACT OF MODERNISATION

Any economic development necessarily involves social and political change, no matter how carefully considered or deterred. Growing political awareness cannot be divorced from the import of technology and especially modern means of information. Expectations of greater participation in political life have always followed modernisation, and failure of the autocratic regimes in the Middle East to pay due regard to such demands could breed tension. Some of these regimes still apparently believe that economic need not involve political and social liberalism, arguing that the area has never practised political liberalism in the Western sense, a system denounced by these regimes as 'neocolonialist'. Many of the rentier states suppose that as long as the government is in a position to buy consensus by distributing goods, services, and income in exchange for little or nothing, it has no need of democratic legitimation.

Modernisation of the region has inevitably transformed its citizens' perceptions of society and expectations from regimes. It is urbanising the region where already 65 per cent of people live in towns, compared with a global average of 45 per cent. Modernisation has produced a change to an almost totally sedentary way of life for the formerly large nomadic populations of Bedouin, changes in the occupation and lifestyles of the majority of the people, significant alterations to family structure, and a rising dominance of Western or Western-style education. Increasing numbers of people receive primary, secondary, and then higher education, either at home or abroad. Geographic mobility is increasing, and many people have established private businesses or entered government services.

The rapid changes that are taking place as a result of modernisation manifest themselves in the rising expectations of the lower strata of population, in the surfacing of new social groupings with distinctive political aspirations, and in the demand for greater participation by the newly emerging middle class which, in contrast to its economic participation, is denied political power. An expanding young population in the cities with wider horizons and expectations has fuelled demands for more political choice and democratisation.

In the meantime, there is the confrontation between the modernisers and the traditionalists. The modernisers believe that society has to change if there is to be a viable long-term future, and they know that the risks of transformation might be extremely painful. For the traditionalists, change is an anathema, indeed a blasphemy, and an acceptance of despised Western materialism and perceived loose moral standards. The struggle against change is then perceived by the traditionalists as the first step in the battle for the rebirth of Islam and its values.

The dilemma facing Middle Eastern autocratic regimes when dealing with the problem of modernisation and its related issues is that it becomes increasingly difficult to develop the nation without accepting sweeping changes, transformations that will ultimately mean political liberalisation and a consequent weakening of central authority. Yet if they do not seek to modernise their societies, they will lose in any case. They learned that when Sheikh Shakbut Bin Sultan Al Nahyan in Abu Dhabi and Sultan Said Bin Taimur Bu Said in Oman consciously took a decision to slow the pace of modernisation, both were thrown out. On the other hand, the Shah's grandiose plans to make Iran the 'Japan of Western Asia' could not be absorbed by the society in the timescale envisaged. The result was a revolution in which the people sought to hold on to the values of their traditional society in the face of a challenge to their basic sense of security.

Yet the main questions for the autocratic regimes in the region remain. How to reconcile the process of rapid modernisation with traditional values while perpetuating the existing monopoly of power and social patterns? Can these regimes manage the new challenges with old tools? What options are open to the governments?

A main difficulty about addressing these questions is that the transition from autocracy to democratically-chosen government is very dangerous. Liberalisation permits political forces to muster, and some of them will be intent on using the new rules of the political game against the regime. The outcome could be a take-over by factions that do not have liberal and democratic values in mind at all, such as the Islamic fundamentalists[1] who seek to attain an Islamic conservative utopia under an integrated political project which is based on a pure interpretation of the Qoran.

ISLAMIC FUNDAMENTALISM

It is Islam that gives fundamentalists in the Middle East a somewhat special position. In theory, Islam is an inherently political religion. Classically, the state's legitimacy depends on its role as protector of the Islamic community (*Umma*) and the preservation of the divine law (*Sharia*) by 'enjoining the good and forbidding the evil'. Thus, fundamentalists have at hand a ready-made indigenous faith that can be used as an ideology to defend the traditional against the modern, and to confront secularism at a time when present regimes do not seem to offer a way forward – only more of the same.

To the Islamic fundamentalists, modernisation implies intolerable social change and an admission that Islam does not contain all the answers to the world of progress. They are not against science as such. But modernisation in its imported form is seen as the West's victory in that it proves that a continued adherence to true Islam is irreconcilable with industrialisation. Modernisation that is insensitive to Islamic culture and heritage is regarded as an undesirable bad development. It harms the traditional foundations of an Islamic state by exposing it to previously unknown challenges and reveals the inadequacy of the tools at the disposal of its government. The West – with whom the imported secularisation and corruption are associated – becomes the target for those discontented with the process. The dependence on the West is thus profoundly irritating. Add to that the long close US affiliation with Israel and American policies towards the Palestinian question and you have an explosive mixture. American policies have been seen not only as being insensitive to the Palestinian cause but as valuing an Israeli alliance above the friendship of the Islamic world.

The dilemma sharpens for many Muslims who would like to advance themselves by taking advantage of Western technology and the spirit of Western democracy without having to absorb what they see as 'Western greed and decadence'. To them, the West is the source of all the evils and maladies that have afflicted the Islamic nation. Readily accepting Western assistance, or even the trappings of Westernisation, do not make them pro-Western. On the contrary, their sense of cultural inferiority, especially among those who are Western-educated, makes them search for their lost identity, self-respect and dignity while seeking a way to give expression to their own authentic way of life. Disillusioned with Arab nationalism, once the most powerful albeit anti-clerical manifestation of Arab protest against the West, more Arab intellectuals are turning back toward an Islamic revival. Islamism is therefore an outlet for airing this bitterness and frustration even if many of those protesting remain non-believers.

The emergence of Islamic fundamentalism is also intertwined with a popularly-induced process of democratisation. For a long time, the issuance of a *Fatwa* (religious edict) in Islamic countries has been controlled rigidly by governments eager to obtain religio–political legitimacy through the 'Islamisation' of their policies and deeds. This way of exploiting Islam for political purposes is not new and can be traced back to the time following the death of the Prophet, when his companions competed against each other using Mohammed's legacy as their weapon. In time, it became standard practice for the political authority to seek legitimisation through the religious authority, institutionalised as a government-salaried clergy. The emergence of Islamic fundamentalism might represent popular protest against discredited and salaried clerics by allowing Muslim activists to choose their own religious leaders without relying on government-appointed clerics. The emergence of fundamentalist leaders in villages, towns, and city neighbourhoods 'democratises' the religious decree-issuing process, providing individual Muslims with an opportunity to seek advice from a leader whom they chose. This undermines the credibility of the Islamic establishment and threatens the governmental sponsorship of institutional interpretation of Islamic texts.

Islamic fundamentalism has been present in the region at least since 1928 in form of movements such as 'the Muslim Brotherhood'. The revival of Islamic fundamentalism received a large measure of reinforcement with the revolution in Iran in 1979, which has become the focus not only for Shia orthodoxy but for a more general return to radicalism and a rejection of secular and Western aspirations. Subsequently, Islamic groupings like *Hamas* (the Islamic Resistance Movement) in the West Bank and Gaza Strip, and *Hizbollah* ('Party of God') in Lebanon (see Box 1.2) have been flourishing, reinforced by militant Islamists (*Mujahiddin*, also called *Afghans*) from various Arab and Islamic states, who had fought the Soviet forces in Afghanistan, and who are now ready to continue the struggle against every 'un-Islamic' regime in the region.

**Box 1.2　Fundamentalists in Action
(Muslim Brotherhood, Hamas, Hizbollah, Afghans)**

The twentieth century's most important Arab Islamist movement, *The Muslim Brotherhood* was founded in Egypt in 1928 by Hasan Al Banna, and has been the model for many later organisations. Al Banna saw the Brotherhood not as engine of radical revolution but of gradual change, and regarded Westernising influences and intellectual emancipation as weakening Islam, while seeking a return to pure Islam and *Sharia* (Islamic law). In 1944 a secret apparatus of the Brotherhood was formed, rationalised as for the *Jihad* in defence of Islam but mainly used to defend the movement against the government.

In the belief that a truly Islamic society will institute an Islamic government and constitution, the Brotherhood has established clinics, schools and other local services conforming to Islamic norms. It has thus highlighted the failure of governments to provide such services.

In Egypt, the Brotherhood has been officially banned, but was sometimes tolerated by the regime especially under President Sadat to counterbalance other political powers or more radical Islamic groupings. During its history, the Brotherhood has also established itself in other countries, including Jordan where it had been for some time the biggest single party in the parliament, Syria where it was crushed by the government army in 1982, and the West Bank and Gaza Strip in the form of *Hamas*.

The radical Palestinian group, *The Islamic Resistance Movement* (better known by its Arabic acronym *Hamas*) found its origins in the Muslim Brotherhood movement in the Israeli-occupied territories. It first appeared on the scene as *Hamas* in February 1988, about two months after the outbreak of the Palestinian uprising. Engaged in guerrilla activity, Hamas has been attacking first 'legitimate' non-civilian targets – like serving members of the Israeli security forces and armed Jewish settlers – before hitting civil goals in early 1996.

In Lebanon, the radical Iranian-backed *Hizbollah* ('Party of God') fulfils a role similar to that of *Hamas* facing Israel in the Shia south of the country, although the Lebanese group is politically more developed. Ideologically, *Hizbollah* has the long-term aim of establishing an Iranian-style Islamic state in Lebanon. Meanwhile, the group has been participating in the democratic process; it currently holds a small bloc of seats in the Lebanese parliament, where it concentrates mainly on domestic issues. *Hizbollah*'s other non-guerrilla activities include construction and lending organisations, and educational and medical operations throughout poor Shia areas. Its involvement in hostage-taking and its

---

Box 1.2   Fundamentalists in Action   *(continued)*

attacks on Western establishments in Beirut in 1983–6 have guaranteed its place in Western demonology. Since the end of the Lebanese civil war in 1990, *Hizbollah* has acquired wide non-community legitimacy as a national resistance movement.

The *Afghans* are militant *Mujahiddin* (who struggle in the name of Islam) from various Arab and Islamic states, who had fought the Soviet forces in Afghanistan, and who are now ready to continue the struggle against every 'un-Islamic' regime in the region. These militants believe they are warriors for the Islamic faith in opposition to forces that seek to threaten or destroy their religious belief. They are convinced that their great honour will be to die in battle defending Islam. Indeed, martyrdom is intertwined with Islamic teaching: no greater martyrdom is possible than that achieved by giving one's life in armed conflict while defending the religious order. The *Mujahid* believes he is performing the highest service for God, and that he need not fear the consequences.

Since the Islamic revolution in Iran, there has been a continuous struggle between liberals and fundamentalists in almost every Middle Eastern country. Even in Iran itself, there has been a political and ideological clash between forces led by *Mullahs* who consider themselves the rightful heirs to the revolutionary Islamic legacy of Ayatollah Khomeini, and the more pragmatic Iranians (also including a number of *Mullahs*). The first group is generally opposed to Western interests and culture, especially those of the USA, attaches highest priority to establishing an Iranian government of their own design, and espouses revolutionary tactics in the Islamic world. The second group believes in access to funds and technologies of the West for the reconstruction and further development of the country.

In Turkey, a state deliberately secularised by Mustafa Kemal Ataturk, fundamentalism is perceived as definite and growing threat with the Islamist Welfare Party (*Refah*) winning the relative majority (around 23 per cent) in the 1995 legislative election, after gaining the majority of seats in 28 cities including the capital Ankara and the commercial centre of Istanbul in the 1994 municipal suffrage. That allowed *Refah* to form a coalition government in May 1996.

In Egypt, an open struggle has been occurring since the mid-1970s between the regime and its Islamic rival, a struggle enhanced by the killing of President Sadat in September 1981. The Egyptian radical Islamic movements seem to be not sufficiently well organised to seize power, although they can make real trouble through riots and bloody attacks.

In Jordan, the strength of fundamentalism has been diminishing through a policy of peaceful containment, followed by a process of side-tracking the Islamic movement. In Syria, a more brutal method was used, especially in 1982 in Hama where as many as 20 000 were reportedly killed.

In the Gulf Arab states, the threat of fundamentalism is increasing but is not yet alarming. In Kuwait, since the liberation in 1991, the Islamic movement has become a powerful influence. Islamic politicians, elected for the parliaments of 1992 and 1996, have been calling for an amended constitution in which *Sharia* will be the sole source of legitimacy.

In the UAE, the role of Islamic fundamentalism was growing for sometime, especially in the federation's only university, situated at Al Ain in Abu Dhabi's eastern province. In 1983 and 1984, the Abu Dhabi government and the UAE's federal authorities quietly moved against the fundamentalist group there. Meanwhile, the chancellor of the university removed several faculty members who strongly favoured the group.

In Oman, a clash in June 1994 opposed security forces and members of the banned Muslim Brotherhood movement, following an apparent bid by the conservative religious group to win greater political influence. Some reports were even talking about a 'fundamentalist plot', following the penetration of members of the Brotherhood into Omani government departments and state bodies.

Saudi Arabia is clearly differentiated from the other Gulf systems by the use that the Saudi regime makes of religion. The Wahhabi regime had a religious dimension from the beginning, and it is still very much alive: 'The Qoran is our constitution' is still a favourite maxim for the dynasty. The Sauds do not claim divine powers. They consider themselves as a temporal authority, charged with sustaining and expanding the world of Islam. Islam has thus become a two-edged political instrument, as the kingdom's primary medium of self-legitimation, and as the main venue of protest for opposition elements.

Following minor challenges from Islamic fundamentalists in form of demonstrations in 1963 and an armed assault on a television station in 1965 by fanatics opposed to that form of communication, the first major fundamentalist shock for the regime in Riyadh was the seizure of the Great Mosque of Mecca in November 1979 by a number of Islamic extremists, mostly Saudis together with some Yemenis, Sudanese, Kuwaitis and others, but led by a Saudi Wahhabi called Juhayman Al Utaibi. There was no evidence that the extremist group received support from outside the kingdom, and the arms which were smuggled into the Great Mosque were bought with money obtained from a merchant in Jeddah. Many extremists were recruited from among students at the University of Medina, a centre for Muslim Brotherhood exiles since the 1960s, where radical ideas mingled with the literalist teaching of Sheikh Abd Al Aziz Ibn Baz, the rector of the university. Sheikh Ibn Baz, who is also the chairman of the Supreme Council of Ulema (SCU), the country's highest religious authority, and the kingdom's general *Mufti* (who interprets the Qoran and thus makes religious laws), once aroused international derision by publishing articles defending a geocentric view of the universe, describing the religious inappropriateness of photography and videos, and outlining the manners in which Muslims are allowed to look, or are prohibited from looking at, or shaking hands with women, particularly non-Muslim ones.

The Saudi authorities did what they could to minimise the significance of the seizure of the Great Mosque, which was brutally terminated after more than five weeks. Riyadh attributed the action to 'purely religious' fanatics whom they term *Khawarij*, taking advantage of the double sense of this term that means an external force (*Kharijiya*) and a specific religious sect of 'people who have left the consensus of the believers'. In reality, there can be no doubt that the action represented a mixed religio–sociological and political protest against the regime, and that the event was extremely serious. This was shown by the fact that all army and security commanders in Mecca and Medina were dismissed and replaced once the danger was over.

In the aftermath of the siege, there were widespread manifestations of religious resurgence, particularly among youth, university students and faculty, assembled under groups committed to religious propagation and puritanical lifestyles. They displayed a distinctive appearance – full beard, short haircut, and short white robe. In view of this challenge, the government in Riyadh sought to prove that it was more fundamentalist that its detractors by reasserting some Islamic orthodoxy and increasing the enforcement of the *Sharia* legislation. Television programmes have been censored, and female singers on television prohibited. Women have been forbidden to travel alone or to work next to men. Newspapers have been forbidden to publish pictures of women, except with their faces concealed.

A new wave of Islamist fervour emerged in the late 1980s. The new fundamentalists consist of outspoken, sophisticated, well organised young, middle-class urbanites in their tens of thousands, led by preachers, teachers, and students, mostly from the religious universities. Their activism and pervasive influence are manifested through the proliferation of publications, bookstores, and clandestine audio-cassettes that are distributed at a nominal charge. Unlike the older, state-sanctioned religious police (*Mutawwa*), the young activists have an agenda to transform social conduct by patrolling the shopping malls, spying on people, and raiding homes in search of 'un-Islamic' conduct. A new source of mass support for the fundamentalists has been a class of recently urbanised Bedouins, whose status of relative deprivation among more affluent urbanites made them eager converts to the activists' cause.

In July 1992, more than a hundred conservative *Ulemas* presented a critical forty-five-page 'memorandum of advice' to King Fahd, deploring 'the total chaos of the economy and society, administrative corruption, widespread bribery, favouritism, and the extreme feebleness of the court', and demanding political, social, and economic reforms. The *Ulemas'* statement caused a stir because it was considered as a clear sign of dissatisfaction among the conservative religious leaders. It upset the Saudi government, which asked the SCU to issue a statement condemning the document's 'lies'. Seven of the eighteen SCU members did not sign that statement – officially on the ground of 'ill health'. A few months later, all seven, together with three of those who did sign the statement, were compulsorily retired from the SCU for 'health reasons'. Shortly afterwards, King Fahd launched an unprecedented assault on clerics in the kingdom who misused their office so that 'pulpits are no longer being used to reveal what has been established by the Prophet or the Qoran. They are now being used for worldly purposes, or for matters unrelated to the public interest'.

In a direct challenge to the authorities, six of the memorandum signatories announced in May 1993 the formation of Saudi Arabia's first human rights organisation – The Committee for the Defence of Legitimate Rights (CDLR). This was a shrewd move, since it placed the Islamist struggle against the regime within the context of the world-wide human rights movement. Two weeks after its founding, the authorities disbanded the Committee, jailed its spokesman, and dismissed five of its members from their jobs 'in the light of the dictates of the public interest', according to an official source. The founders of the Committee have since continued its activities from London. Through a series of communiqués faxed to Saudi Arabia and world-wide, the CDLR has sought to mobilise public opinion against the monarchy by documenting human rights violations. Despite its bitter attacks, the Committee has advocated moderation and peaceful change in the kingdom on the basis of the *Sharia* principles, mounting an unprecedented challenge to the monarchy by becoming the primary channel of opposition for both the Islamist and non-Islamist critics of the regime. Significantly, two dissident Saudi diplomats sought to associate themselves with the Committee.

In September 1993, the CDLR intensified its propaganda war, triggering a government crackdown and the arrest of Sheikh Al Hawali, an opposition leader. That led to a sermon by Sheikh Salman Al Audah, a dismissed member of the SCU, criticising the Saudi government as 'insufficiently Islamic', which put him in jail. Meanwhile, some citizens of the ultra-conservative central town of Buraida mounted a protest by driving a caravan of cars towards Riyadh, only to face arrest.

There is no doubt that the modernisation of Saudi Arabia presents the Al Saud family and the orthodox Wahhabism with a significant challenge. The kingdom has placed great emphasis on economic and technical development while retaining a traditional political system that continues to rest upon the conservative religious and social order of Wahhabism. The survival of Saudi Arabia, therefore, appears to rest on an aspect of Islamic expression that on the one hand rejects innovation and modernisation but on the other promotes progress.

THE ISSUE OF SUCCESSION

Another issue related to the struggle for power in the Middle East consists of the problem of succession, that could become a major destabilising force. In every autocratic state in the region, the question of who will succeed to the present rulers, most of whom are now ageing, remains open. Although usually the leadership remains within the ruling family, there is no hereditary rule and no obvious succession line in any of the region's states.

To begin in the north with Syria, a successor to the pragmatic President Assad was believed to be his son Basil who died in early 1994. Assad's second son Bachar seems now to be prepared to rule after his father, at a time when Rifaat, the president's brother, is thought to still harbour ambitions for the highest power in Damascus. But the objectives of Assad's family would not be easy to achieve in a country where different groups within or outside the regime seek to retain power as soon as President Assad disappears. This is especially true for the Sunni Muslims who want their majority status to be shown in their power within the regime, now controlled by the Alawi minority.

In neighbouring Iraq, the succession to President Saddam Hussein is likely to be lengthy, disorderly, and perhaps bloody whenever and however it occurs. Although Hussein has been grooming his sons Udai and Qusai for leadership roles, no single person is likely to seize and retain power in Baghdad for an extended period after the departure of Saddam. Civil disturbances, a succession of military strongmen, and intervention from neighbouring countries are more likely than an elected government.

In this respect, Iraq is likely to follow the pattern of countries whose fallen dictators have been followed not only by new leaders but also by a changed system of government, aggravated in the case of Iraq by the crucial fact that the unity of the country is also at stake.

In Iran, the political system is characterised by a struggle for succession that began even before Ayatollah Khomeini's rise to power and the establishment of the Islamic republic. A ferocious jostling for power and influence has almost paralysed an already unstable political system. With the death in 1989 of Khomeini, who assumed full control over the state with the sole right to veto anything of which he disapproved, and who dominated practically all spheres of Iranian life through the clerical machinery at his disposal, Rafsanjani has emerged as the most powerful figure in Iran. His overwhelming victory in the July 1989 presidential election reflected his popularity. His previous service as speaker of the parliament has left him with substantial support in that body, and his term as commander-in-chief of the armed forces has given him the opportunity to establish useful relationships within the military.

Despite this wide base of support, Rafsanjani's power has been circumscribed. As pragmatist, his dedication to the principles of Khomeini is doubted by some of that leader's more extreme followers. Thus, to gain the post of president, Rafsanjani was obliged to reach an accommodation under which the power has been shared with the radical Ayatollah Khamenei who was named 'leader of the Islamic revolution,' occupying the post of *Wali Faqih*. Since then, Iran has been immersed in a silent internal political struggle between the two poles of power, a battle that seems to be unresolved and is likely to continue for many years.

Middle Eastern dynasties appear to clarify the issue of succession by naming a heir apparent (crown prince). Although dampening some of the internal debate on succession, such appointments can lead equally to fresh areas of speculation. This is because the crown prince is often the senior member of the ruling family after the ruler and therefore only slightly less prone to ill-health, disability, or death. In addition, the crown prince is sometimes named as an interim measure until the ruler's own sons come of age or gain government experience. At this point, there is room for a new power struggle between two or more competing branches of the family.

In Jordan, the crown prince was Mohammed, the immediate brother of King Hussein (born in 1935), but on the birth of Hussein's first son Abdallah in 1962, the king named the boy as crown prince. However, due to the fact that Abdallah's mother was British, Hussein was forced to reconsider his choice by appointing his younger brother Hasan (born in

1948) as crown prince. But there is doubt whether Hasan will become king when Hussein dies, and considerable doubt whether he will hold the post for long if he does. After Hasan the line is expected to revert to Hussein's family. The second-in-line has been Prince Ali, Hussein's son from his marriage to Queen Alia.

In Saudi Arabia, disputes between princes over the issue of succession have polarised the apparently unified ranks of the Al Saud. It is believed that once the succession issue is settled, devotion of the princes to the survival of the system would transcend any competition between them. When trying to avoid the perennial question of succession, the royal court, including royal brothers and wives, is torn between two unpalatable choices: the absence of an obvious succession line, just as its existence might have unsettling effects. According to convention, a new Saudi king relies upon the other princes, assembled into an *ad hoc* family committee, to confirm his position by swearing the *Baya* (an oath of allegiance). The *Ulemas* must then declare the new king an *Imam* (Muslim leader) on the basis of a *Fatwa* that the succession is legitimate. The approval of the nation's religious leaders not only authenticates the succession on religious grounds, but also serves as a reminder of the historically close relationship between the House of Saud and the Wahhabi Islamic sect.

Fearing the consequences of rift over the ranking positions, the Saudi royal court has striven to establish a system of checks and balances along the line of succession whereby seniority passes horizontally from the eldest brother to the next brother in age – thus from one maternal branch of the family to another – rather than from father to son. But this system of succession means that, before the second generation of grandsons can mount the throne, the last surviving of the 36 sons[2] of King Abd Al Aziz Bin Abd Al Rahman Bin Faisal Al Saud has to be considered first (see Box 1.3). Age and sickness could allow for minor changes but essentially the system points to gloomy prospects for the grandsons.

The system also means that competition will remain fierce in the short term among the two main maternal branches of the Saudi dynasty: the Shamar tribe to whom Prince Abdallah (Crown Prince and Commander of the National Guard) is affiliated; and the Sudairi tribe to whom King Fahd belongs as well as his other influential full brothers – Sultan (Minister of Defence), Nayef (Minister of Interior), Abd Al Rahman (Deputy Minister of Defence), Turki (former Deputy Minister of Defence), Salman (Governor of Riyadh), and Ahmad (Deputy Minister of Interior). There are other branches, including families and cliques of brothers and half-brothers, sons and grandsons which cut across the traditional divisions that

---

Box 1.3   The Thirty-Six Sons of King Abd Al Aziz (Ibn Saud)

Date of Birth

Year			
1900	*Turki* (A)		
1902	*Saud* (A)		
1904	*Faisal* (B)		
1910	*Mohammed* (C)		
1912	*Khalid* (C)		
1920	*Nasir* (D)	*Saad* (E)	
1921	Fahd (F)		
1922	Mansur (G)		
1923	Musaid (E)	Abdallah (H)	Bandar (I)
1924	Sultan (F)		
1924	*Abd Al Mohsin* (E)		
1926	Mishal (G)		
1928	Mitab (G)		
1931	Abd Al Rahman (F)	Talal (J)	
1932	Mishari (K)		
1933	Nayef (F)	Nawwaf (J)	Badr (L)
1934	Turki (F)	Fawwaz (I)	
1935	Abd Al Illah (L)		
1936	Salman (F)		
1937	Majid (M)	*Thamir* (N)	
1940	Ahmad (F)	Abd Al Majid (L)	Mamdouh (N)
1941	Hidhlul (O)		
1942	Mashhur (N)		
1943	Sattam (M)	Miqrin (P)	
1947	*Hamoud* (Q)		

Notes: Each letter in () following the sons names represents a different mother (A for the mother coming from the Mohammed tribe, B for Jilwa, F for Sudairi, H for Shamar...); thus, names with the same following letters are full blood brothers. Sons whose names are in *italics* are deceased.

---

all expect to play a decisive role with regard to the government's policies. In practice neither group is all that homogeneous, especially when the generation gap parallels the education gap between the orthodox conservative tribal chiefs and the progressive, urban, young and ambitious princes. As early as 1963, a small group of these young princes, named 'Liberal Princes', took refuge in Cairo declaring themselves 'republicans'.

The question of the smooth removal of inadequate rulers regarded by the family as acting against the regime's interests has until now been resolved in Saudi Arabia by unanimous decision of the family council. This was the case in 1964, when King Saud was replaced by his brother, Faisal, who had headed the internal opposition. When the latter was murdered in

1975 by a discontented relative, King Khalid took over but, in mid-1977, the family decided that the poor health required that he should go into semi-retirement and, while retaining the royal title, should cede power to the then Crown Prince Fahd. The latter became king with the death of Khalid in 1982 and Abdallah was selected as crown prince. Fourteen years later, in early 1996, the ailing King Fahd handed over the running of the kingdom for around two months to Prince Abdallah, before resuming his responsibilities.

Prince Abdallah (born in 1923), from the Shamar tribe, has strong support among the *Ulema's* tribes within the western Gulf and the National Guard. Considered as a conservative Muslim who is not enthusiastic about modernisation, Abdallah is popular within the kingdom in spite of (and perhaps because of) his stuttering public manner. A committed horseman, the Saudi crown prince is also believed to be very cautious, tending to see procrastination as a virtue. If and when he takes over from Fahd, Abdallah would nominate his Sudairi half-brother Sultan (born in 1924) as crown prince. Sultan's next five youngest brothers were all born before 1936. This leads us to conclude that the kingdom is facing the prospect of having to appoint a new king every two or three years, together with the consequent instability.

In an attempt to clarify the succession process for some, but making it ambiguous for others, and, in either event, giving a tremendous impetus for manoeuvring within the royal family to obtain the kingdom's ultimate prize, King Fahd in March 1992 issued the Basic Law of Government. The Law states that the throne passes to the sons of Ibn Saud, and to their sons. The most upright among them is to receive allegiance in accordance with the principles of the Qoran and the tradition of the Prophet. More significantly, the Law states that the king can choose his heir apparent from among the next generation (maybe his own children!) and can relieve him of his duties by royal order.

Though on a totally different scale to the feuds of their relatives in Saudi Arabia, Qatar's ruling family is another example where persistent disputes remain in practice unresolved, erupting when events matured. In 1960, the ruling emir was deposed by his son, Sheikh Ahmad Al Thani, with British assistance. In 1972, Ahmad was forcefully removed by his cousin Sheikh Khalifa Bin Hamad Al Thani. A struggle had erupted in 1977–8 over the position of prime minister between Sheikh Suhaim, the former minister for foreign affairs and the younger brother of Sheikh Khalifa, and Sheikh Abd Al Aziz, Khalifa's younger son and the former minister of finance and oil, a rivalry that had engulfed other members of the Al Thani family and the armed forces.

In June 1995, another son of the emir, Sheikh Hamad Bin Khalifa Al Thani (born in 1947), then crown prince and minister of defence, overthrew his father in a bloodless coup. Hamad, in one of his first acts, issued in June 1995 a law stating that the throne passes from the emir to one of his sons or, in their absence, to any chosen relative from the Al Thani family. In the October 1996, Doha announced that the ruling family had agreed to appoint the new emir's third son, Jassim, as crown prince.

Elsewhere in the Gulf, succession issues are of lesser magnitude and either have no urgency or are postponed to the days when the question becomes acute, so as to prevent unnecessary internal rifts from surfacing. In Kuwait, the problem of succession line troubled the royal family for a short while following the death of Emir Sabah Al Salim Al Sabah in December 1977. Uncertainty then prevailed as to the way the dynasty would settle the issue of selecting the crown prince. In the past this was based on rotation between the two branches of Al Sabah – Al Salim and Al Ahmad. This model has recently been broken but the issue was settled swiftly according to the old principle. Then, in 1986 the poor health and other weaknesses of Crown Prince Saad (born in 1924) were partly responsible for a constitutional crisis. Some members of the Al Ahmad family wanted to replace him with Deputy Premier Sabah, a full brother of Emir Jabir Al Sabah. As a result, the emir had to dissolve the parliament which Saad alleged was being filled with Al Ahmad followers who threatened his leadership.

The UAE already has a designated crown prince from Dubai but he may have to overcome the rising power of Sheikh Khalifa Bin Zayed Al Nahyan, the crown prince of Abu Dhabi and the ruler's eldest son. In recent years Khalifa has grown more responsible and has assumed more and more control over Abu Dhabi's day-to-day affairs, which makes him the *de facto* leader of the emirate, ultimately controlling plans and expenditures and authorising major projects.

The next crown prince of Abu Dhabi could come from the Beni Mohammed branch of the Al Nahyan family, namely Tahnoun and Surour Bin Mohammed, the sons of the late Mohammed Bin Khalifa, the senior member of the Nahyan family until his death in 1982, although a number of Zayed's younger sons are becoming more important in emirate affairs, particularly the new commander in chief of the air force, Colonel Mohammed Bin Zayed.

In the absence of an heir to the throne, Oman might witness bitter feuding between claimants for succeeding Sultan Qaboos who overthrew his father Sultan Said Bin Taimur in 1970 in a British-supported coup. Indeed, although the sultan enjoys good health and has effectively eliminated political, religious, and family opposition to his rule, he is unmarried – in fact, divorced after a brief marriage in 1976 – and childless, and is likely to remain so. While the Qaboos regime does not embody a strong male relative, the small royal family includes fewer than 50 males, and none of them has significant personal power.

2 Interstate Ideological Cleavages

There are two basic interstate ideological breaches in the Middle East. One is the division between 'pan-Islamists' and 'pan-Arabists' that overlaps but does not neatly coincide with the second cleavage between 'conservatives' and 'radicals'. These two fractures have been highly penetrated by external influences, attracted by the geostrategic location of the region, its straits and waterways, its petroleum resources and the richness of its history and civilisation.

PAN-ISLAMISM VERSUS PAN-ARABISM

Middle Eastern charismatic leaders have had the ability emotionally to appeal to the people of other states in the region over the heads of their leaders on two grounds: the grounds of Islam, Islamic unity and orthodoxy, and the grounds of Arabism, Arab nationalism and brotherhood, like the ones used by regional demagogues such as Nasser of Egypt and Hussein of Iraq.

Pan-Islamism consists of a general call for all Muslims regardless of ethnic, linguistic, or national affiliation to participate in the revival of Islamic political power. Pan-Islamism reached its height during the medieval Islamic empires of the Umayyad and Abbasid. In the latter part of the nineteenth century, Gamal Al Din Al Afghani called for a spiritual rebirth of the Muslim peoples in order to remove the yoke of European domination. Al Afghani's aim was to ensure a more independent spiritual, intellectual, economic as well as political Islamic world by emphasising Muslim values.

In the late 1970s another call for pan-Islamism was shaped by Ayatollah Khomeini, leader of the Islamic republic in Iran which even before the Islamic revolution, under the rule of the Shah, had been adopting an aggressive policy of regional hegemony. After more than seventeen years of revolution, war and political infighting Iran, is now again a power to be reckoned within the Middle East. Tehran's conviction that it is rightfully the dominant power in the region has been a continuing underpinning for its policy, especially with the temporary removal of Iraq as a barrier to its ambitions in the area.

The clerical nature of the Iranian regime and its pan-Islamic aspirations determine Tehran's responses to a variety of external developments. Iran has developed a system of alliances mainly with Syria and Sudan, and has been assisting Islamic political movements throughout the region, even at the sacrifice of long-standing governmental ties. This is especially true in Lebanon and in the Palestinian territories where the radical *Hizbollah* and *Hamas* movements benefit from the open and full support of Tehran.

All this raises the critical question of how far Iran will go toward achieving hegemony over the Middle East and spreading Islamic revolution throughout the region. Tehran might well conclude that the best way will be a combination of religious righteousness and military might. Even if it does not intend to go beyond intimidation to aggression, the conflicting interests between Iran and other Middle Eastern countries could lead to a volatile situation.

Many already believe that pan-Islamism has failed, and for numerous reasons. The size and diversity of the Islamic world make common recognition almost impossible. What may be considered as essential in one region may not be judged so in another. In fact, there is virtually no harmony of outlook in the Islamic world, given its vast differences in cultural and historical make-up; national frontiers also tend to filter out the more emotional appeals of pan-Islamists. Past efforts to sustain pan-Islamism seem to have been unsuccessful, and in the contemporary era, the concept itself has been considered more as a rallying cry than a valid objective.

Pan-Islamism in the Middle East has been confronted by pan-Arabism which departs from the one-ness of the Arab nation and the belief that existing political boundaries are artificial importations, and political fragmentation is a colonial legacy, channelling sentiments of political allegiance from the state to a larger human and social body. Two major factors have stimulated and reinforced the ideology of pan-Arabism in the contemporary world. One is the common experience of colonialism, under first Ottoman and then French and British rule; the other is the creation and existence of Israel in the midst of the Arab world. Both of these factors emphasise common enemies – colonialism (and later neo-colonialism) and Zionism. Thus, one can say that 'negative' factors (what they universally oppose rather than 'positive' and 'integrative' elements unite Arabs.

Symbolic of the cry for Arab unity and for an Arab reawakening is the Baath movement that emerged in Syria in 1953, and is now the official doctrine of the regimes in Damascus and Baghdad, with party branches in Lebanon and Jordan (see Box 2.1). Baath means 'rebirth and renaissance',

---

Box 2.1   The Baath Movement

The Baath movement first emerged in Syria in 1953 as a result of a fusion between the Arab Socialists headed by Akram Hourani, and the Arab Resurrection Party commanded by Michel Aflaq. Aflaq, a devoted Marxist, proved to be the chief ideologue and spirit behind the Baath. The Baath preaches the removal of foreign influence, the nationalisation of industry, and the creation of extensive social services. These are resumed by three vague principles: Arab unity (with the slogan 'One Arab nation from the Atlantic Ocean to the Gulf'), absolute Arab independence, and socialism with a one-party state.

In Syria, the military wing of the Baath movement took control of the country in 1961 and wrote a new constitution establishing the National Revolutionary Council that comprised both civilian and military leaders of the Baath party. In 1969 another constitution was promulgated, making the Baath the only legal party in the country. In 1970, General Hafez Assad seized power, and one year later presented a new constitution to the nation, a document with which he consolidated his power. Assad and his Baath party has since drawn support from army officers, members of the intelligentsia, white-collar workers, and skilled industrial labour.

In Iraq, Colonel Aref gained control of the government in 1963 and formed the National Council of the Revolutionary Command, weighted in favour of the Baathists. However, following some internal political manoeuvres, Aref disbanded the Baath party. In 1968, General Al Bakr seized power and asked the Baathists to help form his government. The ailing Al Bakr stepped aside in 1980 for the younger Saddam Hussein who has been controlling power in Baghdad since then.

---

and it addresses itself to the felt need of Arabs that they can regain their lost stature by joining in collective union. Nevertheless, the Baath movement has neither promoted unity among Arabs nor reduced hostility even among competing Baathist factions.

Another contemporary ideology stressing Arab unity is the Nasserism which is derived from the philosophy of Gamal Abd Al Nasser. Nasser was the first Arab in several centuries to capture the imagination of Arabs everywhere. He became the symbol of Arab vitality, and by any yardstick the leading Arab figure in the post-Second World War era.

Nasserism is more important for its philosophy than for Nasser's work because he did not succeed in most of his practical endeavours. His humiliating defeat at Israeli hands in 1967 made any achievement difficult and sullied his reputation. He never succeeded in uniting more than two or three countries at one time, while he got involved in a misadventure in the Yemeni civil war. Indeed, three and half years after the creation in February 1958 of the United Arab Republic (UAR) by Egypt and Syria,

Damascus decided to withdraw causing a bitter blow to Nasser's Arab unity dreams. That was followed by the dissolution of a loose association agreed in March 1958 between the UAR and (North) Yemen. Even though Nasser had attempted between 1962 and 1967 militarily to defend the republican regime of (North) Yemen, based in Taiz, against the royalist factions, actively supported by Saudi Arabia, which were clustered around Imam Ahmad's power base in Sanaa. Although Nasser decided to withdraw his forces from Yemen in the aftermath of the 1967 Arab–Israeli conflict, the nationalists proved successful and the Imamate was replaced by the Yemen Arab Republic.

Nasser's 'Philosophy of Revolution' is required reading for all aspiring pan-Arabists. He believed it necessary to promote military prowess, and through physical struggle to achieve the modern goals of the Arab world. According to Nasser, the frustrated, restless Arab world requires a great leader, a Salah Al Din (a historic Muslim figure during the Crusades), to rally the population against foreign intervention, and to rid the region of Western exploiters. Above all, Nasserism symbolises the Arab quest for identity, dignity, and national purpose.

Nasserists who emerged following Nasser's death in 1970 had none of his charisma, compassion, or sense of proportion. The primary exponent of Nasserism in the contemporary Arab world is Libya's Muammar Qaddafi who idolised Nasser. As a young man, he believed that Nasser was destined to rehabilitate Arabdom, to strengthen it, and ultimately, to unify it. Qaddafi seized power in Tripoli in 1969 with a view toward fulfilling Nasser's dream of Arab unity, but his idol's death shortly thereafter left a considerable vacuum, and Nasserism quickly degenerated into internecine conflict.

An institutional translation of pan-Arabism has been the Arab League that was formally constituted in 1945, and currently comprises twenty-two member countries (see Box 2.2). Nevertheless, the Arab League has failed to promote the unity that is supposedly its *raison d'être*. As such, it is more a mirror image of divisions within the Arab world. In fact, during the Nasser era, hostility erupted between the Egyptian president and the leaders of Saudi Arabia and Jordan. War over North Yemen in the 1960s pitted Saudis against Egyptians, and the Arab League was hard put to speak of 'Arab unity'. Similarly, wars between Arabs and Israelis in 1956, 1967 and 1973 failed to produce the united front that the League endeavoured to publicise. The Arab League has not been able to moderate differences between rival Arab states, nor could it prevent Iraq from invading Kuwait in 1990.

Box 2.2   The Arab League

The League of Arab States, or Arab League, was formed in 1944 as the first successful expression of pan-Arabism in this century. The Arab League Pact was formally signed in February 1945. The original members of the League were Egypt, Iraq, Syria, Lebanon, Transjordan, Saudi Arabia, and (North) Yemen. The current twenty-two members of the Arab League are: Algeria, Bahrain, Comoros Islands, Djibouti, Egypt, Iraq, Jordan, Kuwait, Lebanon, Libya, Mauritania, Morocco, Oman, Palestine, Qatar, Saudi Arabia, Somalia, Sudan, Syria, Tunisia, United Arab Emirates, and Yemen. Egypt was expelled in 1979 (and then readmitted in 1982) after the signature of a separate peace treaty with Israel, and the League headquarters were temporarily moved from Cairo to Tunis.

The charter of the Arab League calls for the collective protection of the sovereign independence of all member-states. It also emphasises co-operation with other international organisations, and special attention has been given to Afro–Asian activities. The League works closely with the United Nations, and it has won acceptance of Arabic as an official language of that international body and a number of its specialised agencies.

The supreme organ of the Arab League is the Council, consisting of representatives of the member-states. The daily work of the League is managed by the Secretariat under the leadership of the Secretary-General. The Economic Council created in 1950 comprises the Arab ministers of economic affairs or their representatives. The Council of Arab Economic Unity was created in 1964 by the Economic Council. Its aims are the removal of internal tariffs, the establishment of common external tariffs (CETs), the promotion of labour mobility and capital between the members, and the adoption of common economic policies. Specialised agencies of the League include the Arab Educational, Scientific and Cultural Organisation, the Arab States Broadcasting Union, the Arab Labour Organisation, the Civil Aviation Council of Arab States, the Arab Cities Organisation, the Joint Defence Council, the International Arab Organisation for Social Defence, the Arab Postal Union, the Arab Development Bank (or Financial Institute), and the Arab Common Market.

The Arab League's most celebrated activity has been its opposition to the State of Israel. The creation of the Boycott of Israel Office which blacklisted foreign firms doing business with or in Israel was one such recognised activity. In 1948 the League declared war on Israel, but the organisation could not co-ordinate the actions of the several Arab armies engaged in the conflict. Disagreement in different Arab capitals over the conduct of the war and policy toward the displaced Palestinians led to increased tension between the member states that could not be relieved by the League. The Arab defeat in the 1948 war badly hurt the organisation which has since tried, without any success, to implement a collective security pact, signed in 1950. Under that pact, an armed attack on one of the signatories is regarded as an aggression against all of them.

Although the Arab League has failed to perform much of concrete achievement, many believe that its psychological value as the original symbol of Arab unity sustains it, and that the organisation cannot be judged by its performance alone. It is more a promise than a successful enterprise: achievement must be measured in symbols and spirit, not only in purpose and accomplishment.

However, truth to tell, the concept of pan-Arabism suffers from obvious limitations. There are vast discrepancies between the Arab countries, ranging from such factors as size, population and wealth to religious adherence and social custom. There is basically a common language, but even this is not easily comprehensible from one end of the Arab world to the other. Not only do the Arab countries differ considerably from each other, but they are geographically far-flung, and lack a focal leader country and leader chief. This has led to a continuous struggle for the leadership of the Arab world. In fact, since the middle of the twentieth century, rivalry has existed between Damascus and Baghdad about which ruling clique in which city should be recognised as paramount in the Arab world. Cairo entered the arena with Nasser and staked a claim, but then was partly marginalised following the Camp David accords with Israel in 1979. In the oil decades of the 1970s and 1980s, Riyadh threw its hat into the ring of contenders for Arab leadership, based on Saudi protection of Islam's holy places and windfall affluence from surplus oil revenues. The recent conflicts launched by Iraq were, in part at least, wars over leadership in the Arab region.

It seems that an important change has taken place in the Arab world since the 1960s: nationalism has replaced pan-Arabism as the one of most powerful political forces. Even with leaves sacrifices for Arab goals, none of the common objectives has been achieved, and the Arabs, growing weary of political acrobatics, and having had to surrender what little democracy they had to authoritarian governments, are now more than ever before looking inward toward their own nations for their identity.

CONSERVATISM VERSUS RADICALISM

The division between 'conservative' and 'radical' regimes in the Middle East is a political rather than a religious one, encouraged for a long time by the confrontation between the Western countries and the former socialist bloc. Although the Cold War theoretically ended in the early 1990s, the ideological cross-cutting cleavages in the region remain important.

Typical struggles between conservatives and radicals in the Middle East had been the conflicts between the former socialist regime in South Yemen (which merged within the unified Yemen Arab Republic in May 1990) and its traditionalist neighbours, but more particularly the thirty-one-year guerrilla war between the Omani government and the Soviet-backed Dhofari rebels who desired the liberation of the western Omani province of Dhofar, as well as a socio–political revolution which would extend throughout the Gulf. The rebels were aided by communist states, militant groups of the Palestine Liberation Organisation (PLO), and radical Arab countries especially the neighbouring South Yemeni regime. Determined to crush the rebels, the British-backed Sultan Qaboos recruited the support of the UAE and Saudi Arabia, as well as the military backing of the Iranian Shah who wanted to bolster his own regional position. The rebels were subsequently ejected from Dhofar in 1975.

The radical states in the Middle East are usually secular, run by revolutionary regimes, often dominated by the military or having the militaries as important actors, in which socialism in one form or another is declared an objective and in which Islam is often used as a tool of the state. The present major radical states are Iraq, Syria, and Yemen, as well as Iran (although not in the sense of being socialist or secular), and to some extent Egypt. Nonetheless, as a measure of the new post-Cold War era, many of these states are now taking rapid actions to revise and regularise their relations with Western powers, mainly the USA.

The conservative regimes in the region consist of those monarchies, sultanates, and emirates composed of dynastic families established in either colonial or pre-colonial periods. They exercise absolute and autocratic power that is often tempered by a degree of paternalism (see Chapter 1). They have a vested interest in maintaining political traditionalism together with a strong degree of Islamic orthodoxy. They are anti-secular whilst maintaining strong links with the secular West, and indeed are the main source and the main object of Western support in the Middle East.

With the exception of Yemen all states of the Arabian peninsula – Bahrain, Kuwait, Oman, Qatar, Saudi Arabia, and the UAE – fall into this category. These six Arab monarchies have much in common, including a basic similarity in their political, economic, and social systems. Most have maintained close ties for many years, and bilateral relations with Britain and the USA have been close. With the temporary removal of Iraq and Iran from inclusion in the early 1980s during their war, agreement on co-operation among the six regimes was assured. The outlines of an organisation were drawn up by their foreign ministers in February 1981 and a charter was ratified at a summit of the heads of state in Abu Dhabi in the following May. Thus the Gulf Co-operation Council (GCC) came into existence (see Box 2.3).

Box 2.3   The Gulf Co-operation Council (GCC)

Established in Abu Dhabi in May 1981, the Gulf Co-operation Council (GCC) links Bahrain, Kuwait, Oman, Qatar, Saudi Arabia, and the UAE in a political, military, and economic arrangement aimed at protecting their interests in the Gulf region.

The GCC is not a vehicle for merging different sovereignties into one unified state; political integration is not its chief purpose. The GCC is more concerned with issues of common concern and co-operation. The member-states seek the improvement of commercial and technical relationships and have pledged to exchange information and generally promote the well-being of the region. The GCC intends to seek co-operation and standardisation in economic and financial affairs; commerce, customs, and communications; education and culture; social and health affairs; media and tourism; security and defence; and legislative and administrative affairs.

The GCC has a Supreme Council composed of the leaders of the six member states, that meets twice annually for the purpose of establishing policy. The presidency of the Council rotates in alphabetical order by country. A unit of the Council, the GCC Conciliation Commission, is charged with resolving potential disputes among members. In addition, a Foreign Ministers' Council acts as the executive arm, scheduled to meet every second month. A General Secretariat is established in Riyadh by the Supreme Council to insure the implementation of the GCC's decisions. Two Deputy Secretaries General are selected for economic and political affairs.

The GCC encourages economic, financial, and cultural interaction, but it is particularly concerned with the security of its members. Indeed, security concerns were a principal impetus for the council's creation. Although the GCC has been promoting military co-operation, the member states cannot be expected to cope adequately with the entire range of security threats from outside. Thus, they have taken significant steps to acquire the ability to buy time until the arrival of external help. While some additional protection may come from fellow Arab states, such as Egypt or Syria, GCC security essentially depends on a partnership and an alliance with the West, principally the USA. Clearly, the Western or US role is one of backup, to be invited in when the GCC states cannot handle a threat on their own. In military terms, an 'over-the-horizon' partnership is less than ideal, but it is workable. More importantly, it is the only type of partnership that the GCC states can sustain.

For the USA, reassurance of its friends in the region, especially Saudi Arabia that is the linchpin of its Gulf policy, is just as important as deterrence of regional threats. Nevertheless, US policy in the area poses at least two different problems, the first for Saudi Arabia, the second for the Western allies.

The key question confronting Saudi Arabia is related to its current special connection with the USA based on oil-for-security. That very special relationship and close dependence on the Christian USA by an Arab state whose king claims to be the protector of the holy places of Islam presents the kingdom with its most serious and complex dilemma at a time when Islamic fundamentalist movements are gaining strength across the Middle East. An additional embarrassment to Riyadh in its efforts to keep Saudi citizens supportive of American military protection consists of the fact that the USA is the prime guarantor of the independence and security of Israel, still the kingdom's major public enemy. Even more humiliating for the Saudis is the US practice of balancing advanced weaponry for the kingdom against the qualitative edge it promises to reserve for Israel which has been favored over the other countries in the region.

On the other hand, the USA has always tried to co-ordinate its policy in the region with other industrialised states. But there have been repeated instances of discord about the US effort. Although Western states sometimes work at cross-purposes for the same basic objectives, important nuances and divergences emerge on closer inspection. They reflect structural differences in interests and different perceptions of objectives and appropriate strategies, which in turn seem rooted in divergent role expectations and commercial considerations.

3 Peace through more Military and Arms?

Throughout recorded history, the Middle East has been the arena for sweeping military encounters. Enduring geopolitical struggles between the two great river systems – the Nile and the Tigris/Euphrates – date back to the Pharaonic and Babylonian dynasties. As perhaps the world's most important crossroad, the area has been fought over by Greeks, Romans, Assyrians, Persians, Turks Mongols, Crusaders and, latterly, the imperial powers of nineteenth-century Europe. As Islam spread across this area in the eighth and ninth centuries, it was carried, so to speak, in the saddle-bags of Muslim generals.

The Middle East is still one of the most volatile regions in the world. Since 1945, every state in the area has been involved in at least one war. The core conflict has, inevitably, been the Arab–Israeli struggle (and the related Palestinian problem), which has resulted in three regional wars, two major military actions, and several thousand deaths. Opposition to Israel was, up to 1979 at least, a normative factor of foreign policy for every state in the area. Even after Egypt's decision to sign a peace treaty with Israel in 1979, this consideration continued to dominate inter-Middle Eastern politics, as was evinced by Egypt's prolonged exclusion from the Arab League.

The Arab–Israeli conflict was a source of formal concern to all, particularly after the 1967 war when the Golan Heights, Sinai, the West Bank (including Jerusalem) and the Gaza Strip were occupied. It was a source of private irritation to many, particularly when the PLO, in effect a coalition of individual Palestinian movements under a fairly unified leadership, threatened the security of states such as Jordan in 1970, and Lebanon in 1975 as the Lebanese civil war began. It was also the ideal excuse for Israel in 1978 and 1982 to attempt to act as a regional superpower by attacking the Lebanese territories.

Accompanying the Arab–Israeli confrontation have been two spectacular and grisly conflicts initiated by Iraq. The first, the Iran–Iraq war, which raged from September 1980 until a cease-fire in the summer of 1988, was a conventional conflict, with large regular and irregular armed forces confronting each other with very high levels of fire power and means of destruction, including poison gas. The second was the conflict over Kuwait, which started when the Iraqis invaded the emirate in August 1990, and ended (militarily at least) in March 1991 with the liberation of Kuwait by an allied force.

Alongside these major military confrontations, there has been a constant stream of smaller incidents: brief border skirmishes (Bahrain–Qatar, Egypt–Libya, Egypt–Sudan, Saudi Arabia–Qatar, Saudi Arabia–Yemen, Oman–Ras Al Khaimah, Jordan–Syria, Syria–Iraq; and so on) shows of force (Israel versus all its neighbours); invasions of longer or shorter duration (Turkey in Cyprus, Israel and Syria in Lebanon, Iraq in Iran, and then Iran in Iraq).

This simple listing of military conflicts indicates nothing about their causes and motives, which are complex and specific to each particular theatre or conflict. But what is clear is that many states in the region have interests beyond their immediate territory and physical security. Some have allies and commitments, or definitions of interests (such as 'regional stability' or 'strategic balance') for which they are ultimately ready to fight. These elements have been reinforced by the fact that most regimes in the region have been military or quasi-military. Indeed, Middle Eastern societies have experienced prolonged periods of military government that has been the rule rather than the exception in the region. Even when, *de jure*, regimes are headed by civilians, it may be the case that the power wielders are military officers who have left their uniforms in the closet.

The long list of military conflicts tells us that the Middle East has had more than its share of military violence and, predictably, has devoted more of its human and material resources to defence and war-making than have many other regions of the developing world. That is also proved by the figures. In 1970, Middle Eastern states spent $6.1 billion (in constant 1985 $) on defence. By 1975, that figure had increased to $21 billion – a growth of 3.4 times in real terms. By 1980, spending on defence amounted to $38.2 billion: this would mean more than six-fold real increase in about ten years. To put these figures in perspective, the total gross national product (GNP) of all Middle Eastern states did not even double in real terms during 1977–80 in spite of massive transfers of oil wealth to some states.

In the 1980s, the Middle East accounted for between 30 and 40 per cent of the world's arms imports. In 1985, military spending amounted to $57.3 billion, rising to $63 billion in 1990 and to an estimated $74 billion in the mid-1990s, of which around 78 per cent went to Iran, Iraq and the GCC states (see Table 3.1). These figures may be compared to the whole region's petroleum revenues, which amounted to about $82 billion in 1985, around $97 billion in 1990, and some $100 billion in 1995.

In the meantime, the region has become a producer of arms. Turkey, Egypt, Iraq, Syria, and especially Israel have been developing and producing a wide range of armaments. In addition, the area has seen a gradual build-up of chemical and nuclear proliferation. Indeed, to face the nuclear capabilities of Israel (and to acquire regional and international prestige), Iran, Iraq, Syria and Turkey have been working to develop 'civilian' nuclear programmes, while Saudi Arabia announced plans to tie its own programme in with water desalination. Obviously, the arms industries have a significant influence on the level of military spending since they form powerful pressure groups lobbying for greater allocation of resources to military areas. Moreover, long-range conventional or chemical missiles have been developed and/or acquired by countries in the area, such as the

Table 3.1 Defence indicators in the Middle East, 1995

Country	Military expenditure ($ million)[1]	Military expenditure/ GDP (%)[1]	Active armed forces, 1995[2]
Bahrain	247 (1994)	5.5	10 700
Egypt	3500 (1994–5)	8.2	436 000
Iran	10 000 (1995)[3]	20.0[3]	513 000
Iraq	9000 (1995)[3]	na	382 000
Israel	6500 (1995)	9.0	172 000
Jordan	564 (1995)	9.1	98 600
Kuwait	3400 (1995)	13.3	16 600
Lebanon	278 (1994)	5.5	44 300
Oman	1700 (1995)	14.2	43 500
Qatar	294 (1995)	3.8	11 100
Saudi Arabia	17 200 (1994)	13.8	105 500
Syria	2200 (1992)	6.0	423 000
Turkey	14 000 (1994)	5.6	507 800
UAE	1590 (1994)	4.3	70 000
Yemen	1650 (1993)	7.1	39 500

Notes:
1. *Source*: *World Fact Book 1995* (Washington, DC: CIA, 1995).
2. *Source*: *The Military Balances* (London: IISS, 1995/6).
3. Estimates.
na Not available.

Iraqi Scud missiles which hit Israel and Saudi Arabia during the 1990–1 Gulf war. That in itself has been destabilising the military balances and leading to a rethinking of security in global terms.

The greatest growth in military spending in the Middle East has been in Saudi Arabia that, in its 'ceaseless quest for security' (Safran, 1988), accounted for around half of all regional military expenditure in 1979–82 and about one-third in the late 1980s. Saudi spending has also exceeded by far the combined expenditure of the front-line states bordering Israel–Egypt, Syria, Jordan, and Lebanon. In the early 1990s, the Saudi Defence Ministry that soaks up nearly one-third of the kingdom's yearly budget, was given the green light for arms deals against the background of more general budget cuts, while Riyadh had locked up to some 800 000 barrels per day (b/d) for oil-for-arms barter deals.

While Saudi Arabia is undoubtedly the biggest spender in absolute terms, other Middle Eastern countries in the mid-1990s spent just as much, or more, as a proportion of their gross domestic product (GDP). On this base, spending by Iran and Oman exceeded Saudi levels. The ratio of military spending over GDP, together with the disparity in the level of armed forces (see Table 3.1) are usually used to estimate present and short-term potential military threats.

Saudi Arabia, like every GCC state, learned an important lesson from the conflict over Kuwait that financial aid to powerful neighbours does not guarantee long-term security. In fact, during the Iran–Iraq war of 1980–8, Baghdad was the recipient of tens of billions of dollars in aid from the GCC states. Yet, less than two years after that war ended, Iraq invaded Kuwait. The Gulf Arabs also realised that to ensure military security, they would have to bolster their armed forces to a level at which they would be able to hold off potential invaders.

Consequently, serious efforts within the GCC have been made to implement a collective air-defence system, based on Saudi Arabia's radar capabilities, linked to anti-aircraft missiles and interceptor aircrafts. Joint military manoeuvres, largely bilateral in nature, have become commonplace, and an important exercise takes place nearly every year. Meanwhile, a small 'Peninsula Shield' force, composed mainly of Saudi and Kuwaiti brigades with token contributions for other GCC states, has been established at the Hafr Al Batin military base in northeastern Saudi Arabia, for dispatch to any member state requesting security assistance.

However, the GCC states are under no illusion that they will be able to defeat a determined aggressor. Even in combination, the GCC states are far smaller in total population, armed forces, and industrial base than either Iran or Iraq. The combined number of GCC military personnel is less than 260 000. In contrast, Iraq has 382 000 men under arms while Iran totals just under half a million regular troops and *Pasdaran* (Revolutionary Guards), with several million additional paramilitary forces. Even Israel maintains a standing army of 172 000, with additional 370 000 reservists.

More importantly, GCC military establishments are new and untested. While arms acquisitions have skyrocketed in the last two decades, trained indigenous personnel to operate them are in short supply. In fact, the absorption of large numbers of highly sophisticated weapons, the complex mix of various types of arms from a wide variety of suppliers, the intensive competition for skilled manpower and the lack of combat experience, as well as the differences in outlook and policy goals among the defence institutions of the six member states continue to hinder GCC attempts at self-defence.

With all that in mind, the GCC states have started diversifying aspects of security; in other words, rather than relying only on weaponry, they have also signed military accords in order to deter would-be aggressors. During the 1991–3 period, several bilateral defence agreements were reached with Western powers, mainly the USA, Britain, and France. Russia, China, and India were also wooed to provide the GCC with security assistance. Such a system should in principle cause any potential attacker to pause for thought.

Another aspect of Gulf security – albeit a somewhat shaky one – is the 'Damascus Declaration' of March 1991. Coming in the atmosphere of uphoria immediately after the conflict over Kuwait, it envisaged a security system whereby Egypt and Syria would deploy troops in GCC states to protect them from any attack. GCC enthusiasm for such a system has subsequently declined.

A radical remedy to military threats and arms race in the Middle East was proposed in 1991, consisting of arms control and weapons transfer limitation. The issue has emerged as very difficult, however, due mainly to two factors. The disintegration of the Soviet Union means that the governments of the Commonwealth of Independent States (CIS) may lose control of significant non-conventional military technology and human resources, and at the same time may need to export weapons even at relatively low prices to any interested buyer as a way to acquire badly-needed revenues.

Moreover, given the distrust arising from the Arab–Israeli dispute and other regional issues, there is little inclination to expect recipient restraint. This distrust, combined with arm imbalances and build-ups makes a potentially explosive mixture. That is the very combination which exists in the Middle East and which will be a danger both to its inhabitants and to outside powers with a legitimate concern for its affairs.

It seems that present practices do not any longer consist of arms control and weapons transfer limitation, but of forcing Middle Eastern countries, especially those in the Gulf, to purchase weapons in large quantities in the name of self-defence. These practices and efforts by arms producers will almost certainly exacerbate the financial difficulties faced by these countries. What is more, the present practices are ultimately self-defeating because the extra expenditure only adds to the social and political pressures bubbling away under the surface. Thus, a short-sighted interest in short-term gains could threaten to jeopardise the West's long-term economic and political interests.

AMBITION AND STRUCTURE OF ARMED FORCES

Faced with external and internal potential threats, regimes in the Middle East have always attempted to build loyal and strong armed forces and to enhance their military capability. But whether regimes can depend on their armies as pillars of their own systems and prevent them, in spite of constantly swelling ranks, from becoming a threat to their own existence remains an open question.

In the 1950s and 1960s there had been a tendency to look upon military sectors in the region with some favour. Military officers were seen as modernisers, men with a nationalist vision, a strong sense of discipline and organisation, and a commitment to the values of a meritocracy. For many, the military could build nations, just as they had built their armed forces, out of heterogeneous religious, ethnic, or linguistic particles of their societies. They would transform the economy, develop the infrastructure, expand the educational system, and reward hard work and competence with official recognition and advancement.

However, two decades later, neither the military nor their presumptive class allies were viewed with the same enthusiasm. In fact, heavy outlays on defence and war-making diverted scarce resources away from directly productive investment and human-capital formation (education, health, etc.). In addition, the sums used to augment the states' military capability tended to command a large and growing share of the total budget.

A very important aspect of Middle Eastern military complexes is their tendency to become powerful economic enclaves and, because of their strategic nature, not fully accountable to parliaments or auditors. They are in a position to harness important private-sector clients and, indeed, to invade civilian markets. They own property, productive assets, financial institutions, and they can negotiate foreign and domestic loans and put out contracts. Frequently it is alleged that these assets and points of leverage are used by the officer corps to line their own pockets and those of their clients.

Apart from Israel and its northern (Syria) and southern (Egypt) neighbours in war for a long period, as well as Iraq and Iran whose armed forces were always relatively large owing to their mutual fears and to their regional political ambitions, other Middle Eastern states mainly in the Gulf had relatively small and poorly armed forces that were essentially regarded as an internal arm of the central authority. These forces had been nevertheless the cornerstones of the regimes, while foreign powers, mainly Britain, had been the 'protectors' of these entities from external dangers.

With the oil boom and subsequent economic prosperity came a change of emphasis. The excessive wealth and associated sense of both power and vulnerability pushed the Gulf regimes to modernise and to expand their armed forces. Air forces and navies were established. Security needs were redefined to protect the states not only from external threats but also from unadmitted potential internal challenges.

Thus, enormous quantities of advanced weapons have found their way into the area. But absorbing new and sophisticated weapons called for fundamental changes: more soldiers have been recruited, new training systems have been introduced, officers have been sent for instruction abroad, ranks of non-commissioned officers and especially those of technicians have been swelled, and structure of armed forces has been altered accordingly. That has meant that the new armies have ceased to be the bodyguards of the dynasties and have virtually lost much of their previous characteristics.

This military modernisation has been accompanied by an influx of foreign experts and instructors, often with their dependents. In places like Saudi Arabia and Iran, this has irritated the religious establishment because of the effects of such a visible foreign presence and the ensuing process of Westernisation, not to mention continuing military manoeuvres. In November 1995, four Saudis inspired by the ideologies of Islamic fundamentalists fired a bomb at a US-run National Guard training centre in Riyadh that killed seven people. That was followed in June 1996 by a car bomb destroying a military residential complex in the Saudi town of Dhahran, and killing 24 American soldiers.

The diversification of arms suppliers, which aims at diminishing a country's dependence on one sole supplier, with all the attached military and political implications of limiting the patron's leverage over the client, has created additional problems. Not only is that state's military capability seriously affected by the need to grapple with problems flowing from the existence of a number of different kinds of weapons, their absorption and maintenance, but such a process means the influx of even more foreign military experts.

The concentration of large quantities of weapons in the hands of the military grants the armed forces a capability to seize power. Middle Eastern history is full of examples of military overthrows and in the 1950s and 1960s, coups, counter-coups and aborted coups were a yearly, if not a monthly feature in countries like Iraq, Syria, and Turkey. While several of the revolutionary regimes in the region have to confront the related issue of arming civilian militias and party paramilitary groups, Gulf states have to deal with highly politicised, ambitious young academy-trained officers, who have experienced a sad truth, that of the inability of their highly-equipped and generously-financed armies to protect the nation in time of danger, which has necessitated the appeal to foreign forces. Many of these officers, exposed in the course of their instruction to new ideas, might come to represent a real threat to the present regimes. Indeed, officers returning from external military training could cast their lot in with edu-cated civilian revolutionaries of one type or another. Enlarging the officer corps increases the chances of a military coup, and isolating the army from the main centres of population in a number of large and self-contained military cities (in Saudi Arabia, for example those in Tabuk near Jordan, Khamis Mushait near Yemen, or Hafr Al Batin near the Iraqi–Kuwaiti border) may not necessarily enable a regime to stifle disaffection, though it might provide it with much-needed time.

What seems to be another real potential problem for the GCC states is the large proportion of expatriates in their armed forces. Indeed, the small local communities and the lucrative economic opportunities outside the military sector mean that many locals leave and few join the armed forces. Failure to recruit more locals to the army means that the ratio of ex-patriates to locals can only grow. Indeed, when governments find it more difficult to recruit, they have to compromise on the nationality and standard of their new soldiers as well as having to pay enormous salaries to those serving, both to provide an economic incentive and to create a stake for the army in the well-being of the regime.

Lavish inducements, however, cannot buy from foreigners that sense of commitment and reliability for which the reigning dynasties yearn. Lack of loyalty, homogeneity and cohesiveness calls into question not only the army's readiness to defend its paymasters but also its capability to do so. What is more, there is little to stop ideologically-motivated expatriate officers trying to stage, or help others to stage, a coup. They could well be targets for subversion, although, in general, an expatriate-dominated army would constitute less of a security risk as being less politicised.

The figures showing the ratios of expatriates in Gulf armed forces are striking: in the UAE, the 70 000-man federal army is composed mainly of Omanis (around 50 per cent) and Pakistanis (mainly Baluchis), and even the officer corps is dominated by expatriates. Outstanding among them are Jordanians, although contract officers from Pakistan (some of whom form the backbone of Abu Dhabi's air force), Britain and many other nationalities also serve. Non-nationals dominate all technical positions. The implications of such a composition could be far-reaching, especially since one of the UAE's main concerns is a threat coming from Oman, which has never shelved its aspiration for a 'Greater Oman' including large parts of the emirates of Ras Al Khaimah, Fujairah and Sharjah.

Oman also suffers from the problem of a high ratio of expatriate military staff. The sultanate has absorbed many Yemenis and Pakistanis (Baluchis) into its 43 500-man armed forces. The fact that the latter ethnic group forms three separately manned units could prove difficult for the Omani regime if troubles are to erupt in Pakistan and Baluchistan.

On a more modest scale, Qatar's 11 100-strong armed forces include many Omanis, Yemenis, British, Pakistanis and even Iranians seconded or under contract to the government. But Qataris now comprise the backbone of the officer corps. In Bahrain, around 30 per cent of the 10 700-man armed forces are of Jordanian and Yemeni origins, while Bahraini Shias are not allowed to join the military. Many senior advisers at the internal security organisation are expatriates.

Another potential source of instability, especially in states like the UAE, Saudi Arabia, Iraq, and Iran, consists of the fact that armed forces are under separate commands and control. Indeed, power struggles within the military could prove to be just as unsettling as rivalries between the regular armies and internal and/or external forces. In the UAE, each of the seven emirates insists on maintaining its own separate military force and purchasing its own weapons, regardless of the formal military merger that took place in May 1976. The federal troops are stationed under distinct commands which correspond to the sheikhdoms of the federation, although Abu Dhabi supplies 75 per cent of its own troops to the federal forces. This fragile situation could spell disaster if conflicts were to erupt within the federation.

Saudi Arabia maintains separated armed forces which complement yet counterbalance one another. Internal security is assigned to the police, to the small Royal Guard and, primarily, to the National Guard (the 'White

Army') which is a capable and loyal Bedouin force whose task is to defend the monarch and guard the oil fields. The regular army handles the country's external defence. The classification of the Saudi armed forces is reflected in the internal divisions of the royal court: the National Guard is under the command of Crown Prince Abdallah, while the army is the responsibility of his half-brother Sultan, Minister of Defence and Aviation. The struggle over the control of the forces is part and parcel of the issue of succession to the throne among the contenders for power (see Chapter 1). In March 1964, King Saud mobilised his Royal Guard to help him retain power, while his Crown Prince Faisal, who finally won, countered by ordering the National Guard to surround Saud's forces.

The various forces also differ in their composition. Entrusted with the responsibility for the safety of the royal family, the 60 000-strong National Guard is composed of carefully selected regular and semi-regular dedicated Bedouins mainly of Nejdi origin. They are armed essentially with light and medium weapons. The regular army, air force and navy are together about twice (105 500) the size of the National Guard. Many of the recruits to these regular armed services are of urban origin and are generally thought to be less reliable and less attached to the House of Saud.

In Iraq, in addition to the People's Army, or the 'People's Militia', the Sunni-dominated government has established and always supported a military elite called the Republican Guard, a force that has as prime goal the defence of the regime against any internal and external danger. Both the People's Army and the Republican Guard are dominated by loyal officers, but the Baath regime is clearly putting its eggs in the basket of the latter, to which it still owes its survival, especially since the conflict over Kuwait in 1990–1.

In Iran, the Islamic government has been from the beginning suspicious of the military which was, in fact, seriously disorganised following the collapse of the Shah regime in 1979. Lacking spare parts for the sophisticated equipment that had escaped rust, and suffering from mass desertion and low morale, the Iranian army, with its current 380 000-strong complement, was further weakened by the policy of the Islamic regime. Apart from purging the army, the Islamic government set up an independent 130 000-strong military force, the *Pasdaran* (Revolutionary Guards) who are unquestionably loyal to the clergy, and who are commanded by thousands of *Mullahs* who are assigned to all units, serving as political and spiritual commissars. The *Pasdaran* relations with the army have steadily improved, although they still have closer ties to the Islamic activists than to the regular military.

4 Quarrels over God's Identity

The great monotheistic religions, Judaism, Christianity and Islam were all born in the Middle East. The three religions have subsequently splintered into many sects and have been influenced by different philosophies such as Greek thought, Zoroastrianism and Hinduism. This has resulted in a complex mosaic of beliefs as each wave of religious revelation dominated, but did not eradicate, the previous ones.

Nevertheless, the region remains the heartland of Islam although divided between two main sects, the Sunni and the Shia (see Figure 4.1). The two do not differ on fundamental issues since they draw from the same ultimate sources but Shia teachers and interpreters (*Mujtahids*) have, certainly in theory, greater freedom to alter the application of law since they are regarded as spokesmen of the Hidden Imam. Thus, a complex body of doctrinal differences has developed between the two groups making any attempt of reconciliation extremely difficult, though the origins of the split lie in political rivalries surrounding the legitimacy of succession to the Prophet Mohammed.

The Sunni Muslims, followers of the *Sunna*, or the way, course, rule or manner of conduct of the Prophet are the great Islamic majority (probably 80 per cent). Generally called 'Orthodox' the Sunnis recognise the first four Caliphs (Abu Bakr, Umar, Uthman, and Ali) as *Rashidun*, following the right course. The Caliphs were God's vicegerents on earth, required by law to protect the Muslim community (*Umma*), but always recognised to be fallible mortals. By the same token, contemporary reference to the Islamic state emphasises the sovereignty of God, and the governors as his mere servants.

The Sunni Muslims identify themselves with a highly developed juridical order that regulates the totality of the believer's activities and thoughts. They base their Sunna upon the Qoran, God's word as revealed to the Prophet, and the 'Six Books' of tradition (*Hadith*) that represents the Arabian customary law at the time of the Prophet. For them, Islamic law is the ideal legal system, divine, perfect, eternal, and just. It applies to all people, everywhere. They also insist that the divine law takes precedence over society and state, hence the declarations in Muslim countries that laws that are repugnant to Islam are invalid. In other words, governments that

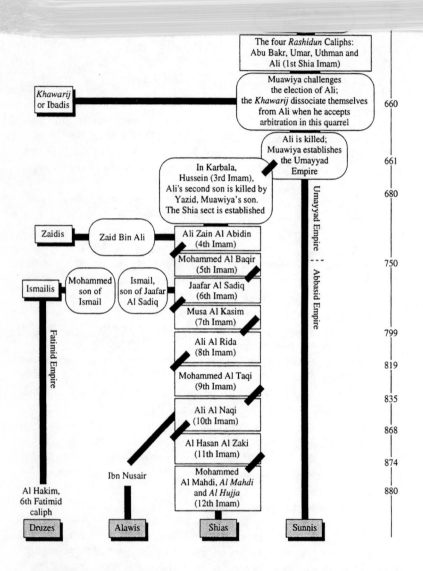

fail to enforce Islamic law are often judged to be beyond the pale and without legitimacy or *raison d'être*.

Controversies in the application of Islamic law produced four major schools of Islamic jurisprudence, which are still in vogue in contemporary

Sunni Islam (see Box 4.1). All these *Mazaheb*, namely Hanafism, Malikism, Shafeism, and Hanbalism, are of equal standing within the Orthodox fold. The four schools were well established by the eleventh century. The *Ijtihad* (discretion or reason) gave then way to *Taqlid* (imitation), accepting the four schools. Sunni Islam has assumed its unchanging character since that period which is known as *Bab Al Ijtihad*, the closing of the door to reason. Subsequent efforts to challenge prevailing doctrine were met with stiff resistance; often the charge of heresy was

---

Box 4.1   The Schools of Sunni Islam

Controversies in the application of Islamic law produced four major schools of jurisprudence, which are still in vogue in contemporary Sunni Islam, namely the Hanafite, Malikite, Shafeite and Hanbalite schools.

The *Hanafite* school (founded by Abu Hanifa, 699–768) is considered to be the most liberal of the four Sunni schools in interpreting the written sources. Abu Hanifa argued that reasoning by analogy (*Qiyas*) is a proper source of law when neither the Qoran nor the *Hadith* (tradition of the Prophet) are helpful in answering a question or resolving a problem. Abu Hanifa's logic especially appeals to non-Arabs who wish to sustain their own characteristic methods and culture. Hanafism was the official rite of the Ottoman Empire, and is now found in modern Turkey and the Indian sub-continent.

The *Malikite* school (established by Malik Ibn Anas, 718–96) is known for its stress on the *Hadith*. The activities of the Prophet as well as the local *Sunna* are presented in the form of *Ijmaa* (consensus of the learned community), which Malik is believed to have spawned. Learned theologians or religious jurists are made responsible for determining the correct path whenever the Qoran is not explicit. The Malikites, however, have their detractors. The opposition argues that *Ijmaa* is a form of man-made law and thus in violation of divine prescription. Nevertheless, Malikite interpretation of Islamic law holds special importance for Muslims in North Africa, Nigeria and Sudan, and it is incorporated in their rituals.

The third school of Islamic jurisprudence is the *Shafeite* (founded by Shafei, 768–820). Reputed to be the most systematic of early Muslim legal theorists, Shafei was critical of local *Ijmaa*, but adopted it when it was possible to have broad community agreement. Shafei rejected that part of the *Sunna* that did not deal directly with, or reflect on, Islamic tradition. He emphasised that only that *Sunna* could be followed which addressed itself to the utterances of the Prophet. Shafei also was more inclined to adopt broad community consensus. Analogy was used sparingly, when none of the other sources of legal performance sufficed. Shafeite doctrine, however, has proved to be weak despite its erudition. The inability to arrive at broad consensus was a key failing, and controversy has followed this school of Islamic jurisprudence to the present day. The Shafeite school is prominent in Egypt, the Levant, south Arabia, and Far Eastern Asia.

Box 4.1   The Schools of Sunni Islam   (continued)

The fourth school of Sunni jurisprudence is the Hanbalite (established by Ahmed Ibn Hanbal) ... ... Taymiyah insisted that only the Qoran and the *Hadith* are acceptable, and sought a return to the pristine purity of early Islam. He condemned any kind of innovation, mystical expression (sufism), lax sexual practices, superstition, or saint worship. The Hanbalite school developed by Taymiyah ultimately gave rise to Wahhabism, the Islamic practice that permeates Saudi Arabia and Qatar.

Wahhabism was founded in the eighteenth century by an austere Muslim theologian and jurist from Nejd, Mohammed Bin Abd Al Wahhab (1703–87) who was influenced by the Hanbalite school of jurisprudence. Wahhab preached a simple return to faith and an absolute obedience to the tenets of the religion. He engaged his son-in-law, Mohammed Ibn Saud, a local leader of a central Arabian tribe, to assist him in spreading a doctrine of discipline, sacrifice, and piety. After many bloody adventures and deceptions, the Wahhabis surfaced again with Abd Al Aziz Ibn Saud who, in the name of Wahhabism, defeated his two rivals, the Rashidies and the Hashemites, in their respective strongholds following the First World War. By the end of 1925, the Sauds already held the Islamic holy cities and Jeddah. They then occupied what is now the Kingdom of Saudi Arabia. Wahhabism is also found in Qatar, where it is the school followed by the Al Thani ruling family.

directed at those who appeared to modify the precepts of Islamic Sunni tradition.

According to the Shia *Hadith*, the Prophet named his cousin and son-in-law Ali Bin Abi Talib as successor before his death. Ali was one of those who had received the dictation of the Qoran, and had been Mohammed's first convert. But in accordance with Arab tribal custom, an election was held and a senior clansman, Abu Bakr, was instead chosen as Caliph. Although Ali refused to yield his claim, he retired from political life so as not to further split the community. The Shias believe that both Abu Bakr and his successor Umar were unsuited to the post and made unwise decisions. The third contest was between Ali and Uthman who, although his father belonged to the Umayyad clan that had opposed Mohammed, was chosen when Ali refused to endorse or accept all the decisions of his two predecessors. After the assassination of Uthman, Ali was elected Caliph in his own right, but chaotic conditions, constant warfare and intrigue eventually resulted in his assassination. For the Shia Muslims, Ali is believed to have been endowed with divine authority, with the secret knowledge to interpret the Qoran, to be the repository of Islamic truth, and special powers were ascribed to his person. In dying, Ali became legendary for his courage, humbleness, wisdom, and generosity to his murderer.

The reign of Ali's successor Muawiya, an Umayyad man, was stormy because he had allegedly made an agreement to restore the Caliphate to Ali's family but failed to honour his promise and named his own son Yazid as his successor. Meanwhile, Ali's oldest son Hasan was mysteriously poisoned. Hussein, Ali's second son, decided to lead a revolt but was seized by Yazid forces and forced to camp on the desert of Karbala in Iraq.

Ten days later (on *Ashura* or the tenth of the *Hejir* month of *Muharram*), the forces of Yazid and Hussein met in battle in Karbala where Hussein was killed. For the Shias, the death of Hussein perverted Islam and prevented the fulfilment of its promise of a just social system. Thus, the focus of Shia Muslims has since been on the perennial conflict between corruption and oppressive tyranny, and has emphasised steadfast dedication to real truth. The legitimist Shias pay allegiance to Ali and Hussein who are accorded exalted positions; some extreme Shia sects even grant them a sort of divinity.

Persecution and death stalked the Shias as successive Sunni Caliphs sought to destroy their faith. The Shia response was to practice quietism or dissimulation (*Taqiyya*)) to hide their beliefs for fear of persecution. Other Shias, however, risked martyrdom in the tradition of Ali and Hussein, and with time martyrdom became the core of the Shia belief system.

The by-far largest Shia school is the *Ithnaashariya* or Twelvers, acknowledging a succession of twelve infallible Imams (see Box 4.2). The last Shia Imam, Mohammed Al Mahdi, disappeared in the year 878 but the Twelvers believe he is still alive and will reappear in the last days before the 'Day of Judgement' as *Al Mahdi* (Guided One) – a sort of Messiah – who will rule personally by divine right. Until the return of *Al Mahdi*, the *Mullahs* serve in his place. In 1502 the Twelvers became the established school in Iran under the Safavid ruler Sultan Shah Ismail who claimed descent from Musa Al Kazim. Twelvers are also found in southern Iraq, Bahrain, the Saudi eastern province, Lebanon, Kuwait, Oman, Qatar and the UAE.

The other schools of Shia are considered to be independent groupings, namely the Ismailis, Druzes, Alawis, Zaidis and Ibadis. The Ibadis are commonly held to have their origins in the *Khawarij* who dissociated themselves from Ali when he accepted arbitration in his quarrel with Muawiya. The *Khawarij* recognised only the first two Caliphs, and claimed the right to elect the Imam from the universality of the Muslim population. Other *Khawarij* rejected all governments and insisted on the rule of God through a Council of Elders. The *Khawarij* were persecuted unmercilessly, and the

---

ʋox 4.2   The Twelve Imams Recognised by the Shia Twelvers

According to the Shia Twelvers, a dozen infallible males served as the legitimate rulers of the Muslim community following the death of the Prophet Mohammed:

  (1) Ali Bin Abi Talib, cousin and son-in-law of the Prophet
  (2) Al Hasan, son of Ali
  (3) Al Hussein, second son of Ali
  (4) Ali Zain Al Abidin, son of Hussein
  (5) Mohammed Al Baqir, son of Ali Zain Al Abidin
  (6) Jaafar Al Sadiq, son of Mohammed Al Baqir
  (7) Musa Al Kazim, son of Jaafar Al Sadiq
  (8) Ali Al Rida, son of Musa Al Kazim
  (9) Mohammed Al Taqi, son of Ali Al Rida
(10) Ali Al Naqi, son of Mohammed Al Taqi
(11) Al Hasan Al Zaki, son of Ali Al Naqi
(12) Mohammed Al Mahdi, son of Al Hasan Bin Ali, known as *Al Hujja* (the Proof), disappeared in the year 878 but the Twelvers believe he is still alive and will reappear in the last days before the 'Day of Judgement' as *Al Mahdi* (Guided One) – a sort of Messiah – who will rule personally by divine right.

---

survivors sought refuge in the southern wastelands of the Arabian peninsula where their descendants, the Ibadis, are found today. Omani Ibadis can be divided into two groups: the more secular, worldly Ibadis who rule Oman, and the more austere hinterland ones.

SECTARIAN MINORITIES

Nowadays, every country in the Middle East, apart from Israel, has a Muslim majority. Based on the fact that the Middle East as a whole is predominantly Sunni, that Iran is the heart of Shia, and that Ibadism is the national religion in Oman, every other Islamic and non-Islamic sect is considered as minority. Statistics on sectarian composition of the region's countries are controversial and those quoted in Table 4.1 must be treated only as estimates.

Islamic Minorities

Shias

Excluding Iran, Oman, Lebanon and Israel, all Middle Eastern states have Sunni regimes governing Shias. In Iraq, Bahrain, and the emirate of Dubai,

Table 4.1　Sectarian composition of Middle Eastern States, 1995 (estimates, %)

Country	Religious grouping[2]											
	A	B	C	D	E	F	G	H	I	J	K	L
Bahrain	40	60	–	–	–	–	–	–	–	–	–	–
Egypt	92	1	–	–	–	–	–	7	–	–	–	–
Iran	7	86	4	–	–	–	–	1	–	1	1	–
Iraq	40	56	–	–	–	–	–	4	–	–	–	–
Israel	12	1	–	2	–	–	–	2	83	–	–	–
Jordan	93	–	–	–	–	–	–	–	7	–	–	–
Kuwait	70	24	–	–	–	–	–	4	–	–	–	2
Lebanon	20	27	–	7	1	–	–	46	–	–	–	–
Oman	25	7	–	–	–	–	75	–	–	–	–	3
Qatar	80	15	–	–	–	–	–	2	–	–	–	3
Saudi Arabia	93	5	–	–	–	–	–	1	–	–	–	1
Syria	74	–	1	3	12	–	–	10	–	–	–	–
Turkey	80	2	–	–	15	–	–	3	–	–	–	–
UAE	75	16	–	–	–	–	–	4	–	–	–	5
Yemen	53	2	1	1	–	40	–	1	1	–	–	1

Notes:
1. *Sources*: *World Fact Book 1995* (Washington, DC: CIA, 1995), and various others.
2. A = Sunnis
   B = Shias
   C = Ismailis
   D = Druzes
   E = Alawis
   F = Zaidis
   G = Ibadis
   H = Christians
   I = Jews
   J = Zoroastrians
   K = Bahais
   L = Others
   – = non-existent

Shias form the majority of population; in Kuwait and in Qatar they constitute around 24 and 15 per cent of the inhabitants respectively. For the bigger
states (Saudi Arabia and Iraq) their importance lies in their populating – like
the Kurds – the sensitive petroleum-bearing regions. The rise of an Islamic
Shia regime to power in Tehran in 1979 inspired this leaderless, scattered
community to voice their protest in a more confident way than ever before.
The Shias thus came to be regarded as a security threat.

Yet the sectarian problem remains at the official level, but also at the popular one considering that since 1979 a growing irritation has been felt between Sunnis and Shias in the region's countries. It could be despair which could make the sectarian issue surface aggressively once again even though the Shia community is far from being a homogeneous group because of their disparate origins and subordinate economic status. That the Shias in one country might join other organisations which would oppose the regimes by championing their grievances remains a possibility much feared by the authorities, who are also worried that tension in one state could spill over to its neighbours. This potential challenge remains great in Bahrain, Kuwait, Saudi Arabia, and especially Iraq.

Bahrain   The Bahraini Shia community (around 60 per cent of the population) is composed of Arabs (mainly of Iraqi origin) and non-Arabic-speaking Iranians who came there either in the nineteenth century or following the discovery of oil. They are not allowed to join the armed forces, and to a large extent are denied access to the country's wealth, despite the fact that many of them form the backbone of the urban middle class. The merchants among them are pushed aside by the preferential positions acquired by a royal family increasingly preoccupied with trade. Moreover, the Al Khalifa Sunni dynasty favours their kin despite the fact that more than 50 per cent of them are illiterate.

The Iranian revolution encouraged Bahraini Shias to break out in demonstrations in 1979 and 1980 when the government was forced to use tough measures to disperse them. But the limited support the authorities then obtained from the more affluent urban Shias reflected the latter's concern at the possibility of this chain of events repeating itself. That what has actually happened since late 1994 following violent riots led by the Shia leader Sheikh Salman and the Islamic Front for the Liberation of Bahrain (IFLB) asking for more rights for the Shia community and for a return to the parliamentary regime (see Chapter 1). The government has again used tough measures against rioters, arguing that 'a foreign neighbouring power' is behind them.

Kuwait   Kuwait's Shia community is fairly small (about 24 per cent of the population), and its history is essentially one of quiescence. In the 1970s, the spreading of Kuwait's wealth meant that there was little in common between its Shia minority and the poor Iranian masses. But the rise of the Islamic republic changed all that, and the Shias who staged large supportive demonstrations in Kuwait during the 1979 occupation of the US embassy in Tehran, and who were linked to the 1984 attack against the US embassy in Kuwait City, came to be regarded as a menace which further complicated the emirate's demographic mosaic.

Precautions have therefore been taken since the Iranian revolution, and the authorities have clamped down on any sign of Shia unease. During the Iraqi invasion, the Kuwaiti Shia had shown true nationalism, and that has allowed them to become more integrated in political life and to be strongly represented in the 1992 and 1996 parliaments.

Saudi Arabia If the Kuwaitis were aware of the seeds of dissent contained in the presence of Shias, the Shia rising in Al Hasa (the Saudi eastern province), which took place in 1979 during the Mecca siege, alarmed the Sauds. This was primarily, though not exclusively, owing to the strategic importance of the eastern province where most of oil fields are located. Indeed, any upheaval in this territory could bring the Saudi oil industry to a standstill, as shown during the Aramco labour strikes in 1953 and 1956 that had concentrated on protesting against working conditions.

The estimated 500 000-strong Shia community in Al Hasa (a very small Shia folk is also living in the Asir region, adjacent to the western border with Yemen) comprises a large share of the workers in oil fields and terminals there. Shias form just over half of the indigenous population of the area which the government are attempting to dilute primarily with Sunnis from Nejd in central Arabia. Although many Saudi Shias are of Bahraini, Iranian and Iraqi origins, they claim to be descendants of the old inhabitants of Al Hasa.

As they did in the mid-1950s and late 1960s, the Saudi Shias protested bitterly in 1979 and 1980 against their inferior economic status, the squalid conditions in which they live and the discrimination they face at being excluded from the bureaucracy and the military. They asked for a better share in the country's wealth, especially since they are responsible for extracting oil and populating Jubail, the new industrial site situated on the Gulf to the north of the Juaymah and Ras Tannura oil terminals.

In 1993, five years after the execution of four Saudi Shias convicted of sabotaging a petrochemical plant in Al Hasa and collaborating with Iran, a limited accommodation was reportedly reached between Riyadh and its Shia minority. That arrangement provided for the safe return of hundreds of Shia dissidents who fled the Kingdom during the 1970s and 1980s. More generally, Riyadh pledged to end discrimination towards those Shias seeking employment in the Saudi public sector. In return, the Shia leaders committed themselves, and their community, to political quiescence. However, the emergence three years later of a Shia militancy which called itself the 'Saudi *Hizbollah*' reflects in part the break-down of the 1993 agreement.

Iraq   In Iraq, the Shia problem is of a totally different magnitude. With the rise of the Islamic republic, Iran and Iraq were on a collision course. The Baath secular Sunni regime feared that its narrow power base might be manipulated by its eastern neighbour's clergy in a way that might foment unrest among the country's Shias, exacerbating the old sectarian rift within Iraq. But Shia dissent did not start with the Iranian revolution and its express and implicit support. Riots in Najaf and Karbala, the Shia's religious centres and strongholds, were common in Iraq's history.

The Shia community is economically backward, although it forms about 56 per cent of Iraq's inhabitants and populates the wealth-producing southern rural part of the country as a demographic buffer between the rest of the Gulf and the 'Sunni Triangle' (the area ranging from Baghdad to Mosul in the north and down to Rutbah in the west and which does not embody any of Iraq's major oil fields). So at the centre of the challenge to the Baathist regime lie not only religious but also economic grievances. Nevertheless, the lack of leadership among Shias made it easier for the Baath to consolidate its position. In addition, Iraqi Shias are not by any means united. They are not monolithic and have various factions. Their clerics are only one of several centres of influence. Moreover, not all Shias are Islamists; some are secularists seeking a separation of religion and state.

One of the latest rounds of repression by the government in Baghdad against the Shias in Iraq dated from January 1990 when the regime carried out a military campaign in which as many as 10 000 people were reportedly killed or injured, although Saddam Hussein acknowledged the fact that Iraqi Shias had remained overwhelmingly loyal throughout the years of his war with Iran (1980–8). Another round of repression occurred in spring 1991 following the retreat of Iraqi forces from Kuwait, succeeded in August 1992 by the UN extension of an air-exclusion zone below the 32nd parallel, denying access for Iraqi aircraft to the southern (Shia) third of the country.

Ismailis

The Ismailis, an Islamic minority living in Iran, Syria, and Yemen, are a group of Shias which do not recognise Musa Al Kazim as seventh Imam, but hold that the last Imam visible on earth was Ismail, son of Jaafar Al

Sadiq. For this reason, the Ismailis are also called the *Sabiya* or Seveners. There is, however, much disagreement among the Seveners as to whether they recognised Ismail himself as seventh Imam or one of his several sons. The Fatimid Ismaili group in Egypt (tenth-twelfth centuries) recognised a son of Ismail's son Mohammed as the seventh Imam. Schismatic off-shoots from the Fatimid Ismaili group are the Druzes, the Nizari Ismailis, of whom Agha Khan is the spiritual head, and the Mustaalians that first settled in Yemen but are now based in Bombay. These sects have an abundant secret literature embodying their esoteric philosophies.

Ismaili groups are socially very active and a large Ismaili institute, sponsored by Agha Khan, was opened in London in 1985. Nevertheless, the Ismailis have not shown any political activity in the recent past.

Druzes

The full origin of the Druze sect and its subsequent expansion are still obscure. The sect is one off-shoot of the Fatimid Ismailis that recognise a son of Ismail's son Mohammed as the seventh Imam. The Druze community acknowledges one god and believes that he has on many occasions become incarnate in man. His last appearance was in the person of the Fatimid Caliph Al Hakim (disappeared in 1020). Al Hakim's *Vizier* (principal advisor) established the ritual and ceremony that are followed by the Druze community today. Their name derives from Al Darazi, a missionary of Persian origin who brought about the conversion of the mountaineers in Lebanon, Syria, and Palestine to the belief of the divine origin of the Fatimid Caliph. Although an off-shoot of Islam, Muslims perceive the Druzes as heretics because for them the Prophet is deemed to be the last of God's messengers.

In 1921, the French mandatory power in Syria recognised the political autonomy of the *Djebel Druze* to the southwest of Damascus. The French refused to honour their agreement, however, precipitating a revolt by the Druze community in 1926–7. In 1939, the Druzes chased all non-Druze Syrian officials from the *Djebel* that was declared independent under the protection of the French Vichy regime. When the Free French forces of Charles de Gaulle assumed power in Syria in 1940, the country was again unified.

Druze opposition to the Syrian military dictatorship of Adib Shishakli led to an uprising in 1953–4 in the *Djebel* under the leadership of Sultan Al Attrach, the Syrian Druze leader, together with some small opposition parties. The government in Damascus subsequently crushed the movement after many weeks of fighting. Druzes were also deeply involved in the family and tribal conflict in Lebanon in 1958, and again during the Lebanese civil war between 1975 and 1990.

Numbering approximately 55 000, the Druzes of Israel have the status of an autonomous religious community with their own spiritual leadership and religious court system. Druzes reside in the Galilee and on Mount Carmel. Unlike Arab Israelis who are not expected to serve in the Israeli's armed forces, the Druzes of Israel have been required to do compulsory service since 1957.

After Syria's loss to Israel in the 1967 war, the 35 000-strong Druze community on the Golan Heights came under Israeli administration. Before the decision of Israel to absorb the Golan, rumours were heard that Tel Aviv contemplated the creation there of an independent Druze state. In the aftermath of Israel's invasion into Lebanon in June 1982, the idea of establishing a Druze state between southern Lebanon and Syria was again surfaced.

Alawis

The Alawis, also called Nusairis (referring to Ibn Nusair), believe that the Prophet Mohammed was a mere forerunner of Ali, and that the latter was an incarnation of *Allah* (God). This Shia extremist sect, established in the ninth century, has also adopted practices of both Christian and pagan origins.

As for the Druzes, there were some plans during the French mandate over Syria to establish a nation for Alawis, which had to be located in the northwestern Syrian region of Lattakia where most of its members live today, mostly incorporated within the Baath regime under the Alawi President Hafez Assad.

Many Alawis, mostly of Kurdish origin, are living in Turkey. Some estimates put their numbers at around 20 million, although this figure seems exaggerated. Like Kurds, Turkish Alawis are deprived of their political and religious rights, a fact that led in 1979, 1980, and in early 1995 to many violent clashes between them and government forces.

Zaidis

The Zaidis are followers of a liberal and moderate sect of the Shia, close enough to the Sunni Muslims to call themselves the 'Fifth School' (*Al Mazhab Al Khamis*). Their name is derived from a grandson of Hussein Bin Ali, called Zaid Bin Ali whom they recognise as the fifth Imam. The

Zaidis, unlike other Shias, do not believe in the Hidden Imam, and reject the religious dissimulation or quietism historically adopted by Shias for fear of persecution.

Zaidism is an important Islamic School in Yemen (around 40 per cent of the population), its main centres being Sanaa and Dhamar. But although they have lived side-by-side with the Sunni Muslims (Shafeites) of the southern Arabian peninsula for centuries, conflicts have not been avoided and carry on down to the present day.

Indeed, the politics of the region is often determined by the Sunni–Zaidi rivalry. The Zaidi Imam Ahmad was associated with the United Arab Republic (UAR) established by Egypt and Syria in 1958, but the experiment failed when Nasser demanded far more than the Zaidis were prepared to grant. When Imam Ahmad died in September 1962, Nasser sponsored a coup that overthrew his successor, Imam Mohammed Al Badr, and established a republican regime in Taiz. Al Badr gathered loyal forces and a five-year war that involved significant numbers of Egyptians started. The Yemeni population was split between the Sunnis (Shafeites) who supported the coup leaders and the Egyptians, on the one hand, and the Zaidis loyal to their Imam, who were assisted by the Saudis, on the other. Although Nasser decided to withdraw his forces from Yemen in the aftermath of the 1967 Arab–Israeli conflict, the nationalists proved successful and the Yemen Arab Republic replaced the Imamate. But although the Sunnis were the technical winners, power in the new government remained in Zaidi hands.

Non-Islamic Minorities

Following the adoption by the Roman Empire of Christianity as official religion in the early fourth century, the Christian Church came to be based on the five leading cities, Jerusalem, Rome, Constantinople, Alexandria, and Antioch. From the divergent development of four ecclesiastical provinces there soon emerged four separate churches: the Roman Catholic or Latin Church (from Rome), the Greek Orthodox Church (from Constantinople), the Syrian or Jacobite Church (from Antioch), and the Coptic Church (from Alexandria). Later divisions resulted in the emergence of the Armenian (Gregorian) Church that was founded in the fourth century, and the Nestorian Church which grew up in the fifth century in Syria, Mesopotamia, and Iran following the teaching of Nestorius of Cilicia (died in 431). From the seventh century onwards, followers of St Maron began to establish themselves in northern Lebanon, laying the foundations of the Maronite Church.

Subsequently, the Uniate Churches were brought into existence by the renunciation by formerly independent churches of doctrines regarded as heretical by the Roman Church, and by the acknowledgement of Papal supremacy. These churches – the Armenian Catholic, the Chaldean (Nestorian) Catholic, the Greek Catholic, the Coptic Catholic, the Syrian Catholic and the Maronite Church – did, however, retain their Oriental customs and rites. The independent churches continued in existence alongside the Uniate Churches.

Thus many Christian minorities are found in the Middle East but from innumerable sects. In Islamic states, these minorities (including Jews) are reduced to a second-class citizenship inferior to Muslims. There is evidence that the recent rise of Islamic fundamentalism has compounded the minority problem, and non-Muslims, such as Copts in Egypt, feel more threatened than ever. The Copts are the most numerous Christian minority in the region, with between 4 and 6 million adherents. The Greek Orthodox are the most important in Syria, Jordan, and the Palestinian territories, while the Maronites and Greek Catholics are most numerous in Lebanon and Israel respectively. Iraq and Iran have substantial numbers of Christians, especially Chaldean Catholics and Armenian Orthodox. The political activism of Christians in the region is limited to some sectarian parties in Lebanon.

Before the establishment of the State of Israel, Jews formed large and old-established minorities in most countries of the Middle East. Since 1948, due to the Arab persecution and the attraction of a Jewish state, there has been a large-scale migration of around 800 000 Jews from Arab countries to Israel, so that only a small number remains, chiefly in Yemen.

The Jews in Israel are divided between the Ashkenazis and the Sephardis, the former originating from east, central, and northern Europe, the latter from Spain, the Balkans, the Middle East, and North Africa. The majority of immigrants into Israel were Ashkenazis, and their influence predominates there due to their role in establishing Zionism and the State of Israel, though the Hebrew language follows Sephardim usage. There is no doctrinal difference between the two communities, but they observe distinct rituals. Some Sephardis accuse the Ashkenazis of discrimination and some of them have established groups calling for co-operation between 'native Middle Easterns' (Sephardis, Palestinians, and other Arabs) against 'Western colonisers' (by which they mean the Ashkenazis).

Zoroastrianism is another non-islamic sect found in the Middle East; it is technically a monotheistic faith, but retains some elements of polytheism, and later became associated with fire-worship. It was developed from the teaching of Zoroaster (or Zarathustra) who lived in Iran some time between 799 and 550 BC. Later adopted as the official religion of the

Persian Empire, Zoroastrianism remained predominant in Iran until the rise of Islam. Some 50 000 Zoroastrians are still living in Iran where the city of Yazd was the ancient centre of Zoroastrianism and was later used as a retreat during the Arab conquest. It is still a centre for the faith (although of minor importance) containing five fire temples. Many adherents were forced by persecution to emigrate and the main centre of Zoroastrian faith is now Bombay where adherents are known as *Parsees*.

Another sect, Bahaism developed in the mid-nineteenth century from the teaching of the *Bab*, or Gateway (to truth), Saiyid Ali Mohammed of Shiraz (1821–59) who was opposed to the corrupt Shia clergy in Iran of his days and was executed. His remains were later taken to Haifa and buried in a mausoleum on the slopes of Mount Carmel. Meanwhile, Mirza Hussein Ali Bahaullah (1817–92) experienced a spiritual revelation while in prison and, in 1863, declared himself to be 'he to whom *Allah* shall manifest' as predicted by the *Bab*. He died at Acre in Palestine and is buried beside the *Bab*. Meanwhile, in 1846, the Bahais declared their secession from Islam, claiming independence from all other faiths.

The Bahais believe that the basic principles of the great religions of the world are in complete harmony and that their aims and functions are complementary. Other tenets include belief in human brotherhood, opposition to racial and colour discrimination, equality of sexes, progress towards world peace, monogamy, chastity and encouragement of family life. Bahaism has no priesthood and discourages asceticism, monasticism and mystic pantheism. The shrine and gardens of the *Bab* on Mount Carmel in Haifa remain the world centre of the Bahai faith. Pilgrims visit this centre and another in Acre, where Bahaullah was imprisoned. Most of Middle Eastern Bahais live in Iran, but since the Islamic revolution there they have suffered from severe official persecution. A 'Guardian of *Allah*'s Command' presides over the elected Bahai assembly of the community (*Bait Al Adli Umumi*), with local assemblies in some 200 countries.

RELIGIOUS RIVALRY

The religious life of the Middle East has brought enrichment and unity but also conflict and persecution throughout the centuries and to the present day. The dividing line between religion and politics in the area is very narrow, and many national leaders have not hesitated to use religion as a populist political ideology.

Apart from Lebanon that has experienced a multi-confessional political regime, but especially from Iran, Oman, and Israel, every rule in the region is predominantly Muslim Sunni. Rivalries between Sunni and non-Sunni regimes have been implicitly but frequently seen within the interstate relations in the area. In addition, the transcendence of religious sects through political boundaries has been the cause of conflicting loyalties, and of political intervention in name of sect protection.

Iran is the centre of Shia in the Islamic world and as such acts as a potential focus of loyalty for Shia minorities in many other countries of the region. At one time Iran was seen, at least by its own advocates, as the model for secularising, modernising and Westernising Islamic states. But, following the success of the Islamic revolution in Tehran in 1979, Iran became the source and driving force of the Islamic fundamentalist revival – a development that posed a potential threat to established governments in the Middle East, especially for those which have secularist and conservative aspirations for their countries.

In Oman, the official religion of the state is Ibadism. The Ibadis, who had often suffered persecution, broke off from the main stream of Islam in the early days, and are usually regarded as *Khawarij* and heretics by the *Ulemas'* chief in Saudi Arabia, among others. As yet, no serious religious conflict has erupted between Ibadi Oman and its neighbours, but the risk remains present and can be used as a catalyst, especially if additional factors are found. Nevertheless, in 1954, the Ibadi Imam of Muscat and Oman (the old name of the Sultanate of Oman), helped by Saudi Arabia, declared the independence of an Ibadi state in the Buraimi oasis and sought membership in the Arab League. The movement was then crushed in October 1955 by forces from Abu Dhabi and Muscat under British command.

The establishment in 1948 of Israel, the world's only Jewish state, in the Middle East, the heartland of Islam, has resulted in the longest-running and most serious regional conflict that has dominated the geopolitics of the area. Apart from the continuing saga of minor incidents, this struggle has turned into three hot wars and many major military actions. The significance of this issue is that it directly interests all Arabs and Muslims and provides them with their most obvious focal point.

The interstate religious rivalries have been aggravated by the location of holy places in different countries of the region. In Islam, Mecca in Saudi Arabia is the most significant centre for pilgrimage. The Qoran commands as a duty of every Muslim to go on the *Hajj* (pilgrimage) to Mecca at least once in a lifetime. In July 1987, murderous incidents opposed Iranian Shia pilgrims in Mecca with Saudi security forces, and officially led to the death of 402 people of which 275 were Iranians. Since then, Tehran has been accusing Riyadh of obstructing Iranian pilgrims wishing to perform the *Hajj*, putting in question the role of the kingdom as the protector of

Islamic holy places. It seems that both countries have since reached an implicit agreement on the number of Iranian pilgrims to be annually allowed to accomplish the *Hajj* as part of a system of national quotas given to each country, computed according to the size of its (Islamic) population.

Following the incidents of July 1987, King Fahd started titling himself 'Servant of the Two Holy Places', referring to both Mecca and Medina, the second Islamic city from where the Prophet Mohammed set out to conquer Mecca. The Islamic holy places in Jerusalem, especially the Dome of the Rock and the famous *Al Masjid Al Aqsa*, have been occupied by Israel, but administered by the Jordanian Hashemite king, a symbolic control increasingly contested by the newly-established Palestinian National Authority (PNA). Other Islamic but Sunni centres include the Al Azhar University in Cairo, and Kairouan in Tunisia.

Every Middle Eastern country has a multiplicity of shrines and saints' tombs held in veneration, except in the Wahhabi states, namely Saudi Arabia and Qatar, which consider saint cults to be polytheism. Due to the Shia's reverence for martyrs and their shrines, Shia holy places are numerous, the most significant of which are not in Iran but in Iraq at Najaf, the burial place and crypt of Ali, and at Karbala, site of the battle where Hussein died and was enshrined. In Iran, Mashad is the site of the shrine of the eighth Imam of the Twelvers group, Ali Al Rida, and Qom is the location of the mausoleum of Fatima, the eighth Imam's sister.

The densest clustering of religious centres in the Middle East probably occurs in Israel and the Palestinian territories. These places are the geographical focus of Judaism and Christianity, while Muslims also revere the sites of the deeds of many commonly accepted prophets, as well as Jerusalem where calls have been heard to turn it into an international city open to all three monotheistic religions. The four main holy cities of Judaism are Jerusalem, Hebron, Tiberias, and Safad, while Christianity regards the sites associated with the actions of Jesus as specially significant (see Box 4.3 and Figure 4.2).

Box 4.3   Religious Holy Places in the Middle East

Islamic Holy Places

Hebron (Habrun) in the West Bank. The Mosque of Abraham, called *Al Khalil*, the 'Friend of God', is built over the Cave of Machpelah that contains the tombs of Abraham, Sarah, Isaac, Rebecca, Jacob, and Leah. The shrine is revered by Muslims and Jews, and is also important to Christians.

Box 4.3   Religious Holy Places in the Middle East   (*continued*)

Jerusalem (*Al Quds* or *Bait Al Maqdis*, the Hallowed/Consecrated) in the West Bank and currently annexed by Israel. Jerusalem is associated with so many pre-Islamic prophets, and Mohammed himself is popularly held to have made the 'Night Journey' there. Jerusalem contains the famous *Al Masjid Al Aqsa* that marks the traditional site where the Prophet left to visit heaven, and the magnificent Islamic shrine, the Dome of the Rock, built between 688 and 691 by the Caliph Abd Al Malik.

Mecca in the Hijaz province of Saudi Arabia. Mecca is centred around the *Kaaba*, the most venerated building in Islam, traditionally held to have been founded by Abraham, recognised by Islam as a prophet. It stands in the centre of the vast courtyard of the Great Mosque and has the form of a cube; its construction is of local grey stone and its walls are draped with a black curtain embroidered with a strip of writing containing verses from the Qoran. In the eastern corner is set the famous Black Stone. Mecca is the centre of the annual pilgrimage, the *Hajj*, for all Muslims in the world. In 1996, around 2 million Muslim pilgrims visited Mecca.

Medina (the city of the Prophet) in the Hijaz province of Saudi Arabia. Medina, formerly called Yathrib, was created as a sacred enclave (*Haram*) by Mohammed who died there in the year 11 of the *Hijra* and was buried in the Mosque of the Prophet. Close to his tomb are those of his companions and successors, Abu Bakr and Umar, and a little further away that of his daughter Fatima.

The following shrines are associated with the Shia and the legitimist sects of Islam:

Baghdad in Iraq, the site of the *Kazimain/Kadhimain* mosque there is a celebrated Shia shrine containing the tomb of Musa Al Kazim, the seventh Imam of the Twelvers.

Karbala in Iraq. The site of the shrine of Hussein Bin Ali (Mashhad Hussein), where he was slain with most of his family.

Mashhad (Meshed) in Iran. The city is famous for the shrine of Ali Al Rida, the eighth Imam of the Twelvers group, surrounded by buildings with religious or historical associations.

Najaf in Iraq. Mashhad Ali, reputed to be constructed over the place where Ali Bin Abi Talib is buried, is a most venerated Shia shrine. The city saw serious riots in 1991 following a Shia uprising in the aftermath of the conflict over Kuwait.

Qom in Iran. It is venerated as having the tomb of Fatima, the sister of Imam Al Rida, and those of hundreds of saints and kings including Imam Ali Bin Jaafar and Imam Ibrahim, Shah Safi, and Shah Abbas II. Following the Iranian revolution, Qom became the religious centre of the Islamic republic.

Christian Holy Places

Bethany (Azariyyah) in the West Bank. A town frequented by Jesus, the home of Mary and Martha and the scene of the Raising of Lazarus.

Box 4.3   Religious Holy Places in the Middle East   *(continued)*

Bethlehem in the West Bank. The traditional birthplace of Jesus is enclosed in the Basilica of the Nativity, revered also by Muslims. The tomb of Rachel, important to the three faiths, is just outside the town.

Ein Kerem in Israel, the traditional birthplace of John the Baptist.

Emmaus (Qubaibah) in the West Bank. It was near this town that two of the Disciples encountered Jesus after the Resurrection.

Ephesus in Turkey. It was in this city, formerly a great centre of pagan worship, where Paul founded the first of the seven Asian Churches.

Galilee in Israel. Many of the places by this lake are associated with the life of Jesus: the Mount of Beatitudes; Tabgha, scene of the multiplication of the loaves and fishes; and Capurneum, scene of the healing of the Centurion's servant.

Jericho in the West Bank, related to the scene of Jesus' baptism.

Jerusalem in the West Bank and currently annexed by Israel. The most holy city of Christianity has been a centre for pilgrims since the Middle Ages. The Church of the Holy Sepulchre stands on the hill of Golgotha in the higher northwestern part of the Old City. Close by is the Rock of Calvary, revered as the site of the Crucifixion. The Way of the Cross is believed to lead from the Roman Praetorium through several streets of the Old City to the Holy Sepulchre. Outside the Old City stands the Mount of Olives, the scene of Jesus' Ascension. At the foot of its hill is the Garden of Gethsemane that is associated with the vigil on the eve of the Crucifixion. The Cenaculum, or the traditional room of the Last Supper, is situated on Mount Zion in Israel.

Mount Carmel in Haifa–Israel. The Cave of St Elie (*Mar Elijah*) draws many pilgrims, including Muslims and Druzes.

Mount Tabour in Israel, the site of the Transfiguration.

Nazareth in Israel, closely associated with the childhood of Jesus.

Samaria (Nablus) in the West Bank. This old town contains Jacob's Well, associated with Jesus, and the tomb of Joseph.

Jewish Holy Places

Bethlehem in the West Bank. The traditional tomb of Rachel is in a small shrine outside the town, venerated also by Muslims and Christians.

Hebron (Habrun) in the West Bank. The Cave of Machpelah, over which a mosque was built, contains the tombs of Abraham and Sarah, Isaac and Rebecca, Jacob, and Leah.

Jerusalem in the West Bank and currently annexed by Israel. The 'Wailing Wall' is the last remnant of the western part of the wall surrounding the courtyard of King Herod's Temple, destroyed by the Romans in the year 70.

Meiron in Israel. The town contains the tombs of Shimon Bar Yohai, reputed founder of the medieval Cabbalist movement, and his son Eleazer.

Mount Carmel in Haifa–Israel. The mountain is associated with the Cave of St Elie.

Box 4.3   Religious Holy Places in the Middle East   (*continued*)

Mount Zion in Israel. A hill southwest of the old city of Jerusalem, venerated particularly for the tomb of David, acknowledged by Muslims as *Abi Dawud*. Not far from the foot of the hill are the rock-cut tombs of the family of King Herod.

Safad in Israel. The centre of the medieval Cabbalist movement, this city contains several synagogues from the sixteenth century associated with the movement's scholars, and many important tombs, notably that of Rabbi Isaac Louria.

Tiberias in Israel. An ancient city containing the tombs of Moses Maimonides and Rabbi Meir Baal Harness. Famous as a historical centre of Cabbalist scholarship, it is with Jerusalem, Safad, and Hebron, one of the four sacred cities of Judaism.

Figure 4.2 Religious holy places in the Middle East

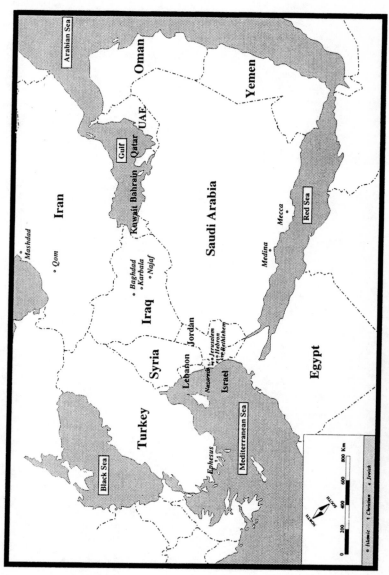

Source: Observatoire Méditerranéen de l'Energie (Sophia Antipolis, June 1996).

5 A Region of Ethnic Mosaic

ETHNIC HETEROGENEITY

The ethnic map of the Middle East shows first the ubiquitousness of the Arabs throughout most of the region. 'Arab' is used in the present context simply and properly to describe all those whose mother-tongue is Arabic. As such, the ethnic distribution represents the consequences of a dynamic and rapid expansion of the Arab population, directly associated with the first century after the rise of Islam, during which they spread from southern Arabia to embrace the whole of North Africa, the Levant and most of the lands between Arabia and the Indus.

The ethnic map of the Middle East shows also that there are non-Arab states as well, namely Iran, Turkey, and Israel, each with a special role to play within the region. Iran, as one of the major non-Arab Islamic states in the area, has seized an ambivalent position in Middle Eastern politics because of its geography, occupying a zone of transition between the region and the Asian world, its pre-modern and contemporary history partly associated with that of the Arabs, and its role in Islamic politics. Iran has a language, culture, and history distinct and separate from that of the Arab nations, and both sides are keen to emphasise that distinction.

Iran has a key and legitimate role to play in the security structure of the Gulf that puts it in contention with the other states in the region, notably Iraq and Saudi Arabia. For a long period during the 1960s and 1970s under the leadership of the Shah Mohammed Reza Pahlavi, Iran acted as a Western, particularly American, agent of influence and interests in the region. After the overthrow of the Shah in 1979 Iran has moved from being a target (and perhaps source) of hostility for the Arabs because of its Western client status to a source of antagonism because of its revolutionary fundamentalist ideology.

Turkey is the other non-Arab Islamic state in the Middle East. Modern-day Turkey is the successor to the imperial Ottoman system which at its height included a large part of the Middle East, what is now Iraq, Syria, Lebanon, Jordan, Israel, the eastern shores of the Red Sea, Egypt, Libya, Tunisia, and Algeria, as well as Greece, Albania, the former Yugoslavia, Hungary, Romania, Bulgaria, Moldova and the Black Sea territories of the former Soviet Union (FSU).

Turkey was, after the dissolution of the Ottoman Empire, the first of the Islamic states to secularise, under the leadership of Mustafa Kemal Ataturk who aspired to modernise his country on the pattern of the European states and to achieve ethno–linguistic homogeneity. Indeed, Turkey has become the model for those secular forces in other Middle Eastern states who would like to bring about such a revolution in their own societies. Turkey also occupies a position that may be regarded as pivotal or ambivalent, depending on which perspective is used. As an Islamic state, Turkey looks to the Middle East, and having borders with Syria, Iraq and Iran it clearly has important interests in the region not only politically but also economically, in particular relating to resources (water and petroleum). But as a secular and Westernised state, Turkey looks also west to Europe, with ambitions one day to become a member of the European Union (EU) after submitting a formal demand in Brussels in 1987. That claim to be European is based not only upon the secular nature of its society but also on the important role Turkey had played during the Cold War as a member of NATO, effectively constituting the southern flank of the Organisation's military strategy against the Soviet Union.

However, in the post-Soviet world, Turkey now finds the tension caused by the contrary pulls of West and East enhanced. The ambivalence of its position on the cultural crisp between Europe and Asia and its pivotal geostrategic position are both reinforced by the rebirth of central Asian republics. The changed political geography of the region means that Turkey has to exert its own influence in the area and further its own interests in the face of competition from other interested parties, such as Iran and Russia.

It is significant to note that Turkey has been engaged in military co-operation agreements with Israel, the other non-Arab state in the Middle East, which has used the renascent Hebrew language as an integrating force amongst its population. The deep political frustrations between Israel and the Arabs have been a cause of conflict, extremism, and terrorism on both sides for more than half century.

The large underlying question that has lain behind Middle Eastern politics is whether it is possible in the long term for Israel to co-exist with Arab and Islamic states in the very centre of the region. It is difficult to set aside the issue of territory since it is at the heart of the problem; but the question does arise as to whether, even from a cultural and religious viewpoint, it is possible for the two cultural systems to co-exist. That will be the future test of the 'Israeli experiment', even when and if a *modus vivendi* is fully achieved on the question of a Palestinian territory.

ETHNIC MINORITIES

Any ethnic map is at once a fascinating and a potentially dangerous document. On the basis of ethnic maps, boundaries of nation-states have been established and justified, at least in Europe, for around two centuries. The force of the argument linking ethnic distinctiveness with a national consciousness and a right to political independence has been so powerful that it continues to form the basis for interference in other states' internal affairs, for demands for boundary modifications, for kindling ambitions for new states, and for political manipulation in order to conceal true ethnic distribution.

Now coming to the fore, the perennial question of ethnic minorities could unsettle the Middle East because, unlike other issues, their claims involve territories. After all, the borders of the relatively new states in the region were generally defined by colonial powers, and some of the minorities have never accepted these lines which they regard as artificial, especially when they separate them from their relatives living on the other side of the borders.

Many ethnic minorities have found themselves living within the states of the region, as shown in Table 5.1, the figures in which are to be considered as estimates because many national data on ethnic variations are not published and in many cases not even collected due to the sensitivity of the issue. Apart from an important Arab minority living in Israel, and small Jewish communities found in some Arab countries, and apart from the migrating labour groups in the Gulf, minorities with distinct identities exist mainly in three states – Iran, Iraq, and Turkey. While the three countries share the Kurds, other important ethnic minorities are found in Iran.

Kurds

With a population ranging between 24 and 27 million contained in five different states (predominantly Turkey, Iraq, and Iran with smaller numbers in Syria and the formal Soviet central Asian republics), living in a hilly region and retaining their tribal way of life, the Kurds have a history of continuous struggle for autonomy. Promised independence by the Treaty of Sèvres (1920) and the unification of independent Kurdistan are probably regarded as their ultimate goals. These goals are perceived by Kurds hosts as aspiring for secession even if they are careful to demand only autonomy within their respective states. Conversely, the regimes of the states where the Kurds live have a common interest: to thwart any

Table 5.1   Ethnic composition of Middle Eastern states, 1995 (estimates, %)[1]

Country	Ethnic grouping[2]								
	A	B	C	D	E	F	G	H	I
Bahrain	73	–	8	–	13	–	–	–	6
Egypt	98	–	–	–	–	–	–	–	2
Iran	6	7	51	–	–	–	26	–	10
Iraq	75	20	–	–	–	2	–	–	3
Israel	15	–	–	1	–	–	–	83	1
Jordan	98	–	–	1	–	–	–	–	1
Kuwait	80	–	4	–	9	–	–	–	7
Lebanon	94	1	–	4	–	–	–	–	1
Oman	90	–	–	–	5	–	4	–	1
Qatar	40	–	10	–	36	–	–	–	14
Saudi Arabia	85	–	–	–	10	–	–	–	5
Syria	90	4	–	2	–	1	–	–	3
Turkey	–	17	–	1	–	80	–	–	2
UAE	42	–	–	–	50	–	–	–	8
Yemen	88	–	–	–	–	–	–	1	11

Notes:
1. *Sources*: *World Fact Book 1995* (Washington, DC: CIA, 1995), and various others.
2. A = Arabs
   B = Kurds
   C = Iranians
   D = Armenians
   E = Asians
   F = Turks
   G = Azerbaijanis/Baluchis
   H = Jews
   I = Others
   – = non-existent

notion of Kurdish (and for that matter any other minority's) separatism. Kurdish aspirations have been regarded as a challenge to these states' own authority, legitimacy, and ability to rule.

Although about half of all Kurds live in Turkey constituting around 17 per cent of the population, or around 11–13 million people, there are officially 'no Kurds' in Turkey but 'separatists in the eastern area of the country'. Ankara has forbidden any political activity in the Kurdish regions and is even trying to 'turkenise' the area by imposing the Turkish language on the population, while at the same time pursuing a continuous and aggressive military campaign against the separatist Kurdish Labour Party (PKK) within its territory and even in northern Iraq, as seen in the spring of 1995 and 1996.

For Iran, the Kurdish question has religious facets (most Kurds are Sunnis) and ideological overtones (part of their leadership is communist). The Islamic republic harbours about one-third of all Kurds who live astride its border with Iraq, and who declared in January 1946 the Kurdish Republic of Mahabad with Soviet encouragement but no military support. The republic survived less than a year before it was conquered by the Iranian army. Until 1979, the Shah regime had followed policies that encouraged Kurds to assimilate into the dominant society. Iranian pressures to absorb Kurds were not as consistent and severe as they have been in Turkey, however. Immediately after the fall of the Shah in 1979, the Iranian Kurds tried to organise themselves as an autonomous region, only to be crushed by the forces of the Islamic revolution. Between the Islamic revolution and 1984, the Kurds and the government in Tehran alternated between negotiation and warfare. By early 1984, the well-trained and well-armed Kurds fell out with *Pasdaran* (Revolutionary Guards) in the rugged mountain terrain.

For the Baath in Iraq, which has been trying to present itself as a socialist popular regime, Kurdish aspirations pose a challenge to Iraqi nationalism, the only ideology that could possibly keep the country united under one leadership. In their attempts to come to terms with the Kurds, different Iraqi governments tried intermittently to crush the Kurdish revolt by force. Failing to achieve this, Baghdad tried to reach political arrangement with them, such as the agreement of March 1970 that acknowledged the territorial gains made by the Kurdish militias (the *Pesh Merga*) and offered the Kurds self-rule. The 1970 agreement was never put into practice, however, due to mutual suspicion and contempt. The major, though certainly not the only, bone of contention has been the oil fields in Kirkuk (around 1 million b/d of Iraqi oil production capacity, and some 35–40 per cent of its oil proven reserves), an area the Kurds regard as their own by virtue of its being predominantly Kurdish; the Iraqi regime naturally disputes this, arguing that Arabs, Turkomans, and Assyrians make it a mixed region. Kurdish leaders have accused the government of trying to dilute the Kurdish nature of the area by 'arabising' it through the imposition of the Arabic language on the education system so as to undermine both Kurdish influence and Kurdish claim over a share of the oil revenues to be carved out for their own development.

While attempting to control their own minority at home, both Iran and Iraq have sought to manipulate each other's ethnic vulnerability so as to increase their own leverage over the other. After a decade in which the Shah had manipulated Iraqi Kurds to advance Iran's regional stand at the expense of its neighbour, and following some military hostilities in 1974 when Iraqi Kurds were pushed back to the regions adjacent to Iran and Turkey, the Kurdish cause received a setback with the signature by Iran and Iraq of the Algiers agreement in March 1975. Under that convention, the Shah agreed to close the Iranian border to support for the Kurds, in return for Iraq conceding Iranian demands concerning borders through Shatt Al Arab (see Chapter 6).

With the weakening of central authority in post-revolution Iran and its unwillingness to respond to Kurdish demands, the problem came on to the agenda of both states again, especially when Iraq started supporting the revived thrust of Kurdish insurgency directed against the regime of Khomeini. So the old pattern repeated itself, but with a different motivation. Whereas the Iranian clerics were trying to promote the plight of their Shia brothers in Iraq in an attempt to subvert the secular Sunni regime there, the latter was striving to cripple the Iranian regime and seeking to profit from its internal struggles by helping Iranian Kurds among other ethnic groups living in Iran. Inside its territories, after relatively quiet years during which it had been preoccupied by war with Iran (1980–8), Baghdad took revenge in the late days of hostilities on what it called 'the Kurdish position against Iraq during the conflict' by bombing Kurdish villages in the north with chemical arms.

The Kurds profited from the setback of Iraq in its conflict with allied forces in early 1991 and invaded the Iraqi Kurdish region including Kirkuk. Following a brutal reply from Baghdad, the UN decided to impose a 'security zone' north of the 36th parallel where Kurds now enjoy a relatively quiet political life after electing a representative council in April 1992. Meanwhile, negotiations with Baghdad over the self-rule of the region intermittently continue, as well as the inter-Kurdish struggles, manipulated as usual by Baghdad and Tehran.

Iran's Other Ethnic Minorities

In addition to the Kurds, Iran has numerous ethnic groups of widely differing origins, reflecting a real ethnic mosaic where Persians, Kurds, Arabs, Azerbaijanis and Baluchis are together forming a country.

Arabs

The 3-million population of Khuzestan on the upper Gulf is primarily Arab in ethnic composition. Khuzestan remains Iran's richest oil-reserve province (more than 80 per cent of the country's proven reserves) where up to 90 per cent of its hydrocarbons have been produced, and where most of the crude is refined in processing plants like the one in Abadan, considered for long one of the largest in the world.

Between 1890 and 1925, the Khuzestanis had enjoyed wide autonomy under one of the tribal sheikhs who managed to maintain close relations both with Tehran and the British. The question of sovereignty over Khuzestan was first raised in the aftermath of the First World War, when Iraq and Iran clashed over the demarcation of their border and the status of Iranian nationals then living in Iraq. In 1925, the Iranian minister of war, Reza Shah, having forcibly suppressed a move for autonomy in Khuzestan, seized the province and began to settle it with Persian-speaking citizens so as to turn the Arab majority into a minority.

In the period immediately following the Second World War, Khuzestan's Arab population renewed their drive for autonomy. An appeal was made to Iraq and the Arab League to grant them citizenship, but the movement was again suppressed by the Iranian government within a few months.

In terms of Iraqi policy, the real change in attitude came following the 1958 Revolution. Until that time, the Hashemite rulers in Baghdad had not pressed the issue out of their desire to maintain close relations with the dynastic leadership in Tehran. It was only within the context of the Shatt Al Arab crisis of 1959–60, when Iraq interfered with Iranian vessels, that the Khuzestan (or Arabistan as Baghdad prefers to call it) issue again emerged as a major point of contention. At that time, the Iraqi Qasim regime not only refused to implement the 1937 treaty concerning Shatt Al Arab, but laid claim to Arabistan.

During another crisis in 1969 on the Shatt Al Arab and Kurdish questions, Iraq again revived the Arabistan issue as part of its campaign against Iran. The Algiers agreement of 1975 made no mention of the dispute, although it was widely acknowledged that one of its tacit provisions (in addition to the settlement of the Shatt Al Arab question and the termination of Iranian support for the Kurdish rebels in Iraq) was the renunciation of any Iraqi designs on the area. With the rapid deterioration in relations between Iraq and Iran after February 1979, Baghdad began a conscious drive to aid and abet the resistance movement within Khuzestan (Khuzestani National Liberation Front). The public articulation of Iraq's conditions for an improvement in bilateral relations included the demand for the provision of self-rule in Khuzestan/Arabistan. It was significant to note that Iraq did not explicitly revive its own irredentist claim to the region (unlike in 1960 and 1969); Iraq instead opted for the adoption of a more indirect, ostensibly pan-Arabic approach to the question, even during its war with Iran between 1980 and 1988. Although the issue has stayed dormant since then, it remains related to the degree of warmth in the relations between the two countries.

Azerbaijanis

The Azerbaijanis (or Azeri Turks as they are commonly called) inhabit the region encompassing northwestern Iran and the adjacent border area within the FSU. In the former area, they constitute the largest ethnic minority, with a population estimated at some 25 per cent of Iran's total. Though retaining a separate linguistic and ethnic identity, they are, unlike Kurds and Baluchis, adherents of the Shia sect.

The modern history of the Azeri Turks has been a turbulent one. In 1907, when Persia was partitioned between the British and the Russians, Iranian Azerbaijanis fell under the jurisdiction of the latter and stayed within the Tsarist sphere until 1918. Following a period of Iranian sovereignty, Iranian Azerbaijanis were again brought under effective Soviet political control with the 1942–6 re-occupation of northern Iran by the Red Army.

The early establishment of the Azerbaijan Soviet Socialist Republic in 1945 was regarded as providing at least some nominal expression to the claims of Azeri nationalism – albeit within the context of a Soviet state structure. In the Iranian sector, the indigenous resistance movements that had staged two abortive uprisings in 1920–1 and 1945–6 were unable to extract any political concessions from the central government. On the contrary, the fear of nationalist fragmentation prompted the government under the Pahlavi rule to proscribe the use of the Azeri Turkish language in educational institutions and media.

The Islamic revolution of 1979 gave the Azerbaijanis a new opportunity to talk about autonomy rights for their region, but without any success. It seems that recent developments in the FSU and the appearance of an independent Azerbaijan have revived Iranian Azeri nationalism at a time when Iran and Turkey are both trying to win influence and control over the whole region. Mass demonstrations early in 1994 in the Azeri region of Iran calling for more autonomy were reportedly supported by Baku.

Baluchis

The Baluchis are a Sunni ethnic group inhabiting some 400 000 km^2 within the territories of Iran, Pakistan, and Afghanistan. In Iran, they constitute around 1 per cent of the total population, and occupy the southeastern region of the country.

Since the late nineteenth century, the Baluchis have pressed for an independent homeland (Baluchistan) with their most recent uprising occurring in Pakistan in 1974. During that crisis, the Shah lent active military support to the Bhutto government in its successful suppression of the movement. The Baluchi question has been on ice since then, but any secession trend in Afghanistan or again in Pakistan would revive the issue in Iran.

6 An Area Divided by Arbitrary Borders

The international boundaries in the Middle East are relatively recent creation. The majority of land borders had been aligned between 1880 and 1930, largely as a result of European intervention, reflecting delimitations agreed by imperial powers in the post-First World War peace settlements.

Even though, when Britain withdrew in 1971 from its two-century formal 'protecting' role in the region, especially in the Gulf area, it left a heritage of *de facto* boundaries. Indeed, London had believed for a long time that if a frontier was causing no immediate problem, it should be left alone, at least while it had responsibility for the area. The last thing to be done was to create work and friction, and 'sleeping dogs should be left to lie' (Schofield, 1994).

A few borders in Middle East roughly coincide with cultural and historic divides, but the majority were arbitrarily superimposed with scant regard for the human and physical geography of the region. Thus, as expressed by Foucher (1988), some borders are now under dispute because they disjoin identical people instead of gathering them in a discrete entity.

The land boundaries in the Middle East vary considerably in legal status and physical characteristics. Most of them are demarcated on the ground by physical or man-made features, or follow geometric guidelines such as lines of latitude or longitude. Most boundary lines subdivide river basins, cut off towns from their natural hinterlands, and interrupt nomadic movements and communications. Many of them are long and straight, constituting a prominent feature on the region's map.

Some of the world's least permeable boundaries are in the Middle East, although the great length of many borders there, often passing through sparsely inhabited regions, leaves ample scope for an illegal border defile. The closure of international boundary crossings that act as filters to the flow of people and goods has been common at times of political tension in the region.

Several territorial disputes over the precise position of international boundaries remain unsettled in the Middle East. The problem concerns, for the most part, the lack of early identifiable permanent surface features. Demarcation of land boundaries across a relatively featureless landscape,

Table 6.1   Land boundaries in the Middle East, 1996

Countries	Length (km)	Status
Egypt–Gaza Strip	11[1]	Undisputed; confirmed by Camp David agreements in 1978
Egypt–Israel	255[1] 228.5[2]	Undisputed; confirmed by Camp David agreements in 1978
Egypt–Libya	1150[1] 1115[2]	Undisputed
Egypt–Sudan	1273[1]	Disputes over Halaib Triangle and Wadi Halfa salient
Iran–Afghanistan	936[1] 885[2]	Undisputed; defined by Paris Treaty (1857)
Iran–Armenia	35[1]	Undisputed; defined by the Treaty of Turkomanchai (1828)
Iran–Azerbaijan	701[1]	Undisputed
Iran–Iraq	1458[1] 1052[2]	Dispute and military hostilities over Shatt Al Arab; less-significant dispute over Khuzestan/Arabistan
Iran–Pakistan	909[1] 904[2]	Undisputed
Iran–Turkey	499[1]	Undisputed; confirmed by Lausanne Treaty (1923)
Iran–Turkmenistan	992[1]	Undisputed
Iraq–Jordan	134[1]	Undisputed; defined by the British mandate in the early nineteeth century and then by a letter exchange in 1932 and an agreement in 1984
Iraq–Kuwait	240[1] 198[2]	Dispute and military hostilities over Kuwait
Iraq–Saudi Arabia	686[1] 861[2]	Undisputed; confirmed by an agreement in December 1981
Iraq–Syria	605[1]	Undisputed; defined by France and Britain in 1926
Iraq–Turkey	331[1] 352[2]	Although confirmed by Ankara Treaty (1926), Turkey questioned it in 1995
Israel–Gaza Strip	51[1]	Defined by the peace agreement of September 1993
Israel–Jordan	238[1]	Defined by the peace agreement of October 1994
Israel–Lebanon	79[1]	Although undisputed, part of south Lebanon has been occupied since 1978
Israel–Syria	76[1]	Dispute and military hostilities over Golan Heights

Table 6.1   *Continued*

Countries	Length (km)	Status
Israel–West Bank	307[1]	Final borders including the issue of Jerusalem to be defined by an agreement expected in 1996–7
Jordan–Saudi Arabia	742[1]	Undisputed; defined by Amman Treaty in 1965
Jordan–Syria	375[1] 351[2]	Undisputed; defined by Sykes–Picot agreement in 1916 and then the Protocol of Paris (1931)
Jordan–West Bank	97[1]	Final borders including the issue of Jerusalem to be defined by an agreement expected in 1996–7
Kuwait–Saudi Arabia	222[1] 163[2]	Undisputed; confirmed by an agreement in December 1969
Lebanon–Syria	375[1] 313[2]	Undisputed; defined by the French mandate in September 1920
Oman–Saudi Arabia	676[1] 724[2]	Undisputed; confirmed by an agreement in March 1990
Oman–UAE	410[1] 430[2]	Disputes with Ras Al Khaimah over the towns of Dawra and Rims; with Abu Dhabi over Buraimi oasis; many common administered enclaves together with the emirates of Ajman, Fujairah, and Sharjah
Oman–Yemen	288[1]	Undisputed; defined by an agreement in 1992
Qatar-Saudi Arabia	40[1] 69[2]	The application of a 1965 agreement defining the border has led to quarrel and military hostilities
Qatar–UAE	20[1]	Dispute over Khaur Al Udaid inlet
Saudi Arabia–UAE	586[1] 512[2]	Part of the border with Abu Dhabi defined by an agreement in July 1974, and remains undefined for the other part, and for the neighbouring UAE's emirates
Saudi Arabia–Yemen	1458[1] 1384[2]	Dispute over the application of the Taif Treaty (1934) concerning the western part of the border, the other parts of which are still undefined
Syria–Turkey	822[1]	Dispute over the province of Alexandretta/Hatay
Turkey–Armenia	268[1]	Claims evoked by Armenia to the Armenian region east of Turkey
Turkey–Azerbaijan	9[1]	Undisputed; confirmed by Lausanne Treaty (1923)

Table 6.1   Continued

Countries	Length (km)	Status
Turkey–Bulgaria	250[1] 241[2]	Undisputed; confirmed by Lausanne Treaty (1923)
Turkey–Georgia	252[1]	Claims evoked by the FSU of 230 km of land on shore of the Black Sea, as well as the region of Kars–Ardahan given to Turkey by the treaties of Kars (1921) and Moscow (1924)
Turkey–Greece	206[1]	Undisputed; confirmed by Lausanne Treaty (1923)
Inter-UAE	–	Neutral Zone between Abu Dhabi and Dubai; disputes between Dubai and Sharjah, and between Fujairah and Sharjah; many enclaves commonly administered by different emirates

Notes:
1. *Source*: *World Fact Book 1995* (Washington, DC: CIA, 1995).
2. *Source*: *Cambridge Atlas of the Middle East and North Africa* (Cambridge: Cambridge University Press, 1987).

as in the desert, or following geometric guidelines, obviously poses difficulties and is considered to be hypothetical. Even if a border line is settled on the map, its exact position on the ground leads most of the time to dispute. From an international law perspective, these is no convention governing land borders.

Another particular issue posed with regard to the drawing of international boundaries in the Middle East consists of the fact that the position of a border line at the surface can be critical for the extraction of water and petroleum, the two key resources on which the region's life and wealth depend. In most cases, international boundaries in the area were not constructed to reflect the distribution of subterranean resources; thus, they only exacerbate the resource geopolitics.

Since they are no respecters of international boundaries, oil and gas reserves straddling boundaries tend inevitably to lead to maximum production, for what is not produced by one country will be produced by its neighbour. Recent developments in horizontal drilling allow producers to take even greater advantage of their neighbour's subsurface hydrocarbon

Figure 6.1   Land and maritime borders under dispute in the Middle East, 1996.

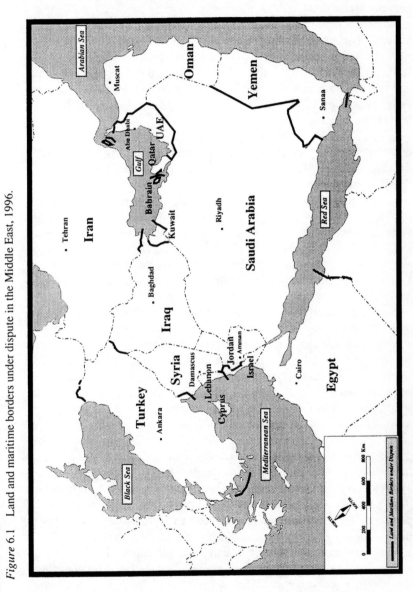

Source: Observatoire Méditerranéen de l'Energie (Sophia Antipolis, June 1996).

deposits than was previously the case. The issue is whether the parties concerned will co-operate to ensure optimum reservoir drawdown or risk damaging potential output with competing attempts to push flows up quickly from the field. Differences over exploration and development can provoke at best disagreement and at worst military conflict.

Many frontiers have witnessed strife – varying from a war of words between Saudi Arabia and Yemen to Iraqi military invasion of Kuwait – with real or potential cross-border petroleum reserves as a contributing factor. Other fields, such as that between Qatar and Iran, or between Oman and Iran, or those straddling the Saudi Arabia – UAE boundary, have not yet provoked problems, but differences could emerge as development leads to production.

In turn, border disputes in the Middle East have, until now, slowed down or completely paralysed petroleum exploration and development in the disputed areas. Petroleum operations represent long-lived, large and fixed investment projects. To ensure adequate financial return requires clear-cut property rights which are impossible to get if the concession is the subject of a border dispute. The disputed areas in the region are believed to contain about 37 billion barrels of oil reserves and between 2.8 and 4.3 trillion cubic metres of recoverable natural gas, especially in the southeastern and southwestern parts of the Arabian peninsula, and off-shore the Gulf and the Red Sea. More could be found if the disputes were settled.

Nevertheless, cross-border reserves do not always result in dispute. Saudi Arabia has peacefully shared petroleum reserves in border regions with Kuwait (Neutral Zone structures) and Bahrain (Abu Safaa field), while Qatar is sharing the resources of the Bunduq oil field with Abu Dhabi. The revenues of the Mubarak field, offshore of Abu Musa Island, are split evenly between Iran and Sharjah which then passes on smaller shares to Ajman and Umm Al Qaiwain. Mubarak's revenue-sharing agreement has even been unaffected by the dispute over Abu Musa.

The presence of oil and natural gas on the seabed of the Gulf has provided a strong incentive for the formal delimitation of some of the earliest maritime boundaries in the region, that began seriously only in the 1960s and is still far from complete (see Table 6.2). In fact, questions like the settlement of the 'continental shelf' become imperative when various petroleum concessionaires refuse to proceed with drilling operations in disputed zones until such time as the disputes have been resolved.

The problems of maritime boundary delimitation are basically in geographical aspects such as the definition of a base line, what constitutes an 'opposite' coastline and what is the 'natural' prolongation of land.

Table 6.2   Maritime boundaries in the Middle East, 1996[1]

	Coast line (km)	Continental shelf	Territorial sea (nautical miles)	Exclusive economic zone (nautical miles)	Contiguous zone (nautical miles)	Status
Bahrain	161	ns	12	ns	24	Dispute with Qatar over Zubarah strip and Hawar Islands; agreements with Saudi Arabia (1958) and Iran (1971); Iranian claim to Bahrain?
Egypt	2450	8	12	ns	24	Dispute with Sudan over Halaib maritime boundary in the Red Sea; agreement with Israel in 1978
Gaza Strip	40	ns	ns	ns	ns	Defined in September 1993
Iran	2440	9	12	50[2]	ns	Dispute with the UAE over Abu Musa and the Tunb Islands; disputes with Iraq and Kuwait?; agreements with Abu Dhabi (1971?), Bahrain (1971), Dubai (1974), Saudi Arabia (1968), Qatar (1969), and Oman (1974)
Iraq	58	ns	12	ns	ns	Disputes with Iran and Kuwait
Israel	273	3	12	ns	ns	Boundaries with Gaza Strip and Jordan defined in September 1993 and October 1994 respectively; boundaries with Lebanon remain to be confirmed
Jordan	26	ns	3	ns	ns	Agreements with Saudi Arabia and Israel in 1965 and October 1994 respectively
Kuwait	499	ns	12	ns	ns	Disputes with Iran?, Iraq, and over the maritime boundaries of the Neutral Zone with Saudi Arabia, including the rights over Qaru and Umm Al Maradim Islands
Lebanon	225	ns	12	ns	ns	Maritime boundaries with Israel remain to be confirmed
Oman	2092	ns	12	200	24	Disputes with Ras Al Khaimah and Sharjah; agreements with Iran (1974), Saudi Arabia (1990), and Yemen (1992)

Table 6.2   Continued

	Coast line (km)	Continental shelf	Territorial sea (nautical miles)	Exclusive economic zone (nautical miles)	Contiguous zone (nautical miles)	Status
Qatar	563	ns	12	200	ns	Dispute with Bahrain over Zubarah strip and over Hawar Islands; part of the continental shelf with Saudi Arabia remains unsettled; agreement with Saudi Arabia (1965), Iran, and Abu Dhabi (both in 1969)
Saudi Arabia	2640	ns	12	ns	18	Part of the continental shelf with Qatar remains unsettled; dispute over the maritime boundaries of the Neutral Zone with Kuwait including the rights over Qaru and Umm Al Maradim Islands; maritime boundaries with Yemen still undefined; agreements with Bahrain (1958), Iran (1968), Oman (1990), Qatar (1965), and Sudan (1974)
Syria	193	ns	35	ns	41	Dispute with Turkey over the maritime boundaries of Alexandretta/Hatay province
Turkey	7200	ns	6–12[4]	[5]	ns	Dispute with Syria over the maritime boundaries of Alexandretta/Hatay province; dispute with Greece in the Aegean Sea; agreement with the FSU (1973)
UAE	1318	[6]	12	200	24	Dispute with Iran over Abu Musa and the Tunb Islands; disputes of Ras Al Khaimah and Sharjah with Oman; agreements of Abu Dhabi with Iran (1971?), and Qatar (1969); agreement of Dubai with Iran (1974)

Table 6.2 Continued

	Coast line (km)	Continental shelf	Territorial sea (nautical miles)	Exclusive economic zone (nautical miles)	Contiguous zone (nautical miles)	Status
Inter-UAE	–	–	–	–	–	Maritime boundaries agreements between Abu Dhabi and Dubai (1968), Sharjah and Dubai (1981), and Sharjah and Umm Al Qaiwain (1981)
Yemen	1906	6	12	200	18–24(f)	Maritime boundaries with Saudi Arabia still undefined; dispute with Eritrea over Greater Hanish Island north of Bab Al Mandeb; agreement with Oman (1992)

Notes:
1. *Sources: World Fact Book 1995* (Washington, DC: CIA, 1995); and various others.
2. In the Gulf of Oman; continental shelf limit, continental shelf boundaries, or median lines in the Gulf.
3. To depth of exploitation.
4. 6 nautical miles in the Aegean Sea, 12 nautical miles in the Black Sea and the Mediterranean sea.
5. In the Black Sea only, to the maritime boundary agreed upon with the FSU.
6. 200 nautical miles depth, or to the edge of the continental margin.
7. 18 nautical miles in the North, 24 nautical miles in the South.
8. 200 metres depth, or to the depth of exploitation.
9. Natural prolongation.
ns not specified.

Besides, there is no way in which a maritime border line can be marked other than on charts. Moreover, state jurisdiction offshore is more complicated than on land because differing degrees of state control are recognised, usually embracing internal waters, territorial seas, continuous zones, continental shelves, and exclusive fishing zones. Where the ownership of islands that are entitled to their own territorial water is also in contention, drawing an offshore boundary is nearly impossible, as between Kuwait and each of Iraq and Saudi Arabia, and between the UAE and Iran.

After nine years of negotiations, the UN Convention on the Law of the Sea regulating maritime boundaries finally emerged in 1982, but, as at the end of March 1996, it was ratified by only seven of the fifteen Middle Eastern states, namely Bahrain, Egypt, Iraq, Jordan, Kuwait, Lebanon, and Oman. The Convention gives states the right to exercise the same degree of sovereignty over 'internal water' as over the land. Internal water includes bays, estuaries, and water lying behind any straight baselines that may be drawn along highly indented or island-fringed coasts. These, or in their absence the low-water mark, provide the baseline from which the 'territorial sea' is measured. Within the territorial water limits, states exercise absolute sovereignty over the air space above, the waterbody, and the seabed, although ships of other states have the right of innocent passage. Middle Eastern states have claimed various breadths of territorial sea in the past, but under the Convention it must be standardised at 12 nautical miles. Beyond territorial seas, 'contiguous zones' are sometimes declared for specific purposes such as the enforcement of sanitary, fiscal, and customs regulations. Seven such zones have been declared in the region, to distances of 18 (Saudi Arabia and North Yemen), 24 (Bahrain, Egypt, Oman, and South Yemen) and 41 nautical miles (Syria).

Under the UN Convention, coastal states have the right to exploit all the resources of the territorial sea; they are also entitled to the resources of the seabed of their continental shelves beyond territorial water. The Convention proposes a 200-nautical mile 'exclusive economic zone' (EEZ) extending from the baseline from which the territorial sea is measured. In the EEZ, coastal states have the right to the exclusive exploitation of all living and non-living resources. In the Middle East, only Oman and Yemen have the full entitlement of 200 miles. Elsewhere, the region's narrow seas have to be partitioned between opposite states.

A recent revival of border disputes reflects a new political environment in which major threats have been replaced by less-than-vital concerns. Whereas the reduction of major threats has diminished the need for regional cohesion and unity and has led to states feeling able to pursue past claims, domestic problems and the delicate process of political adjustment and transition in some states may have increased the incentive for playing the nationalist card and trumpeting the claims of state. The surfacing of border and territorial disputes is also symptomatic of far deeper political differences in the region. Territorial disputes as surrogates for other conflicts are thus becoming the barometers of political relationships, which they reflect or foreshadow.

At the last resort, the border disputes are time-bombs and are poisoning relations between the countries of the region. With an explosive mixture of resource interests and political ambitions, these disputes constitute a serious threat to political stability in this part of the world. While every unsettled land and maritime boundary in the Middle East remains a potential territorial conflict, the border disputes in the region can be classified as active or dormant, according to the date and degree of eruption. An 'active' border dispute is defined as an effective and vigorous struggle still erupting, while a 'dormant' one consists of a latent and sleeping dispute, inactive for a reasonably long time but not definitely settled yet.

ACTIVE BORDER DISPUTES

Many conflicts have erupted over boundaries in the Middle East. To begin with, Bahrain and Qatar have been in dispute over the delineation of their territorial waters. Tensions have risen between Egypt and Sudan concerning the potentially petroleum-rich Halaib region. Iran has been disputing the Shatt Al Arab with Iraq and has been in conflict with the UAE over the island of Abu Musa and the two inlets of Tunb. Kuwait and Iraq have been opposed on the delineation of their borders and the division of the Rumaila/Ratqa oil field. Israel and some of its neighbours are still in state of war as a result of territorial disputes. Saudi Arabia has been in active border conflict with Yemen, just as it is with Qatar.

Bahrain–Qatar

The two sheikhdoms of Bahrain and Qatar, both members of the GCC, have long disputed the ownership of the Hawar Islands on the west coast of Qatar. The islands, sixteen in number with a total area of 19.3 km^2, are 18 miles away from Bahrain's coastline and 1 mile from the coast of Qatar where the Dukhan oil field is thought to extend as far as Hawar. The dispute over the islands was cited as the principal reason why Bahrain and Qatar failed to join the UAE federation in 1971.

Bahraini ownership of the islands has long been recognised by third parties. In 1939, Britain ordered Qatar to relinquish sovereignty over Hawar, and in December 1947, London included a provision excluding the islands from the demarcation of the median line of the continental shelf of Qatar. Nevertheless, Doha has continuously claimed that the Hawar Islands lie within its territorial sea, proclaiming its sovereignty over them as well as the two coral reefs of Fasht Al Dibal and Qitat Jardah.

Disputes over the islands and the reefs resulted in a military confrontation between the two countries in April 1978, taking them to the brink of a full-scale war. At that time, Qatar attacked and destroyed the equipment and installations of a Dutch oil company that was invited by Bahrain to drill on Fasht Al Dibal. Saudi mediations kept the two countries from going to war, but failed to solve the problem. Subsequently, Qatari troops landed in April 1986 in some of the disputed islands and jailed foreign workers building a coast guard station for Bahrain, but they left 2 months later.

Qatar submitted the dispute over Hawar in July 1991 to the arbitration of the International Court of Justice (ICJ) in The Hague, but Bahrain opposed the move, arguing that such an application had to be made jointly by the two countries concerned. While the ICJ has been waiting to receive a joint request, Qatar issued a decree in April 1992 regarding its territorial sea, fixing its limits at 12 nautical miles. Bahrain rejected the Qatari decree and claimed a 24-mile contiguous zone where it can exercise many rights.

The two countries have also been in dispute over Zubarah, a north-western coastal strip on the Qatar Peninsula. The Bahraini government's claim to Zubarah is based upon a settlement which Al Khalifas established on that site in 1766 after migrating from Kuwait, and was used 17 years later in their conquest of the island from the Persians – the first Al Khalifa ruler is even buried there. During the Ottoman suzerainty over Qatar, Bahrain relinquished control of the strip. Then in 1937, Qatar asserted its full sovereignty over the Zubarah settlement and its environs along the coast.

Much less has been heard recently of the dispute over Zubarah, yet it will be surprising if Bahrain does not evoke the historical claim to the strip in some form in the event of the Hawar dispute reaching international arbitration.

Egypt–Sudan

Egypt and Sudan have been disputing since the early 1990s over the 10 304 km^2 Halaib Triangle on the eastern borders between the two countries. The problem is related to 'political' and 'administrative' boundaries, recognised by Cairo and Khartoum respectively, and which one has the status of international border. The dispute has a repercussion on the maritime boundaries in the Red Sea, where according to a study financed by the World Bank in 1989–90 important resources of hydrocarbons can potentially be discovered. The 'political' boundary came into effect with the Anglo–Egyptian condominium agreement of 1899, defining the border at the 22th parallel. Three years later, in 1902, an 'administrative' boundary was agreed upon, running north of the political border where Sudan was given administrative responsibility, and south about half-way between the Red Sea coast and the Nile where Egypt acquired administrative rights.

In addition to Halaib, both states have been claiming the Wadi Halfa salient, a small piece of territory which is now under the waters of Lake Nasser in southern Egypt.

Iran–Iraq

The border dispute between Iran and Iraq remains one of the most pernicious boundary conflicts in the Middle East. It was on 4 July 1937 that the Iraqi–Persian Treaty designated the low-water mark on the eastern bank of the Shatt Al Arab as the frontier and conferred on Iraq control over the waterway with the exception of areas adjacent to the Iranian ports of Abadan, Khoramshahr, and Khosrowabad, where it was fixed at the *Thalweg* (deepest line). That treaty followed an Ottoman–Persian agreement in 1847 giving Iraq full control of the whole Shatt Al Arab. The 1847 agreement was confirmed by a protocol in Constantinople in 1913. The Shatt Al Arab issue emerged again between November 1959 and January 1960, when Iraq interfered with Iranian vessels in an attempt to assert the prerogatives ostensibly conferred to it under the 1937 treaty. A hardening in the Iranian position prompted Baghdad to reassert its claim to the 3-mile territorial water around Abadan that had been conferred to Iran in one of the provisions of the 1937 agreement. Intermittent diplomatic exchanges between the two countries following the episode had fostered a modest improvement in the political atmosphere.

Following disputes and consequent military hostilities over the Shatt Al Arab between 1969 and 1974 as a result of the Shah's denunciation of the 1937 treaty in April 1969 and a subsequent mediation by the then Algerian President Boumedienne, an agreement was signed between the Shah and the then Iraqi Vice-President Saddam Hussein during an OPEC meeting in Algiers in March 1975. The agreement 'that completely eliminated the conflict between the two brotherly countries' aimed at 're-establishing security and mutual confidence along their common frontiers' and undertook to exercise a strict and effective control with the aim of finally putting an end to 'all infiltrations of a subversive character from either side'.

The 1975 agreement conceded Iranian demands for a *Thalweg* boundary throughout the Shatt Al Arab, and delimited the land frontier (where many oil fields are located) between the two countries on the bases of the Protocol of Constantinople of 1913. In political terms, the agreement embodied a straightforward *quid pro quo*: whereas Iraq acceded to a revision of the 1937 treaty, Iran was bound to cease its assistance to the Kurdish nationalist movement within Iraq.

Following the success of the Islamic revolution in taking power in Tehran and the subsequent open hostilities between the two Gulf states, President Saddam Hussein took the formal step of abrogating the Algiers agreement on 17 September 1980 (in fact, tearing his copy of the accord to pieces before an Iraqi television audience), 5 days before the outbreak of the eight-year Iran–Iraq war. But, ten years later, in September 1990, after occupying Kuwait, the same Saddam Hussein announced that his country again accepted the terms of the 1975 agreement. There remains in mid-1996 no evidence that both countries have signed any document to formalise Hussein's latest concession, however. Meanwhile, the continued deadlock over where the border between the two countries lies has led Iraq to consider diverting the Shatt Al Arab away from the border. But such a diversion is likely to result in a noticeable reduction of the water level in the waterway, jeopardising the Iranian ports.

Another territorial issue between Iran and Iraq has been the question of the Khuzestan/Arabistan region on the upper Gulf, which is Iran's richest petroleum-producing province where more than 80 per cent of the country's proven oil reserves and where up to 90 per cent of its hydrocarbons have been produced (see Chapter 5). The question of sovereignty over Khuzestan/Arabistan where the 3-million population is primarily Arab in ethnic composition was first raised in the aftermath of the First World War when Iran and Iraq clashed over the demarcation of their border and the status of Iranian nationals then living in Iraq. The region was seized in 1925 by Reza Shah, then Iranian minister of war. The issue was again evoked in 1959–60, in 1969, and in early 1980 on the eve of the war between the two countries. However, it seems that much of the issue's significance has since been lost.

Iran–UAE

On 30 November 1971, the Iranian Shah ordered his troops to land on the three strategically located islands near the Strait of Hormuz, namely Abu Musa, Tunb *Al Kubra* and Tunb *Al Sughra* (the greater and lesser Tunbs) which were then under the respective titular authority of the emirates of Sharjah and Ras Al Khaimah. The Iranian landing came only two days prior to the inauguration of the UAE and immediately after the end of Britain's direct rule in the Gulf. Iran maintained its historical rights to the islands on the basis of continuous Persian occupation until the last quarter of the nineteen century when they were evicted by Britain, and argued that the freedom of navigation into the Gulf was dependent upon control of the islands by 'a power committed to the stability of the region'.

The landing of Iranian troops came one day after the conclusion of an agreement with Sharjah concerning the status of Abu Musa Island (with the first clause of the accord reading as follows: 'Neither Iran nor Sharjah will give up its claim to Abu Musa nor recognise the other's claim'!). While both continued to maintain their respective claims to sovereignty over the island, they were able to agree that the Iranian troops would be stationed in part of Abu Musa where Iranian flag would be flown and full Iranian jurisdiction would be exercised, and Sharjah would retain full jurisdiction over the remainder of the island. The two countries recognised a 12-nautical mile limit of territorial sea around the island and agreed to share equally any revenue accruing from oil exploration and production. In fact, since 1974 when the Mubarak offshore field first came on stream, its revenues have been split evenly between the two countries (with Sharjah passing on smaller shares to Ajman and Umm Al Qaiwain), unaffected by the dispute over the island.

It was against this background that Abu Musa returned to the headlines in April 1992. It appeared that Iran, in the name of the island's security, was impeding foreign nationals employed by Sharjah from entering to the island, a step considered by the UAE as a *de facto* occupation. That was followed by a multilateralisation of the issue with the UAE taking it to the GCC and to the UN Security Council. Nevertheless, tension has since eased between the two countries with Tehran still proposing the continuation of bilateral negotiations with the UAE, but without 'pre-conditions'. The UAE agreed to resume the talks, provided that they also included the issue of Tunb inlets.

In fact, no agreement has been reached between Iran and Ras Al Khaimah over their contending claims of sovereignty on the Tunb Islands, like the one signed with Sharjah on Abu Musa. Consequently, the UAE is still considering the Tunbs as occupied since 1971.

The invasion and continuing occupation of Abu Musa and the Tunb Islands have precluded the conclusion of continental shelf boundary agreements between Iran and many emirates of the UAE. Nevertheless, it was reported that Abu Dhabi had actually initialled an agreement with Tehran in the period prior to the occupation in 1971. Dubai which has always sought to foster closer ties with Tehran so as to serve as a counterbalance against Abu Dhabi paramountcy within the federation, concluded an agreement in August 1974 with Iran, extending the maritime boundary line for a distance of 39.25 nautical miles with endpoints which coincided with those of the 1968 lateral offshore boundary line between Abu Dhabi and Dubai, and the unilateral declaration made by Sharjah in 1964 concerning its continental shelf border with Umm Al Qaiwain.

Iraq–Kuwait

On 19 June 1961 Kuwait became an independent state following the mutually-agreed termination of the 1899 bilateral agreement that had established it as a British protectorate. Within a week, the then Iraqi President Major General Qasim laid claim to Kuwait, declaring that it constituted 'an integral part of Iraq', based on the fact that it had been a district of the Ottoman Empire under the indirect administration of the governor of the Basra's *Wilayat*. Qasim asserted that with the dissolution of that empire in the aftermath of the First World War, Iraq had legally succeeded to the Turkish territorial sovereignty (or suzerainty) over Kuwait. The then Iraqi president observed that during the 1938–61 period (after the discovery in 1938 of the large Burgan oil field in Kuwait), Iraq's King Ghazi and King Faisal and Prime Minister Nouri Said had all moved to demand outright Kuwait annexation in various public statements.

Following Qasim's declaration a contingent of British troops was dispatched to Kuwait on 30 June 1961. In the following October the British forces withdrew, and in their place a 3000-strong Arab League contingent was positioned in the country. Two years later, in October 1963, Iraq under the pro-Baath government of Colonel Aref officially recognised the independence of Kuwait and confirmed the borders as defined in the 1932 exchange of letters between the Iraqi prime minister and the ruler of Kuwait.

In April 1969, Iraq was granted permission to temporarily station forces on the Kuwaiti side of the border so as to permit a forward defence of the

Iraqi city of Umm Qasr against Iranian threats. These forces withdrew in 1977, two years after the conclusion in Algiers of an Iranian–Iraqi agreement.

Meanwhile, Iraq continued to insist that Kuwait agree to cede or to lease the two islands of Bubiyan and Warbah and the coastal area adjacent to them in order to improve its access to the Gulf, if it wanted Baghdad to reciprocate by agreeing to the final delimitation of the land boundary further west. Bubiyan and Warbah Islands, formed by the Mesopotamian mud, are sparsely inhabited and located little more than a kilometre from Iraq's 16-km stretch of coastline along the Gulf. An Iraqi proposal for a long-time leasing of Warbah Island was already advanced in 1953, in return for the supply of water from Shatt Al Arab through a projected waterway, but was rejected by the Kuwaiti government. There were also reports in 1989 that Iraq had suggested a scheme to Kuwait whereby Bubiyan and Warbah Islands might be ceded or leased in return for unspecified inland Iraqi desert areas west of the Batin region. That would have been similar to the Jordanian–Saudi land-swap agreement of 1965, under which Jordan's narrow coastline on the Gulf of Aqaba was lengthened to the southeast of the port. In return, Saudi Arabia was granted a substantial area of inland desert.

The issue of the Iraq–Kuwait border was quiet until August 1990, when Saddam Hussein sent his troops and occupied Kuwait, proclaiming it as the '19th Iraqi *Wilayat*'. One reason given for the invasion was the 'irregular' extraction of Kuwait of oil from the Rumaila/Ratqa field that straddles the border, together with other justifications such as the petroleum policy adapted by the emirate at that time, and the problem of Iraqi debts to Kuwait. Kuwait was subsequently liberated in March 1991 by allied forces, and UN forces have since been positioned on a buffer zone between the two countries.

In May 1993, the UN Security Council approved the report of the UN Iraq–Kuwait Boundary Demarcation Commission (UNIKBDC) established in April 1991 to determine the land and maritime borders between the two countries. The Commission recommended the frontier in the Safwan area be moved northwards by some 570 m, giving Kuwait a larger part of the Rumaila/Ratqa oil field. The Commission also gave the emirate a fraction of the Iraqi port of Umm Qasr. It was not until early November 1994 that Iraq *de jure* recognised the sovereignty of Kuwait within the borders determined by UNIKBDC, while it noticed that the new border determination has in itself 'the seeds of future conflicts'.

Israel and its Neighbours

At least until a happy end is reached in the peace process between Israel and its neighbours, the borders between the Hebrew state and Arab countries with whom it is still officially in state of war remain sources of dispute and instability in the region.

While the boundaries of the West Bank (including Jerusalem) and Gaza Strip, occupied in June 1967, must be clearly defined by an agreement expected in 1996–7, Jordan and Israel in October 1994 reached a complex accord that allows the kingdom to reassert its sovereignty over Israeli-occupied territories (some 380 km^2 between the Gulf of Aqaba and the Dead Sea, about 5 km^2 between Aqaba and Eilat), while allowing Israel to lease two small lands for a 25-year period, the first near the Sea of Tiberias (0.83 km^2) and the second in Wadi Araba, south of the Dead Sea (1.3 km^2) This unusual arrangement could become a precedent for Israel's negotiations with Syria.

Indeed, since June 1967 Israel has been occupying the Golan Heights on the Syrian border, that strategically overlooks Israel, Syria, Jordan, and Lebanon. The Golan, where UN forces have been positioned in a buffer zone, currently supplies around 30 per cent of Israeli fresh water. In south Lebanon, Israeli troops have been stationed since June 1982, creating a self-declared 'security zone', north of which a UN force (UNIFIL) is positioned. Even though many border skirmishes have occurred in the border's region, the latest round of which dates from April 1996. The Israel–Lebanon boundary is in principle still governed by the terms of the Armistice agreement of 1949.

Qatar–Saudi Arabia

The inlet of Khaur Al Udaid at the southeastern base of the Qatar and its adjacent coastal area which gives access to the Gulf waters south of the peninsula have been the subject of dispute between Qatar and Saudi Arabia as well as Abu Dhabi. The inlet has only shallow water but Riyadh considers it to be of strategic importance. In December 1965, Qatar and Saudi Arabia concluded an agreement – rejected by Abu Dhabi – delimiting their land and maritime boundaries, and giving the sovereignty of the strip to Riyadh. However, following an incident in September 1992 at the border post of Al Khofous, the government in Doha announced that it no longer recognised the 1965 agreement.

Following mediation by Egypt, Qatar and Saudi Arabia agreed on a programmed settlement of the dispute in December 1992 by setting up a joint committee in accordance with the 1965 agreement, responsible for enforcing all its provisions. The committee was also to be responsible for marking the border points in accordance with the accompanying map and was to be assisted in this task by a specialised surveying company chosen jointly by the two parties. The committee was to draw up a definitive map, signed by both parties, and this map was to be deemed an integral part of the 1965 agreement. The committee, that should have completed its assignments by end-1993, has let nobody hear any news since the beginning of that year. Meanwhile, Qatar has reported several border clashes with Saudi forces.

On another hand, although an agreement delimiting the continental shelf boundary between Saudi Arabia and Qatar in the Bay of Al Salwa, west of the Qatari peninsula, was reportedly reached in December 1965, it has been neither officially ratified nor published.

Another dispute over the border area of Jabal Naksh which had been claimed by Saudi Arabia in the 1930s was accentuated by rumours that sizeable oil deposits lay under the zone. These proved false and the Saudi claim lapsed after the Second World War.

Saudi Arabia–Yemen

The major part of the border between Saudi Arabia and Yemen, particularly through the Rub Al Khali and Hadramout, as well as the maritime boundaries, have not yet been delimited. The territories between the 17th and 18th parallels are widely believed to be under Yemeni sovereignty, although Saudi Arabia still considers the strip between the 17th and 20th parallels to be under dispute and the subject of negotiations. Serious border incidents already occurred in 1969 when South Yemeni forces crossed the 18th parallel at one point.

The western part of the border, from Ras Al Muwaj on the Red Sea to Jebel Thar in Najran, was fixed in 1934 in accordance with the Treaty of Taif under which Yemen ostensibly dropped its claim to the 'Greater Yemen' of the seventeenth century which embraced most of southwest Arabia from the mountains of northern Asir on the Red Sea to the Dhofar coast on the Arabian Sea. The Taif Treaty, renewable every twenty years and called 'the Treaty of Islamic Friendship and Brotherhood', confirmed Saudi control over the territories of Asir (with its small Shia population), Jeysan, and Najran, while allowing Yemen to exert its authority in the regions of Jawf and Marib which both proved to be rich in petroleum.

Early in 1992, the unified Yemen Republic announced that it opposed the renewal of the 1934 treaty which was due to expire in May 1994. In the meantime, Saudi Arabia, whose drilling suggested that the western region of the border could contain important petroleum reserves, sent notes in March 1992 (and again in August 1993) to foreign oil companies that were awarded concessions by Yemen on this border area to end their activities in 'disputed regions'. Subsequently, a Saudi–Yemeni joint committee on the demarcation of borders between the two countries was established.

Meanwhile, in December 1994, Yemen accused its northern neighbour of violating its border by erecting observation posts and building roads on its territories. That led to increased tension which resulted in border clashes in January 1995. Following a resumption of negotiations, a memorandum of understanding was signed in Mecca in February 1995 between the two countries. Under the memorandum, both sides reaffirmed their recognition of, and adherence to, the legality of the 1934 treaty, while the remainder of the border, including maritime boundaries, was to be delineated 'scientifically' under the supervision of the committee representing the two states.

DORMANT BORDER DISPUTES

Around many borders in the Middle East, latent and sleeping but not yet definitely settled disputes are still present, although inactive for a reasonably long time. This is the case in the territorial question between Bahrain and Iran, and the boundary conflict opposing the latter to Kuwait. Kuwait has had some problems with Saudi Arabia over the delimitation of the offshore boundaries of the Neutral Zone. Within the UAE federation, and between the UAE and both Oman and Saudi Arabia, many border issues remain to be solved. The same applies to the Turkish boundaries with both Iraq and Syria.

Bahrain–Iran

In the early seventeenth century, Persia expelled the Portuguese occupiers from Bahrain. Then, in 1783, the Arab Utaibi rulers of Zubarah on the Qatari coast, related to the present Al Khalifa leading family, wrested Bahrain from Persian control. Nevertheless, Iran has since 1880 confirmed its claim to Bahrain. In 1927, Tehran brought the claim before the League of Nations, and protested in 1930 and 1934 when the Al Khalifa ruler had granted oil concessions to Western companies.

In May 1970, following a renewed Iranian claim to the island after the announcement of Britain's decision to withdraw by the end of 1971 from its positions east of Suez, the UN decided to organise a plebiscite which found that virtually all Bahrainis wanted a fully independent sovereign state and that the great majority wanted an Arab one. The results of the referendum were approved by a large majority by the Iranian parliament in the same month.

The Bahraini question re-emerged with the Iranian revolution. In February 1979, Ayatollah Rouhani, a prominent leader in the Islamic republic, considered Bahrain with its Shia majority as Iran's '25th province', a declaration considered by Tehran not to represent the 'official view'. The issue has been dormant since then, although Iranian involvement in two unsuccessful Bahraini coups in December 1981 and February 1996 as well as in internal riots since late 1994 has been widely suspected.

Although the bases of Iran's intermittently voiced claim to Bahrain have been both historical and sectarian in origin, it is significant to note that the emphasis accorded to either in Iranian policy has been largely a function of the nature and character of the regime in Tehran at any given point. Thus, whereas the dynastic rulers tended to highlight ancient Persian ties to the island as a justification for its position, the present theocratic regime has sought to frame the issue primarily in term of the special affinity between Iran and the archipelago's Shia majority.

Iran–Kuwait

A joint Iranian–Kuwaiti committee to determine the continental shelf boundary between the two countries was established in June 1965 and was followed by the initialling of an accord between the two parties in January 1968. The agreement provided that one of each country's prominent nearby islands (Iran's Kharg and Kuwait's Failaka) should be considered part of the onshore baselines which would be used to determine equidistance. A compromise on this point allowed both parties to confer to its island 'full effect' and to incorporate them into their respective baselines.

Iraq angrily denounced the Iranian–Kuwaiti accord on the ground that it grossly infringed its own considerable continental shelf rights in the Gulf. Accordingly, and due to the failure to officially confirm the maritime boundary line between Iraq and Kuwait, and that between Saudi Arabia and Kuwait's Neutral Zone, the January 1968 agreement was never confirmed in treaty form.

Iraq–Turkey

Just as the Turkish army announced in early May 1995 the winding up of its six-week offensive against Kurdish militias in northern Iraq, the Turkish President Demirel called for a redefinition of the border with Iraq, shifting it towards the plain lying behind the Iraqi mountains in a bid to stop the infiltration of rebels. Demirel also claimed that the Iraqi province of Mosul had belonged to Turkey and 'should be returned to it', as no provision had been made for its incorporation into Iraq by the Lausanne Treaty of 1923 which recognised the state of Turkey after the break-up of the Ottoman Empire.

In fact, it was not in 1923 but two years later that the League of Nations under British pressure recommended that the district of Mosul – where the huge oil fields of Kirkuk were later discovered – to which the Turks had laid claim, be incorporated into the new kingdom of Iraq, a decision fully implemented in the Treaty of Ankara in July 1926 between Britain, Turkey, and Iraq.

Iraq, together with many Arab countries, reacted angrily to Demirel's call for modifying the border, and the suggestion was even opposed by the USA, Britain, and France. That led Demirel to stress that Turkey had no expansionist ambitions, and was not planning to alter the border unilaterally or by force but through dialogue and in co-ordination with 'the countries concerned'. Meanwhile, in mid-1996, Turkey was planning to establish a 'security zone' in the Iraqi region adjacent to the border.

Kuwait–Saudi Arabia

The land boundary between Kuwait and Saudi Arabia was delimited by the Treaty of Uqair in December 1922. One provision of this agreement established the Kuwaiti–Saudi Arabian Neutral Zone to facilitate the movements of Bedouins in the region. In July 1965, the two countries agreed to terminate the temporary provision of the 1922 treaty, and to partition the Neutral Zone equally. Revenues from the area's oil and other natural resources have been shared by the two countries ever since.

An agreement in December 1969 confirmed the July 1965 demarcation of the land boundary in the Neutral Zone; this agreement was not extended to include the lateral offshore border, however, due to the ongoing jurisdictional dispute over the islands of Qaru and Umm Al Maradim. Saudi Arabia apparently considers the two islands to be subject to the same co-sovereignty status as that of the Neutral Zone, whereas Kuwait considers them to be its own. In September 1949, Kuwait had to cancel an oil concession covering the two islands, awarded to the US American Oil Company of California, following strong protest from Riyadh. Though the length of this offshore lateral boundary line has yet to be determined, it seems that the segment which passes through the Safaniya and Khafji oil fields has been accorded *de facto* recognition for a number of years.

In another development, Kuwaiti sovereignty was acknowledged in the mid-1980s over the island of Kubr, which had previously been another point of contention with Saudi Arabia.

Oman–UAE

Oman has periodically circulated the idea of a 'Greater Oman' that would include large parts of the UAE emirates of Ras Al Khaimah, Fujairah, and Sharjah so as to establish a direct territorial link with Musandam, the Omani enclave on the tip of the peninsula which governs the Strait of Hormuz.

On the southwest of Musandam, Oman has claimed some 16 km of land between the villages of Dawra and Rims in Ras Al Khaimah, which had been administrated by Oman for centuries. That claim turned into a long-term source of confrontation, the most recent incident of which occurred in November 1992. The maritime border with Ras Al Khaimah adjacent to the disputed stretch of territory emerged as a source of contention in 1977–8 following the start of offshore petroleum exploration. On the northeast of Musandam, the town of Diba Al Hisn is politically divided into three component settlements under the respective authorities of Oman, Fujairah, and Sharjah.

The boundaries between the Omani mainland and the UAE have not yet been exactly defined. One enclave along the Wadi Hadf on the border between Oman and Ajman is ruled by a common administration from the two countries; authority over another enclave west of the Hajar range of mountains is shared by Oman and Sharjah. Moreover, both Abu Dhabi and Oman have claimed sovereignty over the Buraimi oasis, based upon their continuous occupation of the area and its environs since 1869. The disputed territory consists today of six Abu Dhabi and three Omani villages immediately adjacent to the town of Al Ain, the area traditionally associated with Abu Dhabi's ruling Al Nahyan family. That town and the surrounding mountains which are contiguous with Oman remain of vital importance to Abu Dhabi as they are at present its primary source of fresh water, and are considered to be potentially rich in hydrocarbons. It seems that both Oman and Abu Dhabi want to maintain the territorial *status quo* at the oasis and its environs, at least for the time being.

Saudi Arabia–UAE

Like a large part of its boundary with Abu Dhabi, the land and maritime borders between Saudi Arabia and its neighbouring UAE emirates remain undefined.

As mentioned earlier, the Khaur Al Udaid inlet at the southeast base of the Qatar peninsula and its adjacent coastal area have been the subject of a dispute between Abu Dhabi and Saudi Arabia as well as Qatar. Abu Dhabi's claim to sovereignty over the inlet, supported by British declarations to that effect in 1878 and 1937, was based upon the occupation of the strip by a certain section of the Bani Yas tribe between 1869 and 1880. In December 1965, Qatar and Saudi Arabia concluded an agreement delimiting their land and maritime boundaries, giving the sovereignty of the strip to the kingdom, but without the consent of Abu Dhabi.

In 1970 when Aramco made a very promising oil strike at Shaybah, Saudi Arabia claimed all the territories south of Abu Dhabi's Liwa oasis (the Shaybah field is part of the larger 7-billion barrel Zarrara structure on the other side of the border). Four years later, in July 1974, Abu Dhabi and Saudi Arabia concluded an agreement under which the emirate pledged not to exploit the small portion of the Shaybah/Zarrara field lying within its own boundaries. The agreement that provided for exploration and development of the whole field by Saudi Arabia granted the kingdom access to the Khaur Al Udaid inlet through a territorial corridor across its frontier with Qatar.

In return, Saudi Arabia under the July 1974 agreement renounced its claim to the Buraimi oasis, disputed by both Abu Dhabi and Oman. Riyadh had claimed its historical connection to the oasis and its adjacent territory, and in August 1952 it dispatched a small police contingent to the area, which was able to assert civil Saudi authority over the village of Hamasa. Saudi Arabia, meanwhile, helped the Ibadi Imam of Muscat and Oman (the old name for the Sultanate of Oman) to declare the independence of an Ibadi state in Buraimi in 1954 and to seek membership in the Arab League. The movement was subsequently crushed and Saudi forces were ejected from the oasis in October 1955 by forces from Abu Dhabi and Muscat under British command. That was followed by an agreement which led to a standstill situation, kept until the signing of the July 1974 treaty. The whole border between Oman and Saudi Arabia was subsequently defined in an agreement concluded in 1990.

Syria–Turkey

The border between Turkey and Syria was confirmed by the Treaty of Lausanne in 1923 which considered the province of Alexandretta as part of the Syrian territory, although governed under a special regime. Nevertheless, Turkey pressed in the 1930s for a separate agreement concerning the status of the province. In 1937 the League of Nations decided that Alexandretta should be fully autonomous. Meanwhile a treaty between France, the then mandatory power, and Syria was signed in 1936 envisaging the emergence of a unitary Syrian state that included Alexandretta. The treaty was never ratified, but instead, and under the pressure of international tension, the province of Alexandretta was ceded to Turkey in June 1939 and was renamed Hatay, while the city of Alexandretta was renamed Iskenderun.

The territory is still in dispute, although not actively, at a time when Syria considers the province of Alexandretta as part of its territory, still shown on the official maps of the country. As a consequence, the maritime boundaries adjacent to the province have also been disputed.

Inter–UAE

Territorial arrangements within the UAE have always been complex, reflecting political units derived from tribal relationships. Many small enclaves within the country are still commonly administrated by different emirates. Moreover, only Abu Dhabi and Umm Al Qaiwain of the seven emirates of the federation comprise territorially integral units. By way of contrast, the smallest emirate, Ajman, with a total area of approximately 300 km^2, is sub-divided into three component territorial units.

In addition, several internal boundaries between members of the federation are still undefined or disputed. After Abu Dhabi's claim in 1946 to nearly half of Dubai and the subsequent military action, the dispute was provisionally settled in 1969 through the creation of a neutral zone in the contested area. The two parties also agreed to share the revenues equally from any future oil find at that location.

Another emirate, Fujairah, was considered until 1901 as part of Sharjah. It had been recognised as autonomous by the British protectorate until 1952, when it became independent. Following the establishment of the UAE in 1971, fighting erupted between Fujairah and Sharjah over an oil field. The dispute was provisionally resolved by granting both emirates equal access rights to the field's wells.

Dubai and Sharjah have had a long-standing dispute over the demarcation of their border. In 1981, the issue was settled by an arbitration award by a select group of international lawyers. A dispute was raised between Sharjah and Umm Al Qaiwain in 1968 over drilling rights following the discovery of a major new field off the coast of Abu Musa Island (then under the sole control of Sharjah). The dispute was resolved in 1981, and the land border between the two emirates was defined by an agreement concluded in May 1994.

7 Disparity in Growth and Economic Constraints

DISPARITY IN ECONOMIC DEVELOPMENT

A continuing source of disaffection and conflict in the Middle East, especially among neighbouring countries, consists of the great disparity between those which have vast wealth as a result of petroleum deposits and those which have virtually no economic resources at all. Numerical comparison shows the striking differences in the level of economic development.

As indicator of a country's wealth and level of development, *per capita* gross national product (GNP) is the most widely used and is usually thought to be a better indicator of living standards than gross domestic product (GDP). The latter takes account only of the value of domestic production, while the former includes income from abroad. In the Middle East, the latter is significant for both the major oil exporters and the poorer, more populous states. The remittances which Egyptian workers earn in the Gulf or Turkish workers get in Germany are taken into account in the GNP figure. For the petroleum exporting countries, the income on overseas investments is an important element in GNP, but not in GDP. Kuwait earned more from its overseas investments than it did from oil exports in the 1980s when one-third of Saudi Arabia's revenue was accounted for by interests, profits and dividends on foreign financial assets.

Per capita GNP for different countries has to be denominated in terms of a common unit of account if international comparisons are to be made. It is usually in US dollars, the usual conversion, because of its widespread recognition and use. If a currency depreciates, however, this lowers the value of its GNP when measured in dollars, and appreciation increases its value. Exchange rates have generally been stable in the GCC but as Israel and Turkey, among other Middle Eastern countries, devalue their currencies several times a year, the choice of a conversion rate poses a problem. When a country has multiple exchange rates, as is the case with Syria, the conversion factor is also a matter for debate. This type of issue means that GNP figures, although good for comparison purpose, are far from being precise, and must be interpreted with caution. For these reasons, some analysts prefer to use the *per capita* GNP in current international dollars (CID). The CID is obtained by special conversion factors designed to equalise the purchasing powers of currencies in the respective countries. The special conversion factor, or the purchasing power parity, is defined as the number of units of a country's currency required to buy the same amounts of goods and services in the domestic market as one dollar would buy in the USA.

Per capita GNP figures (in usual US$ conversion, and in CID) as reported in Table 7.1 show the huge disparity in the level of economic

Table 7.1   Disparity in economic development in the Middle East, 1976, 1985, and 1994 (*per capita* GNP, US $)[1]

Country	1976[3]	1985[3]	1994[3]	1994[4]
Bahrain	na	na	7460	13 200
Egypt	280	610	720	3720
Iran	1930	7400[2]	2820[2]	4720
Iraq	1390	7500[2]	800[2]	2200[2]
Israel	3920	4990	14 530	15 300
Jordan	610	1560	1440	4100
Kuwait	15 480	14 480	19 420	24 730
Lebanon	1080[2]	1700[2]	1500[2]	4360
Oman	na	6730	5140	8590
Qatar	na	na	12 820	19 100
Saudi Arabia	4480	8850	7050	9480
Syria	780	1570	1300[2]	5000
Turkey	990	1080	2500	4710
UAE	na	19 270	23 000	22 480
Yemen	250/280[5]	550/530[5]	280	1955

Notes:

1. *Sources*: *World Development Report* (Washington, DC: World Bank, various issues).
2. Estimates.
3. In US$, usual conversion.
4. In current international dollars (CID), obtained by special conversion factors designed to equalise the purchasing powers of currencies in the respective countries. The special conversion factor, or the purchasing power parity, is defined as the number of units of a country's currency required to buy the same amounts of goods and services in the domestic market as one dollar would buy in the USA.
5. North Yemen/South Yemen.
na=not available.

wealth and development between the countries of the Middle East, from a very low income (Yemen) to one of the highest in the world (the UAE). Countries with *per capita* GNP (in usual US$ conversion) of less than US $725 such as Yemen and Egypt are classified as low income, and are considered by the World Bank to be amongst the least developed countries in the world, although the situation in Egypt seems to be recovering. Those countries with *per capita* incomes of up to $2900 are classified as lower middle income. This band is wide, and includes countries such as Iran, Iraq, Jordan, Lebanon, Syria, and Turkey.

The sparsely-populated petroleum exporting countries are in a category of their own; a state such as the UAE enjoys close to the highest *per capita* GNP in the world, at around $23 000 in 1994 (although still far from the topmost in the world, that of Switzerland with $37 930, but comparable to the $25 880 of the US and the $23 420 of France). In 1994, Kuwait (even following a disastrous war) and Qatar enjoyed high *per capita* GNP of $19 420 and $12 820 respectively. A more populous exporting country like Saudi Arabia recorded in 1994 a *per capita* GNP of $7050.

The *per capita* GNP for the Gulf states is, however, a striking instance of the inadequacy of this indicator as a measure of living standards. Although the oil exporting countries are prosperous by Third World standards, and food and housing conditions for local citizens are generally adequate, living standards remain well below those enjoyed by the majority in Western Europe, Japan or North America. In fact, *per capita* GNP merely reflects the level of petroleum production. Moreover, a high level of petroleum output increases current national and personal income, but reduces future potential income as petroleum reserves are depleted more rapidly.

The large gap between rich and poor countries in the Middle East has been the engine for pragmatic calls for more equal distribution of wealth in the area, which could be imposed by force. This has increased the tension between the countries with different living standards, which often border each other, creating a kind of polarisation between the poor and indignant on one side, and the rich and complacent on the other. This contrast in wealth has already exacerbated the conflagration in the upper Gulf between Kuwait and Iraq.

The windfall affluence of petroleum wealth has thus created a paradox for the GCC capital rich states, increasing their own political isolation in the region. The ruling families of these states have learned that although both internal and external political support can be bought in the short term, survival will ultimately depend either on a more equitable sharing of oil revenues, or on a continued recourse to outside assistance to defeat regional challenges to the *status quo*, a recourse that could prove to be worse than the alternative.

SOCIAL IMPACTS OF ECONOMIC CONSTRAINTS

Middle Eastern states bordering Israel have experienced economic problems partly due to their enormous spending on defence. Considering that these countries have never lived through an economic boom like those seen in the region's oil producing states, their government subsidies and benefits systems have always been of minor importance. Consequently, impacts of economic recessions have not been so clearly felt by the nationals whom 'better life' expectations have remained relatively modest. Some exceptions must be mentioned, however, such as in 1977 in Egypt, where economic constraints due to large increases in food and other prices adopted in a programme of economic reform dictated by the International Monetary Fund (IMF) led to violent social riots.

Nevertheless, together with the high growth in population and the advances toward peace with the Hebrew state, 'better life' expectations of nationals in these countries are likely to grow. If these expectations for 'peace dividends' are for one reason or another not met, serious unrest can be awaited. That is exactly what happened in Jordan in August 1996. Already a decline in the economic activity in oil exporting states of the region is creating unemployment in these countries, many of whom depend heavily on the Gulf absorbing their surplus manpower, and is hampering their own economic growth by depriving them of enormous transferred earnings and generous financial aid.

In fact, the oil producing countries in the Gulf had had a very prosperous economic and financial situation, mainly as a result of large oil wealth compared to the absorption capacity of these states, and they consequently spent beyond their income for around two decades from the early 1970s. Nevertheless, their economic and financial situation has recently become more of a problem due to many factors, including the marginalisation of OPEC and Gulf supplies, the decline in oil prices, and the costs and consequences of two major conflicts in the region within one decade.

Indeed, after the eight-year war between Iran and Iraq, during which billions of dollars were spent, both countries have been urgently in need of external capital for reconstruction. Iraq's requirements have substantially increased as a result of the conflict over Kuwait, which has been concentrating on ways to finance its huge and expensive reconstruction programme after paying dearly for its own liberation. For its part, Saudi Arabia's past strength in internally satisfying the investment requirements of its economic sectors has now been weakened by the government's heavy arms purchases and its contribution towards the costs of liberating Kuwait. The UAE, while not so badly affected by the military developments in the region, has had to bear the financial difficulties of its Bank of Credit and Commerce International (BCCI).

The economic and financial constraints of the Gulf have been aggravated by the weak oil markets and prices since the mid-1980s, which are expected to remain flat throughout the 1990s, at a time when the region's countries are still almost totally dependent on oil as source of revenue and means of economic development. As an example of that impact, each fall of 1 dollar per barrel in oil prices in 1995 meant a loss of over $2.8 billion in annual Saudi oil export revenues, around $1 billion for Iran, $850 million for the UAE, and some $750 million for Kuwait.

In economies like those of the Gulf oil exporting states, high revenues generated by successive oil price increases have led to expenditures that are not necessarily needed. Then, theoretically, a decrease in oil prices would stimulate a reduction in expenses, which would not be of real damage to the economy. Obviously, much will depend on the rate of decline in oil price and revenues. However, one of the main problems for these governments is that current expenditure has proved politically sensitive and therefore very difficult to prune back. There are huge costs involved in running and maintaining the activities already established by development project capital inputs, in social services as well as physical infrastructure. What is even more important is that these states could be vulnerable to domestic unrest if they were forced to decrease the funds for politically sensitive sectors such as defence and security, and to curtail the benefits and subsidies they bestow on their populations.

In fact, the Gulf Arab states have been pursuing a number of spending policies and items of business and social legislation, designed to pump real personal wealth into the hands of citizens while giving non-nationals enough to induce them to stay and perform their useful work, but no more. The enrichment of nationals was an end in itself, leading to a real personal sense of having the world's highest disposable incomes and living in the world's most generous welfare states. Any attempt to curtail this generosity could prove to be deadly. Riots sparked by higher prices for petroleum products in Iran in early April 1995 exemplify what could happen elsewhere in the Gulf.

As a way to overcome their economic and financial constraints, the Gulf governments started to disinvest some of their overseas assets and reserves. Kuwait and Saudi Arabia can exemplify this process. Until the eruption of the conflict with its northern neighbour, Kuwait had enjoyed a relatively healthy economy. In every year during the 1980s, the country had registered a current account surplus higher than those reached by any neighbouring state. That was partly due to growing income from the country's overseas investments. It was said that the Kuwaiti economy before the conflict with Iraq effectively existed outside its own territorial borders except for some refineries, petrochemical, and desalination plants, and that the emirate since 1986 had earned more from its overseas investments than it had directly from oil exports.

Kuwait's overseas investments consist mainly of bank deposits and holdings of stakes and bonds in industrialised countries, in addition to upstream and downstream oil activities abroad, including hydrocarbon exploration and production, oil refining and distribution, and petrochemical production in more than forty foreign countries. Although there are wide discrepancies between published estimates of Kuwait's available foreign assets, conservative estimates of its liquid foreign investments at the time of the Iraqi invasion in August 1990 were of the order of $70–100 billion, including reserves held in the Fund for Future Generations (FFG). The FFG was set up in 1976, and by law receives 10 per cent of all Kuwait's oil revenues; although it was not supposed to be drawn on until 2001, money from the fund was used in the aftermath of the Iraqi invasion. Indeed, liquidation of some of Kuwait's foreign assets was necessary after the conflict with Iraq in order to pay for coalition military costs – estimated at around $47 billion – and defray reconstruction costs. In mid-1995, the volume of Kuwait's foreign assets was estimated at $32 billion.

In neighbouring Saudi Arabia, budget deficits have been partly covered by drawing on foreign reserves and assets. Riyadh was the first in the Gulf to adopt this policy, between 1986 and 1991. Official Saudi assets consequently declined from around $171 billion in 1981 to around $28 billion in 1995, of which some $20 billion are non-performing loans to Iraq and African countries. Accordingly, there has been some questioning about the liquidity of the overall reserves figure, with the major part representing loans that could be recovered only with great difficulty, and a minor part representing subscriptions to international agencies.

The divestment of overseas assets and reserves is considered as a perverse approach due to the fact that, in principle, depleting government-led foreign assets, apart from making disposals of non-core investment assets in appropriate circumstances, could disrupt the investment strategy and affect the profits expected from these investments. In any case, depleting overseas assets and financial reserves is by nature limited. That has led to recourse since the mid-1980s to large-scale borrowing (see Table 7.2). Most of the area's governments are borrowing, based on the assumption that higher oil prices will eventually come. However, this approach is storing up problems for the future, due to the uncertainties (and the consequent adverse effects) related not only to oil prices, but also to exchange and interest rates. Moreover, foreign debts aggravated by the financial costs, primarily interest, are placing a heavy burden on the region's economies. If the borrowing continues for a long time, it could be used as a pretext for foreign political domination and control of the debtor resources (Mexico in 1995 is a very recent example), and could lead to a subsequent loss of independence. That was the case with the occupation of Egypt by Britain in 1882, and the French protectorate on Morocco and Tunisia in the early decades of the twentieth century.

Table 7.2   External debt in the Middle East, 1994[1]

Country	External debt ($ billion)	Debt/GNP (%)
Bahrain	2.6[2]	61
Egypt	33.4	79
Iran	22.7	18
Iraq	82.0[2]	370
Israel	25.9	37
Jordan	7.1	122
Kuwait	9.0[2]	40
Lebanon	2.0	21
Oman	3.1	31
Qatar	1.5	21
Saudi Arabia	50.6[2]	41
Syria	20.6	105
Turkey	66.3	51
UAE	11.6	30
Yemen	6.0	162

Note:
1. *Sources*: *World Debt Tables 1996* (Washington, DC: World Bank, 1996), and various others.
2. Estimates.

8 Divergence in Petroleum Policies

Every petroleum producing country in the Middle East is deeply concerned with the fact that petroleum is a diminishing resource. They are equally aware that petroleum is more or less the only natural resource they have. Therefore, it goes without saying that the first and biggest economic preoccupation for the producers consists of the value of their petroleum reserves, and how to extract the highest possible price for them and conserve them for as long as possible. A standard producer rhetoric has always spoken of managing the national asset as 'a trust for the generations yet unborn'.

These issues are matched by an equally obsessive concern with petroleum income that accounts for nearly all revenues and all but a fraction of the countries' foreign exchange receipts, although many producers have been trying to diversify their sources of income from non-petroleum sectors. In 1995, and according to OPEC statistics, petroleum exports were still representing 81.4 per cent of the total value of exports in Iran, 93.7 per cent in Kuwait, and 84.7 per cent in Saudi Arabia. Future evolution of the economic situation in petroleum producing and exporting countries thus remains largely dependent on petroleum prices.

At the same time, however, Middle Eastern producers, especially in the GCC, have been pursuing a policy that can only make diversification of income sources more difficult and put off the day when their economies might be self-sufficient without petroleum revenues. This policy has consisted of the wholesale enrichment of their own citizens. But the richer the populations become, the more dependent they are on a high petroleum income to maintain the standard of living to which they have made themselves accustomed. One might say that petroleum producers have set themselves the almost impossible task of not only diversifying the sources of revenue, but diversifying while maintaining their populations as some of the richest in the world.

With that in mind, petroleum policy, and especially the issue of price (and revenues), becomes critical. In an attempt to consolidate a strong petroleum policy and to co-ordinate with other producers in form of an international cartel, governments of petroleum producing countries in the region together with few from other areas established the Organisation of Petroleum Exporting Countries (OPEC) in September 1960 (see Box 8.1).

Box 8.1   The Structure of OPEC and OAPEC

OPEC Structure

For the Organisation of Petroleum Exporting Countries (OPEC), supreme authority is vested in the *Conference* that consists of the heads of delegation of member countries, usually the ministers of oil or energy. The Conference, which meets at least twice a year at a venue of its own choosing, and operates on the principle of unanimity, is responsible for the formulation and implementation of the Organisation's policy. It also decides on applications for membership, and on recommendations made by the Board of Governors on the affairs of the Organisation. The Conference approves the appointment of the OPEC governor for each member country, elects the chairman of the Board of Governors, appoints the Secretary General and the Deputy Secretary General, and decides on the Organisation's budget, as submitted by the Board of Governors.

The effective management of the Organisation is carried out by the *Board of Governors*, each of whose members is appointed for a period of two years, but can be reappointed. It is the Board that implements the resolutions of the Conference, approves the annual budget, decides on reports submitted by the Secretary General, and ensures the proper and timely preparation of reports and recommendations to the Conference.

The *Secretariat* (in Vienna, Austria, with around 250 staff) carries out the executive functions of the Organisation in accordance with the provisions of the OPEC statute and under the direction of the Board of Governors. It provides the Conference with support facilities of various kinds, and carries out research into energy, economics and finance; prepares reports and statistics; provides information on the Organisation and its activities in the shape of publications, and organises seminars, briefings and lectures. The Secretariat is financed by member countries, each paying the same amount of contribution irrespective of its size or oil production.

The chief executive of the OPEC Secretariat is the Secretary General, who is the legally authorised representative of the Organisation. He can delegate some of his authority to the Deputy Secretary General. The Secretary General is appointed, either on merit or by rotation, by the Conference. If on merit, he is appointed for a period of three years, which term may be renewed once for the same period. The appointment is made on nomination by member countries and based on the qualifications, experience and background of the nominee. If by rotation, the Secretary General is appointed alphabetically, for a term of two years, without prejudice to the required qualifications.

The Secretary General is assisted in the discharge of his duties by the Deputy Secretary General, who is appointed by the Conference for a term of three years, which term may be extended for a period of one year or more on the recommendation of the Board of Governors. The Deputy Secretary General is responsible to the Secretary General for the co-ordination of the research and administrative activities of the Secretariat.

Box 8.1   The Structure of OPEC and OAPEC   (*continued*)

The functions of the different departments are also exercised under the supervision of the Deputy Secretary General, who naturally acts for the Secretary
General when the latter is absent from headquarters. It is the Secretary General
that appoints the heads of departments, subject to the approval of the Board of
Governors.

The *Economic Commission Board* (ECB), created in 1964, is a specialised
body operating within the framework of the OPEC Secretariat. The ECB
consists of the Deputy Secretary General of OPEC (who is *ex officio* the Board's
chairman), the national representatives appointed by member countries and
a commission co-ordinator (who is *ex officio* the director of the OPEC
Secretariat's research division). The ECB assists the Organisation in promoting
stability in international petroleum markets and deals with oil- and energy-
related questions such as production, supply and demand, and pricing. It also
studies reports submitted by the OPEC Secretariat, makes recommendations to
the Conference, and reviews developments in the international economic and
financial spheres. The ECB meets at least twice a year.

The Conference is assisted by a number of other special committees, some of
which were created to deal with issues of particular complexity emerging in the
early 1980s. The most important of these committees is the *Ministerial
Monitoring Committee* (MMC). The MMC was established by the Conference
in March 1982, with a brief to meet periodically to monitor the market situation
and recommend measures to be taken. From time to time, *ad hoc Committees*
are set up to look into particular issues of concern to the Organisation, after
which they are disbanded. For example, an *ad hoc* committee was set up in
December 1971 to renegotiate posted oil prices following the effective devalu-
ation of the US dollar.

OAPEC Structure

The highest authority of the Organisation of Arab Petroleum Exporting
Countries (OAPEC) is the *Ministerial Council* that draws up the general policy
of the Organisation, directs its activity and makes the rules governing it. The
Council decides on applications for membership and approves invitations to
petroleum exporting countries to attend its meetings; decides, recommends and
advises on matters to the Organisation's general policy and its positions – or the
position of one or more of its members – toward specific issues; approves draft
agreements reached by the Organisation and issues the necessary regulations
and amendments thereto; approves the draft annual budget, the budget of the
Judicial tribunal, and the end-year accounts; and appoints the Secretary General
and Assistant Secretaries General.

The Council is composed of the oil ministers or comparable officials from
each of the member countries. It convenes twice a year, and the chairmanship
rotates annually among the representatives in alphabetical order of their
countries.

Box 8.1   The Structure of OPEC and OAPEC   (*continued*)

The *Executive Bureau* assists the Ministerial Council in supervising the Organisation's affairs by preparing the Council's agenda, approving and amending as necessary the regulations applying to the General Secretariat staff, reviewing the Organisation's draft annual budget as prepared by the Secretary General and submitting it to the Council for approval, and submitting suggestions and recommendations to the Council on matters related to the agreement and to the execution of the Organisation's activities.

The Executive Bureau is composed of one representative from each of the member countries. The Bureau convenes at least three times a year to prepare the agendas for the Council meetings and to review the Organisation's budget. The chairmanship rotates annually in the order followed by the Council.

The *General Secretariat* (in Kuwait City) plans, administers and executes the Organisation's activities in accordance with its objectives and with the resolutions and directives of the Ministerial Council. The Secretariat is headed by a Secretary General, who is also the Organisation's official spokesman and legal representative and is answerable to the Council. The Secretary General, aided by up to three Assistant Secretaries General, directs the Secretariat and supervises all aspects of its activities.

The *Judicial Tribunal* was formed in 1981 according to a special protocol that is attached to the Organisation's agreement. Nine part-time judges are serving on the Tribunal; their terms of office are subject to rotation every three years. The Tribunal has compulsory jurisdiction in disputes relating to the interpretation and application of the OAPEC agreement; disputes between two or more member countries concerning petroleum operations, so long as they do not infringe on the sovereignty of any of the countries concerned; and in disputes that the Ministerial Council decides are within the competence of the Tribunal. With the consent of the disputing parties, the Tribunal may also rule on disputes between a member country and a petroleum company operating in its territory; disputes between one member country and a national oil company of another member; and disputes between two or more member countries, apart from the compulsory jurisdiction above.

The Tribunal also has advisory jurisdiction enabling it to give its opinion on issues referred to it by the Ministerial Council. Rulings of the Tribunal are considered to be final and binding on the disputing parties, and in themselves carry the authority of executive power in OAPEC member countries.

Established by Iran, Iraq, Kuwait, Saudi Arabia, and Venezuela, OPEC today also includes Algeria, Indonesia, Libya, Nigeria, Qatar, and the UAE. Ecuador and Gabon decided to withdraw in 1992 and 1996 respectively. Prompted by an inadequacy to manage petroleum resources on an individual basis, OPEC sought at the start to present foreign oil companies with a unified front. The Organisation was somewhat successful in preventing further cuts by the oil companies in posted prices from which their taxes were calculated in the early 1960s, while seeking to acquire higher revenues for its petroleum.

OPEC tried to punish Israel's supporters in the 1967 Arab–Israeli war by cutting off sales to the West. At that time there was, however, an oil glut in the world, and the boycott lasted only one week, costing Saudi Arabia about $30 million and Kuwait around $7 million. In 1968, OPEC issued a declaration of principles insisting that the right to control oil production and prices rested within the producing countries. 1968 also saw the establishment of the Organisation of Arab Petroleum Exporting Countries (OAPEC), currently composed of ten Arab producers, namely Algeria, Egypt, Iraq, Kuwait, Libya, Oman, Qatar, Saudi Arabia, Syria, and the UAE (see Box 8.1)

It was the revolution in Libya in 1969 that provided OPEC with new strength and increasing leverage against foreign oil companies. Libya under Muammar Qaddafi initiated actions to restrict production and increase revenues earned from petroleum exploitation. In February 1971 Abu Dhabi, Iran, Iraq, Kuwait, Qatar, and Saudi Arabia met in Tehran with members of the foreign oil companies. Using Libya as their example, they pressed for greater rewards, and the companies eventually yielded to their demands. Still another agreement was concluded in April 1971 by Libya and Iraq that brought even more handsome dividends. In December 1971, however, US President Nixon devalued the dollar, and the gains achieved by the oil producing countries were virtually wiped out. OPEC thereupon insisted on further increases, which were again granted by the companies. In June 1973 another price adjustment was won by the Organisation. Moreover, future posted prices were to follow a formula reflecting fluctuations in the dollar's value.

In addition to these victories, oil producing countries began to nationalise many of their foreign holdings. Algeria seized the French operations, and Libya nationalised British Petroleum's interests in 1971. Iraq followed suit in 1972, and Iran, which had taken possession of its fields in 1951, effected total control in 1973. Saudi Arabia, Kuwait, Qatar, and the UAE sought a more moderate course, but by the mid-1970s they too had gained control over their installations. Management, however, continued under company's control.

The Arab–Israeli war in October 1973 emboldened OPEC to insist on higher prices for their petroleum. The Organisation called a meeting in Kuwait in mid-October, when the Arab members insisted on tying the sale of petroleum to the degree of support the consuming nations were prepared to give the Arabs in their war against Israel. The Arab members called for a 5 per cent reduction in production each month until Israel was forced to return the territories seized in the 1967 war and to respect the rights of the Palestinians. Libya imposed an embargo on the USA. Saudi Arabia, represented by its petroleum minister Sheikh Ahmad Zaki Yemeni, quickly increased the pressure by cutting oil production by 10 and then by 25 per cent, and by terminating all shipments to the USA. The USA was called upon to cease supplying Israel with military supplies, but Washington decided against yielding, and in fact increased its arms transfers to Tel Aviv.

These events played havoc with the world oil market. Fear of vast shortages forced prices to unprecedented levels, with premium oil rising to $20 per barrel. Oil was judged a potent political weapon as well as a means toward fulfilling the financial needs of the producing countries. Arab political objectives were not realised but OPEC got an economic advantage. OAPEC was divided, and despite verbal displays of unity against a common foe, the member states could not agree on a uniform policy or measures, especially with reference to their relations with the USA. The oil embargo was finally lifted in mid-1974.

The collapse of the Shah's administration in 1979 through the Islamic revolution in Iran, and the Iran–Iraq war that started in September 1980 seriously damaged OPEC and OAPEC. The shortfall in oil supply brought on by the two events forced oil prices to astronomical heights in the early 1980s, with best quality petroleum selling for well in excess of $40 per barrel on the spot market.

Despite such high prices, OPEC and OAPEC were less and less able to act as effective organisations. Saudi Arabia refused to follow the dictates of the other members, and its superior production, further exaggerated by the loss of Iranian and Iraqi crude, placed it in a pivotal situation. Furthermore, because of the high cost of petroleum, conservation efforts in the industrialised states and belt-tightening elsewhere dramatically reduced the world-wide demand for oil. In 1981–2 an oil glut occurred, forcing a slight reduction in the posted price. Efforts by OPEC were aimed at cutting production, and Saudi Arabia, after first delaying its decision, began to cut back sales in order to stabilise prices, playing the role of 'swing producer'. A decline in oil prices started in early 1986 following a decision by OPEC members, especially Saudi Arabia who removed Sheikh Yemeni from the ministry of petroleum, to defend their market shares by producing freely. The quota system was re-established in the late 1980s but the weakness in oil prices has remained, although prices saw some temporal upward movements especially in the early days of the conflict over Kuwait in 1990–1.

Nevertheless, after many decades since their formation, there is little indication that OPEC and OAPEC are coherent organisations capable of acting as unified for specific goals, although OPEC represents the most influential cartel in the contemporary world and, whether directly or indirectly, the economies of the world's nations have been deeply affected by its activities.

OPEC has in effect found it very hard to achieve its objectives, and the real prices of oil in 1994–5 found the same levels as in the earlier years of this century (see Figure 8.1). One of the reasons for the failure of OPEC to attain its objectives has been its eroding market share due to the increasing share of non-OPEC output, although development and production costs in the member countries, especially those in the Gulf, are considered to be the lowest in the world. However, there is a consensus in the oil industry that technological progress has been reducing the cost of developing and expanding production in almost every producing area. A great deal of effort and funding had already been put into research and development (R&D) following the oil price hikes of 1973 and 1979–80. The industry was able to focus on the most promising innovation for technological and cost reduction potential. Indeed, since the early 1980s, new technology has transformed the business of finding, developing and producing oil. Innovations such as the introduction of three-dimensional (3-D) seismic analysis, improvements in horizontal drilling techniques, and major advances in cost-effective development strategies have all enabled companies to bring new (mostly non-OPEC) oil fields on stream at lower costs.

Other reasons for OPEC failure are partly related to the difficulty of maintaining sufficient solidarity and discipline among its member countries in order to follow a consistent policy on market share, production and pricing. This is primarily because many of the members have conflicting interests and are susceptible in varying degrees to domestic and international pressures that inhibit their ability to conform with the organisation's policy.

Among the main factors preventing OPEC solidarity are the disparities in petroleum revenues between the members and the disparities in the respective populations that those revenues have to serve. Algeria, Iran and Iraq have relatively large populations to satisfy whereas Kuwait, Bahrain, Qatar and the UAE have very small populations. There have also been disparities regarding the purposes to which petroleum revenues have been put. In most of the GCC states, there has been some internal development but very little industrialisation other than refining and petrochemical installations. Most of the oil revenues have been invested in foreign

132

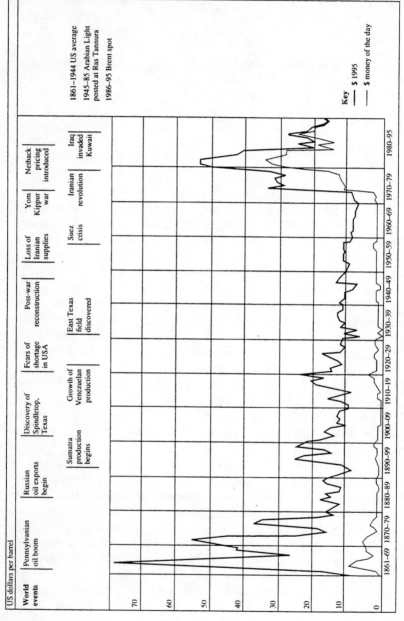

Figure 8.1   Crude oil prices since 1861

Source: BP Statistical Review of World Energy 1996 (London: British Petroleum, 1996). Reproduced with permission.

countries, thus providing even more revenues, allowing a large proportion of the indigenous populations to live easily and rely on immigrant labour to do the less savoury work.

Iraq, on the other hand, with its booming population, has attempted to invest in internal industrialisation and development as well as spending a large proportion of its revenues on military equipment both from the West and from the USSR. In addition, for eight years from 1980 Iraq was engaged in a war with Iran that consumed much of its revenues and put a drastic strain on its economy before being involved in a conflict over Kuwait. Given this situation, it is clear that Iraq would be much more sensitive to price and revenue fluctuations than Gulf states.

Iran also is very sensitive to prices: with a population as large as that of all the GCC states combined, its urgent need is for petroleum revenues as a form of economic warfare against the West and as a means of development and reconstruction after the war with Iraq. Indeed, the Islamic republic, since its revolution in 1979, has always been regarded as a price hawk.

What seems important to highlight in this context is the policy of Saudi Arabia regarding petroleum price and revenues. Due to its huge reserves and its ability to adjust output over a broad range, the kingdom comes closer than any other nation to being able to influence the oil price. Two explanations have been applied to Saudi Arabia's oil price policy since the mid-1980s. The first is that the policy consists of increasing volume and accepting the consequent lower prices. The other is that the policy resides simply in pursuing low prices *per se*.

The first version argues that Saudi Arabia's policy is aimed at maximising the kingdom's share of the oil market to gain revenue for a cash-short treasury and to position for negotiations on possible cutbacks in the future. A further explanation is that Saudi Arabia used volume to display to OPEC its power to enforce discipline and enable itself to regain the sort of control enjoyed in the Organisation's meetings in the 1970s and the first half of the 1980s.

The second version of Saudi Arabia's policy objective, which does not necessarily contradict the first, is that the country simply wants low oil prices. In the longer term, the view is taken that the kingdom, with its huge reserves, seeks to protect the role of oil in the world energy markets. The second oil shock of 1979–81 is now perceived by Riyadh to have been a disaster that led to a substantial reduction in the role of oil in the world's energy balances and which threatened the country's future. The view is that cultivating low prices and low price expectations would encourage a demand recovery, inhibit the development of other, more costly, oil supplies, and would help the recovery of Western economies, especially that of the USA, Saudi Arabia's closest ally, while a high price would badly affect pro-Arab support in the West, encourage the development of other sources of energy (and costly oil), reinforce the power of potential neighbouring enemies for the kingdom, and lead to an ultra-rapid economic growth in the country, creating internal tensions and overthrowing traditional equilibrium.

Although both versions of Saudi Arabia's policy objectives lead to lower prices, there are plausible reasons why in the future policy may switch to seeking higher oil prices. These include the ever-growing requirements for revenue, the consumer governments' avowed intent to reduce oil consumption for environmental reasons, and the hostility to the kingdom's position on low prices that is likely to grow and may well force Riyadh to an accommodation. In fact, low prices are causing difficulty in the rest of the Middle East, and have generated increasing hostility to the kingdom that is seen by many as the cause.

Kuwait and the UAE tended during the 1980s to support Saudi Arabia's public stance on price moderation. While the UAE's motive for price moderation was in part linked to the unwillingness of the rulers of Abu Dhabi to pursue any policy too divergent from their more powerful northern neighbour, (not to mention strife over petroleum policy between Abu Dhabi, the largest UAE producer, and Dubai), Kuwaiti policy stemmed from its expanding role as an integrated international oil producer and refiner seeking markets. Low crude prices protect the future role of oil in the energy equation, and negative revenue effects could in part be offset by increased refining margins. In any case, Kuwait had always had excess capacity to boost revenue if needed, and had faced relatively limited revenue pressures. Since the early 1990s, as a result of financial pressures, both Kuwait and the UAE have switched to a policy of higher prices, however, so that divergences between low and high price adherents have currently diminished. Apart from Saudi Arabia, there is a consensus for higher prices although there are differences as to how high prices should, or could, go.

Nevertheless, although financial needs have a major impact on oil price policy, other factors such as domestic, regional and international politics and alliances (in or outside OPEC), and the size of reserves play an equally decisive role in elaborating such a policy. Obviously, the high-reserve countries are more interested in increasing their market shares and in long-term prices. This position contrasts with that of low-reserve countries which are more immediately concerned with actual and short-term prices.

The divergence between low and high price adherents has proved to generate dangerous repercussions. In early 1990, overproduction by Kuwait (and the UAE) led to a reduction in the price of oil by nearly 40 per cent (from a peak of around $22 in January to about $13 in June). In the context of fixed oil output, that represented a very serious reduction in revenue for Iraq in the face of severe economic difficulties and a heavy debt burden. It was probably the anger, frustration and sheer desperation on the part of the Iraqis in the face of drastically reducing oil revenues that was the most probable immediate explanation for Iraq's invasion of Kuwait.

Another important factor which could lead to disputes concerns the divergence in interests between countries with large crude oil and (associated) gas reserves (Iraq, Kuwait, Saudi Arabia) and those with huge non-associated natural gas resources only. In the region, Qatar represents the only country with minor oil reserves, but with large natural gas resources; Iran's natural gas reserves are the second largest in the world, while the country's oil resources are relatively big although produced with the help of secondary and enhanced recovery techniques from ageing and maturing fields. The question is to evaluate the position of neighbouring countries with huge oil resources towards the states that are developing their natural gas reserves, or are planning to do so in the future.

In fact, developing an alternative energy source as important as natural gas could affect the long-term interests of countries with huge oil reserves in the region. Saudi Arabia is a typical example in this case. Indeed, Riyadh has resisted to every scheme for pumping natural gas originating from countries such as Qatar, Oman, and Yemen through its territories. Because the price of gas is structurally related to that of oil, it has even been thought that the policy of low oil price adopted by some countries is partly aimed at handicapping the development of natural gas.

9 Is not Water more Precious than Oil?

Water in the Middle East is as scarce and precious as oil is plentiful. The region is among the least blessed areas on earth with respect to the availability of water resources. Vast areas in the region are even bedevilled by hyperaridity.

The Middle East is not the only place where water crises and disputes exist, but it is the region in which the potential for conflict over water is at its most extreme. The disputes that divide the area over borders, religion and race today may pale into insignificance against the potential future conflicts over water. Water is so vital in this most volatile of the world's troubled regions that it could be a force for peace, inducing old enemies to co-operate for the common good; but history shows that it is more likely to be a disruptive cause of conflict. Indeed, for those who possess water, it is usually a means of leverage and a way of projecting power; to those who lack adequate supplies, a prime concern of national security consists of increasing what is available. Those two concerns often collide.

Discrepancy in water availability in the Middle East is basically caused by the great variation in annual average precipitation which ranges from well below 100 millimetres (mm) in the Arabian desert and in lower Egypt to 2000–2500 mm along parts of the Turkish coasts of the Black Sea and the Caspian coastlands of Iran. Other areas with an average annual precipitation of more than 750 mm, a volume that can be described as abundant by Middle Eastern standards, are limited in extent and include the coasts of southern Turkey and the Levant, and the mountain zone running northwest – southeast from Lake Van in Turkey into the Zagros Mountains of Iran. Areas of moderate annual rainfall between 500 and 700 mm include most of Turkey, Lebanon – the only country in the region that lacks extensive arid areas – and most northern and western Iran.

The uneven distribution of precipitation over the land areas of the Middle East constitutes a major influence on the agricultural potential of various countries and on the distribution of cultivated land. There is also some correspondence between the rainfall map and that of population density – though with major anomalies where agriculture is supported by the irrigation of desert lands, as in the valleys of the Nile, Tigris and Euphrates rivers.

Middle Eastern populations, concentrated on coasts, riverbanks and oases, have learned over time to live with meagre water resources. They adapted their socioeconomics and their relations to the available water which, until recently, was sufficient to cover their demands. But as a result of population growth, urbanisation, higher standards of living, industrialisation and other activities as well as inefficiency (up to 50 per cent in some countries!) in urban water distribution networks due to poorly constructed, maintained and managed systems, which have all accelerated the exhaustion of available resources, the spectrum of water use has widened and the intensity of water needs increased.

But the principal cause of the rise in water use is national water policies. More than 80 per cent of water in the region is allocated to irrigated agriculture although the marginal value-added of water used in agriculture is low compared with that in the municipal or industrial sectors. Over-ambitious agricultural schemes continue to receive a high level of attention from governments fearing dependence on food imports and seeking – not to say dreaming of – food security in staple crops (like wheat in Saudi Arabia, 1 ton of which requires 2000 tons of water, and where agriculture – now aimed to meet the domestic demand and no longer oriented towards export – accounted for 90 per cent of water use in the late 1980s), or due to other security considerations. Some examples from actual sociopolitical life help to clarify the picture.

In the Southeastern Anatolia Development Project in Turkey, also called Great Anatolian Project (GAP), the integration of the Kurdish areas into the rest of the country is a prime concern, with the aim of making it difficult for the Kurdish Labour Party (PKK) or other radical groups to operate in the future. By offering greater prosperity to all, Ankara hopes to remove the water in which the separatist fish can swim. In Egypt, graduates and veterans of the 1973 Arab–Israeli war were given plots of reclaimed land designated for increased food crop cultivation despite their lack of farming expertise; more important than ensuring high production, the process aimed to remove potential dissidents, to relieve chronic unemployment and to transfer population away from the densely-populated areas in the Nile delta and valley. In Syria, priority has been given to irrigation in the Euphrates valley, though it might be better used elsewhere; but the valley is a major recruiting ground for the armed forces.

Most of the countries in the Middle East are at present using or over-using all their annual renewable water resources. If a minimum acceptable annual supply of 1000 cubic metres (cu m) *per capita* is taken as an indicator, only Egypt, Iran, Iraq, Lebanon, Oman, and Turkey had in 1992 an acceptable level of water supply. By the year 2025, only Iran, Iraq, and Turkey will retain this standard (see Table 9.1).

While renewable water supplies have already reached problematic levels, ground water resources in many areas of the region, including renewable and non-renewable supplies, are approaching exhaustion with the over-pumping of the risky and short-term expedient use resulting in saline incursions and spring desiccation. The worse is yet to come: together with the peace process in the Middle East, many countries have begun to put great hopes on tourism, the most water-intensive industry of all. According to the UN Food and Agriculture Organisation (FAO), the same quantity of water needed to keep 100 luxury hotel guests going for just 55 days can irrigate 1 hectare of high-yielding rice and support 100 urban families for two years.

The fragile water situation in the Middle East is aggravated by the fact that the major water resources of the region are shared. Many countries receive high proportions of their water supplies from other territories. The highest ratio of dependency on foreign water is registered in Egypt

Table 9.1 Availability of renewable water in the Middle East, 1960, 1992, and 2025 (cu m/year/*per capita*)[1]

Country	1960	1992	2025
Bahrain	0	0	0
Egypt	2251	1100	645
Iran	5788	1900	1032
Iraq	14 706	5200	2000
Israel	1024	450	311
Jordan	529	240	91
Kuwait	0	0	0
Lebanon	2000	1350	809
Oman	4000	1220	421
Qatar	100[2]	60	0
Saudi Arabia	537	140	49
Syria	1196	520	161
Turkey	5000[2]	3190	2000[2]
UAE	3000	180	113
Yemen	481	200	72

Notes:
1. *Source*: *World Resources 1994–95* (Washington, DC: World Resources Institute, 1995).
2. Estimates.

(98 per cent), followed by Iraq (66 per cent), Israel (65 per cent), Jordan (36 per cent), and Syria (34 per cent). These ratios show already how deep and explosive is the issue of water in the Middle East.

As yet, there is not internationally recognised legal regime for the exploitation of surface or ground water shared by several states. Various international juridical bodies, such as the International Law Association (ILA) and the International Law Commission (ILC) of the UN have proposed guidelines based on principles of 'good neighbourliness'. The ILC draft articles on the non-navigable use of international water systems (1991) advocate 'equitable and reasonable utilisation' and joint environmental monitoring. Upstream states should not divert rivers without consultation and cause appreciable harm to their downstream neighbours.

A main concern in the Middle East, however, is the realisation that regulations and recommendations by the ILC are not binding, and that there is a great deal of confusion over the interpretation and meaning of 'water rights', especially if there is an interstate use of one water resource, either a river or underground source, extending across national borders. The members of the ILC admit that conflict between obligations makes it inevitable that rules must enjoy some kind of elasticity, giving an impetus towards negotiations between interested parties. Negotiations could lead to agreements, but there is no international institution that can implement or control the execution of such accords.

The main river basins in the Middle East, namely Jordan, Nile, and Tigris/Euphrates (see Box 9.1) are the subject of riparian disputes. The lack of clear interpretation of international law will only help to aggravate the already tense situation around these basins and perpetuate the existing imbalances in the exploitation of water, often based on certain states being the military and politically dominant powers.

THE JORDAN BASIN

The most obvious dispute over water in the Middle East is between Israel and its Arab neighbours. One of the most difficult problems to be resolved, if efforts for a peaceful settlement to the Arab–Israeli conflict are to succeed, is the allocation of the small quantities of water available in the Jordan river, the lowest in the world, and its tributaries.

The political complexity of the Jordan basin is illustrated in its geography. There are three main water heads of the river: the Hasbani, rising in Syria and Lebanon; the Banias, with springs in the Syrian and Israeli-occupied Golan Heights; and the Dan, wholly within Israel. The major tri-

River	Length (km)	Average annual flow (million cu m)	Sources	Countries concerned
Jordan	360	550 (south of Lake Tiberias)	Hasbani in Lebanon and Syria, Banias in Syria, and Dan in Israel	Jordan, Israel, Syria, Lebanon, and the Palestinian territories
Nile	6648	74 000 (at Aswan)	Highlands of Ethiopia, Lake Victoria, and Lake Albert	Rwanda, Burundi, Tanzania, Zaire, Kenya, Uganda, Ethiopia, Sudan, and Egypt
Tigris/ Euphrates	1900/ 2700	42 000/ 32 000 (at the southern Turkish borders)	Guneydogu Toroslar Mountains and Zagros Mountains in Turkey	Turkey, Syria, and Iraq

Box 9.1   The Three Main Rivers in the Middle East

butary, the Yarmuk, provides the boundary successively between Jordan and Syria, and Jordan and Israel. The river Jordan itself forms the border between Israel and Jordan and, to the south, the West Bank and Jordan. In the Jordan valley, Syria and Lebanon are upper to Israel, while Israel is the upstream country to Jordan. Along the Yarmuk, Syria is upper to Jordan, and Jordan to Israel. The most crucially interested states, from the point of view of water supply, are Israel, Jordan, and the Palestinian territories of the West Bank and Gaza Strip. As yet, power resides largely in Israel, however.

The complex water geopolitics of the Jordan basin has exercised a considerable limiting influence on development. Since 1951, with the draining of the Huleh Marshes, there have been incidents connected with water. The most serious accidents arose as a result of Israeli plans to divert water from the Jordan above the Sea of Tiberias, and of attempts, following the Arab Summit of 1964 to divert the Hasbani, the Banias, or both, wholly through Arab territories. Since 1967, from its occupied positions in Golan Heights, Israel has been able to protect the Jordan water heads and control some half of the course of the Yarmuk. The occupation of southern

Lebanon since 1978 has resulted in a complete Israeli control of the Hasbani and an indirect access to the Litani river.

Meanwhile, the Hebrew state which, prior to 1967, obtained some 60 per cent of its fresh water from the ground resources of the West Bank, had increased this figure to around 80 per cent, extracting some 650 million cm per year from the region, whereas the Palestinians received less than 160 million cu m. In the meantime Tel Aviv has been proposing a canal to carry water from the Mediterranean to the Dead Sea, opposed by Jordan that planned a canal from the Red Sea to the Dead Sea.

In the peace agreements signed in 1994 between Israel on one hand, and the Palestinians and Jordan on the other, the Hebrew state asked for limitations in water use and exploitation by the Palestinians, while agreeing to increase their annual share from the West Bank ground water by around 120 million cu m. Tel Aviv also agreed to guarantee 215 million cu m annually for Jordan from the Jordan river. The two countries agreed to pursue joint projects, such as water storing and dams.

However, without a global and final agreement on the water issue in this part of the world, the situation is likely to deteriorate further as the water crisis in Israel, Jordan, and the Palestinian territories worsens. Facts show just why: at a time when the water requirements of the Palestinian territories are expected to steeply increase together with moves towards autonomy (or independence), many expect the Gaza Strip to run totally dry by 2005; meanwhile, Israel is already consuming 95 per cent of its renewable water resources, and by the year 2000 Jordan's need may exceed its resources by 30 per cent. Significantly enough, King Hussein in 1990 delivered a solemn public warning to Israel (and others?), declaring that 'the only issue that will bring Jordan into war is water'.

THE NILE VALLEY

The situation in the Nile Valley also led to a similar warning in 1979 from the then Egyptian President Sadat: 'the only matter that could take Egypt to war again is water'. But this warning was not directed at Israel but at the upstream Nile countries, especially Sudan and Ethiopia.

The Nile, father of African rivers and the longest stream in the world, passes through Rwanda, Burundi, Tanzania, Zaire, Kenya, Uganda, Ethiopia, and Sudan, before flowing majestically on through Egypt to the Mediterranean. The Nile is made up of three main rivers and several smaller tributaries. The largest of the main rivers, the Blue Nile, accounts for about four-sevenths of the total Nile flow. Almost all the water in the

Blue Nile comes from Ethiopia. The White Nile, the longest branch, contributes two-sevenths of the total stream. Most of its water originates from the region of Lake Victoria and Lake Albert, and from the Sobat, a tributary that rises mainly in Ethiopia. A major scheme to dramatically enhance Nile supplies by reducing the loss of water evaporation through the construction of a canal from where the Sobat joins the river to Jonglei in south Sudan (called the Jonglei Canal) was abandoned in the 1980s as a result of the Sudanese civil war. The Blue and White Niles meet at Khartoum, north of which the third main river, the Atbara, joins the Nile and contributes the remaining one-seventh of the flow. The Atbara also rises mainly in Ethiopia.

It is generally agreed that Ethiopia accounts for between 80 and 90 per cent of the Nile flow and is therefore the key source, while between 10 and 20 per cent is contributed by the East African Lake Plateau System. At the opposite end of the Nile basin Egypt, with a burgeoning population, is the key consumer. The Nile is literally the life of Egypt, its only source of water, and around 96 per cent of its population lives astride it. The river is considered by the Egyptians as so vital that President Sadat, under popular pressure, had to withdraw plans proposed in the late 1970s to supply Israel with water from the Nile through a canal.

There is hardly any rainfall at all in the territory between north of Khartoum and Cairo, and so any agriculture in most of Egypt's length and northern Sudan is through irrigation from the Nile. Therefore, the river is also important to Sudan, although the degree of dependence is less since the country has considerably more precipitation than Egypt.

In the late 1950s, Egypt decided to build a dam on the Nile at Aswan in the south, with the intention of increasing irrigated acreage in line with the rapidly growing population, controlling seasonal flooding, and ensuring that Egypt's southern neighbours did not divert the precious water to the detriment of the Egyptian population. The dam was finally completed in the early 1960s through Soviet technical and financial assistance. Meanwhile, in November 1959, Cairo signed an agreement with Khartoum, under which the river water collected in the Lake Nasser (an artificial lake caused by the damming of the Nile) on the border was to be divided one-quarter (around 18.5 billion cu m/year) to Sudan and the rest (some 55.5 billion cu m/year) to Egypt.

The Aswan dam has indeed increased agricultural yields in Egypt, provided water in time of severe drought, electrified village communities, and managed water during flood stages. However, many problems have developed from the dam construction and use. Lake Nasser has been filling up with rich Nile silt at a rapid rate, preventing the nourishment of agricultural lands further down the river, and destroying the fishing industry. Vegetation in the lake is also growing so rapidly that it cannot be dredged effectively, clogging the irrigation channels and creating stagnant water and a breeding ground for a variety of disease-bearing insects and sea urchins. More significantly, the dam gave Egypt a vulnerable monument which, if attacked or destroyed, will generate catastrophic consequences. That had been in the heart of Israeli thought during the October 1973 war, when Tel Aviv reportedly ordered its long-range missiles to be ready to hit the Aswan dam if the conflict had escalated further.

At present, the chief concern of Egypt focuses upon Ethiopia, the main source of discharge, which is in desperate need of greater food production. This is likely to be achieved only through irrigation and construction of around thirty-three dams, seven of which have already been built (with the help of Israeli experts). The implementation of any serious development plan by Addis Ababa will most probably require more water supplies. But abstraction in the water heads in Ethiopia would clearly reduce the possibilities for development lower down the valley. Although Egypt has alternately courted and threatened Ethiopia in its search for a formal agreement on the Nile, no accord has as yet been reached. Meanwhile, the Egyptian High Military Command has prepared contingency plans for armed intervention in each of the countries around the Nile basin in case of a direct threat to the flow of the river.

THE TIGRIS AND EUPHRATES RIVERS

Elsewhere in the region, the mighty Tigris and Euphrates rivers stretching from the snow-capped mountains of eastern Turkey to the warm waters of the Gulf, have been down the centuries a cause of tension between the nations and states that have depended on them. The main segment of the Iraqi region between the two rivers was known in antiquity as Mesopotamia, and was the location of Assyria, Babylonia, and Sumer.

None of the three riparian states, Turkey – the major source of discharge – Syria, and Iraq, is facing an imminent water shortage, but they all are fast-developing economies and are involved in a number of major water projects. Over the past three decades, dam construction by the three states has poisoned relations. For the most part, the war had been confined to words and the three states have fought shy of open conflict.

Hydropolitical activity already occurred in the basin in 1974 when the filling of the lakes behind the Turkish Keban and the Syrian Al Thawrah dams coincided, causing a temporary but significant drop of some 75 per cent in the discharge of the Euphrates. Iraqi troops were moved to the border, but following some mediations leading to the release by Syria of additional water, the situation was defused in June 1975. In January 1990, the stream of the Euphrates was again greatly reduced as the reservoir behind the Turkish Ataturk dam was filled in an action representing an interesting piece of geopolitical symbolism. Although the governments of Syria and Iraq had been both warned in advance and flow had been enhanced prior to the one-month cut-off, alarm over water security was immediately expressed.

The Keban and Ataturk dams as well as the shortly-to-be-built Kargamis dam (only 4.5 km from the Syrian border) are three components of the ambitious Southeast Anatolia Development Project, or Great Anatolian Project (GAP), under which nineteen other dams are to be built by the year 2006 on the Tigris and Euphrates and their tributaries, with the double goal of irrigating 1.7 million hectares of land, and generating 27 billion kilowatt-hours per year of electricity. The GAP, when completed, is expected to divert as much as half of the Euphrates flow into Turkish dams and irrigation canals. The most pessimistic forecasts in Damascus and Baghdad are that the GAP could cost Syria 40 per cent and Iraq 90 per cent of the Euphrates flow. The truth is that much of the water will get back into the river, but after irrigating Turkish fields it will be saltier when it reaches the Syrian and Iraqi farms downstream.

The three riparian states have never reached a formal agreement on the sharing of the water of the Tigris and Euphrates, although Turkey in 1991 unilaterally gave firm pledges that it would release from the Euphrates a minimum of 500 cu m per second across the border, while noting that future supplies could be increased in return for further Syrian help against Kurdish separatists. Ankara remains a hard-liner, an attitude reflected by the famous declaration of the then Prime Minister Demirel in 1990 – confirmed by Premier Yilmaz in early 1996 – saying that

neither Syria nor Iraq can lay claim to Turkey's rivers any more than Ankara could claim their oil. This is a matter of sovereignty. We have a right to do anything we like. The water resources are Turkey's, the oil resources are theirs. We don't say we share their oil resources, and they cannot say they share our water resources.

The Head of Middle East Department in the Turkish Foreign Ministry added to this in early 1996 by saying that 'Syria should indeed be grateful to Turkey for regulating the Euphrates flow and thus preventing seasonal floods'.

By controlling the water resources of its southern neighbours, Turkey feels strong enough to dictate its point of view, and even to promote since 1986 some grand ideas for piping surplus supplies to the Gulf through a 6-million cu m/year, $21-billion (1991$) pipeline scheme which could run from the Seyhan and Ceyhan rivers to as far south as Mecca in Saudi Arabia and east to the other Arabian peninsula monarchies. The so-called Peace Pipeline Project (PPP) has aroused only limited interest from its supposed beneficiaries as they are clearly un-enthusiastic about putting their fate in hands of others. Another scheme, the already-half-completed Manavgat water export project on the Mediterranean coast near Antalya consists of shipping water at $0.45/cu m to any buyer, a price compared to an average incremental cost for ground water of about $0.40/cu m.

On the other hand, the Shatt Al Arab waterway, which runs around 180 km from the confluence of the Tigris and Euphrates with that of the Iranian Karun river down to the Gulf, has been the subject of bitter dispute between Iran and Iraq (see Chapter 6). It is the outlet from Iraq's port of Basra to the sea, while on the Iranian side lie the ports of Abadan, Khoramshahr and Khosrowabad. The continued deadlock over where the border between the two countries lies has led Iraq to consider diverting the Shatt Al Arab away from the border. But such diversion is likely to result in a noticeable reduction of the water level in the waterway, jeopardising the Iranian ports.

Nearby, Iraq had long claimed Bubiyan and Warbah – the two sparsely inhabited Kuwaiti islands located little more than a kilometre from Iraq's 16-km stretch of coastline along the Gulf – and the coastal area adjacent to them, arguing that the two islands are composed of sediments deposited by the Tigris/Euphrates system, and therefore constitute a natural prolongation of its territory (see Chapter 6).

THE GULF

In the northern Gulf, Iran lies across a wide range of rainfall zones. The western and northern peripheries receive moderate and generally reliable precipitation, much in the form of snow. However, the bulk of the land surface, including the central plateau and much of the south and the east, is in the arid or semi-arid zones and has a permanent water deficit. In addition, the combination of rapidly increasing demographic numbers and a burgeoning urban population is putting increasing strains on available water supplies.

In the southern Gulf, well known as one of the most arid areas on earth, ground water resources are rapidly depleting and becoming polluted in urban areas. Waste water is creeping into surface supplies and deeper drilling is yielding water of brackish and non-potable quality. Therefore, the countries there have increasingly placed their reliance on desalination to supply fresh water. Around 60 per cent of the world's desalination capacity in early 1994, or about sixty units with a total output potential of more than 1.5 billion cu m per year, were operating in the Gulf. More than a third of the Gulf desalination plants in 1994 were located in Saudi Arabia, the largest country in the world without a river. The annual requirement of Gulf countries for desalinated water is expected to grow to 5.4 billion cu m by the year 2030.

Desalination plants are tremendously expensive to instal and costly to run ($1–2/cu m). They can produce only a limited amount of fresh water and have to depend on a constant supply of energy. Their output is also limited by the amount of mineral salts contained in the water input. Although the region's countries have the energy resources to keep the plants going, their ability to finance new schemes is currently constrained and is likely to remain depressed throughout the 1990s. In fact, the cost of new desalination projects will be a big burden on the Gulf exchequers unless consumers are obliged to pay the full cost of provision, or if the construction, operation, and maintenance of plants are hived off into the private sector. Another issue related to desalination plants is their vulnerability and easy exposure to any terrorist or external attack (even in the form of an oil spill), especially since they are rightly considered to be of strategic importance.

The Gulf Arab countries have until now been satisfied to place their reliance on desalination plants, turning their backs on the possibility of importing water from available sources nearby. The argument has always been that imported water would give the supplying country a stranglehold over the importing state, and that in a literal sense the supplier would have his hand on the tap and could turn it off at any moment. One of the earliest suggestions for importing water was made in 1930, when Kuwait was suffering from a shortage that was leading to unrest among its population. Iraq offered to divert water from the south through an extension of the Khor Abdallah Canal, but Kuwait turned down the offer, and continued to rely, as it had for decades, on importing drinking water from Basra and the surrounding areas supplied by tankers driven across the border and sailing down the Shatt Al Arab.

Efforts to revive the project were made in 1953 when the idea was to construct a waterway from the Shatt Al Arab to Kuwait in return for a long-term leasing of Warbah Island to Iraq. This time, the Kuwaitis were worried that a canal could be used for military purposes. They commissioned an expert study, which suggested a pipeline instead. But an agreement between the Iraqis and the Kuwaitis to pipe around 3 million cu m per day from the Euphrates was signed only in the late 1970s. At that time, the Kuwaitis felt more secure, because in return for Iraqi water they would supply electric power. The scheme was never carried through, however, and was left on ice until August 1990 when Iraq occupied Kuwait and announced that plans to pipe water to the '*Wilayat* of Kuwait' would go ahead. Not surprisingly, once Kuwait was liberated in 1991 the government of the emirate decided there should be a ban on all talks about projects linking its country with Iraq.

In addition to the PPP scheme from Turkey, a project to pipe water from the Karun river in southwest Iran by a submarine line to Qatar has been considered since the mid-1980s, with the two countries signing in 1991 a memorandum of understanding on the project, but without taking any concrete steps. Another scheme consisted of diverting water in a pipeline from Pakistan through Baluchistan to a pumping station on the Iranian coast. At first, tankers would have carried the water across the Strait of Hormuz to Ras Al Khaimah, the rest of the UAE, and Oman; later, pipes would have been laid on the sea bed. The UAE, which was to finance the scheme, finally decided against it, however.

10 Demographic Explosion and Population Disparity

It took thousands of years for the world's population to reach 1 billion, in 1830, but it took less than 100 years for another billion to be added to this figure, in 1925. Since then the numbers have swollen rapidly, so that in 1962 the world had 3 billion people. Thirteen years later, in 1975, the global population reached 4 billion. Currently about 5.9 billion, the world's population is expected to exceed 6.4 billion in 2000 and 8.5 billion in 2025. The nations of today's OECD would then account for about 10 per cent, down from the current 16 per cent, with more than half of their people likely to be over 50 years old, while half of the seven billion 'poor and semi-poor' would be aged under 20.

For most of the Middle East's history prior to the early nineteenth century, its population rose and fell in long and short cycles with little incremental growth. Population increases during 'good' years were offset partially or completely by high mortality during periods of epidemics, wars, and famine. During the nineteenth century, the region's population grew slowly, adding 15 million people in 100 years to reach 43 million in the year 1900. In that year, Turkey, with 14 million people, was the most populous country in the region. Egypt had about 10 million inhabitants and Iran contained nearly 8 million. The Arabian peninsula was home to some 6 million people. In contrast, Syria and Iraq had each around 2 million inhabitants, while Lebanon, Jordan, and Palestine had a combined total of 1 million.

Middle Eastern population started growing in the first half of the twentieth century, partly because of increases in immigration to Palestine (later to Israel) and the Gulf region, and to declines in mortality. Mortality declined among urban residents in response to better urban housing and sanitation, sand filtration of water, and improved nutrition. The UN estimated the region's population at 80 million in mid-1950, about double the estimated size in 1900. But the truly explosive population growth did not begin until after 1950. The region's rapid growth was the result of a substantial decline in mortality triggered by the increasing use of anti-biotics, insecticides, vaccinations, and disease control and sanitation programmes. Immigration to the region also increased during that period, following the independence of the area's countries, the creation of Israel, the activation of economic life, and the development of petroleum resources in the Gulf countries.

With an annual average growth rate of approximately 3 per cent between 1950 and 1980, the Middle East had had one of the highest demographic growth rates in the world – second only to Africa. Iran's population is now increasing by an extraordinary rate of 3.7–4 per cent a year and is projected to reach over 152 million in 2025. Egypt would see its population reaching more than 100 million in 2025 from a current 62 million. Turkey would have in 2025 as many inhabitants (around 101 million) as Italy and Britain put together. The aggregate populations of Iran, Egypt and Turkey in 2025 would constitute around 63 per cent of the region's total, a fact showing the increasing weight of these three poles within the area.

The Middle East is thus collectively experiencing a demographic boom, although the growth can be classified into four main groups: a persistent high fertility and declining mortality in an intermediate-to-low socioeconomic setting (Jordan, Oman, Syria, Yemen, and the Palestinian territories); a declining fertility and mortality in an intermediate level of socioeconomic development (Egypt, Lebanon, Turkey, and Iran); a high fertility amid rapidly declining mortality in a high socioeconomic setting (the 'Gulf Transition': Bahrain, Iraq, Kuwait, Qatar, Saudi Arabia, and the UAE); and a low fertility and mortality in an above-average socioeconomic development (the 'European-Style Transition': Israel).

The main reasons behind the generally high population growth in the region are the provision of modern medical services – sharply lowering death rates – combined with the limited use of contraceptive methods, the family role of women (still very important in the region) and some voluntary and highly-incentive pronatalist policies in most of the countries.

In fact, in sharp contrast to some countries like Egypt, Turkey, and Yemen that have officially support family planning policies, the governments of Iraq, and Kuwait and Israel promote policies to raise fertility. In Iraq, the government planners have been trying to raise the birth rate from about 3.2 per cent in 1988–9 to more than 4 per cent during the 1990s. Iraqis receive interest-free housing loans after the birth of a fourth child, and mothers are entitled to one year's maternity leave on full pay. Iraqi posters reading 'bear a child and you pierce an arrow in the enemy's eyes' displayed during the Iran–Iraq war leave little doubt as to the government's position on fertility. The government of Kuwait provides generous cash benefits by way of child allowances, maternity benefits, and housing subsidies to families. Israel promotes four-child families as the optimum size. Family benefits include one-time birth grants, child allowances, and special allowances for third and subsequent children, while sterilisation is permitted only for health reasons. Even so fertility in Israel remains the lowest in the region.

The governments of other countries, such as Saudi Arabia, the UAE, and Qatar, do not have explicit policies to raise their fertility. However, many of their social policies and benefits – such as free health care, education, and guaranteed government jobs – may be viewed as pronatalist.

Iran's demographic policies have changed dramatically over the past decade. After the 1979 revolution, the Islamic government adopted pronatalist policies and dismantled family planning programmes started in previous decades. The government advocated higher fertility 'to produce more Muslims who will spread the Islamic revolution' throughout the world. The minimum legal age at marriage for girls was lowered – although there is no evidence that the average marriage age actually declined during the 1980s.

As Iran began to rebuild its economy after the end of the Iran–Iraq war in 1988, however, rapid population growth came to be viewed as a major obstacle to economic development. The government reversed its policy, and is now favouring lower fertility and slower population growth, arguing that 'one literate Muslim is better than ten illiterate ones'. The government now distributes contraceptives free of charge to low-income families and provides free sterilisation services in government clinics. In May 1993, the Iranian parliament ratified a bill to encourage couples to stop at three children by refusing certain privileges to fourth or higher-order children born after May 1994.

Regardless of their views on fertility levels, most governments in the region recognise the need for family planning as a health measure for women and children, and consider the access and practice of contraception to be a human right. Only Iraq and Saudi Arabia expressly limit access to contraceptive information, guidance, and materials.

There are opposing points of view as to whether or not Islam allows family planning. Many present-day Muslim theologians sanction modern contraceptives using the juristic venue of analogous reasoning (*Qiyas*). Indeed in the early days of Islam, companions of the Prophet practised *coitus interruptus*, the method known at that time. Neither the Prophet nor the Qoran prohibited the practice explicitly. Some other theologians, however, oppose the family planning programmes mainly because they associate them with a Western conspiracy to limit the size of the world-wide Muslim population. They also fear that contraception would invite promiscuity among young Muslims.

Nevertheless, the great majority of Muslim theologians agree that Islamic law permits the spacing of pregnancies and the prevention of health hazards due to repeated or poorly timed pregnancies. Contraception is also normally permitted to protect a breastfeeding child from the impact of a new pregnancy on the quality of the mother's milk, to avoid economic embarrassment to the family from too many children, and 'to safeguard the wife's beauty and to keep her fit and in good form' (a justification advocated by Al Ghazali, a celebrated eleventh-century theologian). However, permission to use contraception is subject to the sanction of the wife (or husband, when a female method is used). In addition, contraception is voluntary, and should not be enforced by law; nor should there be a specific quota for the number of children. Contraception is not acceptable if practised to avoid female children, or to shirk the maternal role.

Sterilisation is available to a majority of women in the region. Abortion, however, is relatively restricted, although it is technically permissible for health reasons under Islamic law. With a strong health justification, abortion is allowed before the fourth month in some legal schools, such as the Hanafite school. After the fourth month of pregnancy, abortion is prohibited by consensus except when the pregnancy threatens the survival of the mother. Turkey is the only country in the Middle East where abortion is allowed on request. In a majority of countries, abortion is allowed only to save a mother's life. However, anecdotal evidence suggests that illegal abortion is widespread in the major cities of the region.

What must be said is that Middle Eastern culture, religion, and politics tend to encourage large families, and – although trends vary among countries – high fertility is common throughout the region. On average, Middle Eastern women give birth to five children by the age of 45. Women here have about three children more than women in developed countries, and one more than the average for women in all developing countries.

It seems that strong kinship bonds and large families are highly valued in Islam, the dominant religious and cultural force in the region. It is interesting to notice that Muslim communities throughout the world tend to have large families. Albania, for example, with its large Muslim population, has the highest level of fertility in Europe. Muslims in Malaysia have higher fertility than other major religious groups in that country.

Although some analyses emphasise the egalitarianism inherent in the Qoran, Islam (and some prefer to say the Arab mentality that was tempered by Islam) seems indeed socially restrictive for women. There are stringent practices of female seclusion and sex segregation, born within the social context of Arabia in the seventh century. Islamic law defines women as juridical minors, familial 'goods', and individuals less valuable and important than males who have always all the social prerogatives; each man can marry up to four wives on the condition that each wife should be treated equally (some Islamic schools rule out polygamy on the ground that this condition is impossible to comply with); men can easily divorce women, whereas the reverse is not true; the father, not the mother, typically gets custody of the children. Some Muslim women try to have large families as a kind of 'insurance policy' against divorce: a man might be more reluctant to divorce the mother of six than the mother of only one child.

High fertility in the Middle East also reflects the economic and social value of children in the Islamic culture. In both urban and rural areas, children contribute to the family income by working within or outside the household. Part of the economic utility of children is prospective, as well. Children, particularly sons, are a source of economic security for parents in their old age because social welfare systems for the elderly do not exist in most countries of the region. Women who bear more children (especially sons) achieve a more stable position in the family and greater social recognition.

Nearly all the signs point to a continued expansion of the population of the Middle East for the next 30–40 years. The centrality of the family in society, young age at marriage, universality of marriage, early child-bearing, relatively low educational attainment for women, and low level of female labour force participation, all point to continued high fertility within the region.

The estimates in Table 10.1, provided by the UN, show demographic developments in the Middle East in the years 1994 and 2025. Some figures for 1994 must be taken with reservation and restraint, due to the tendency in some countries either to inflate or to deflate their population estimates for political and economic objectives. For the year 2025, the table refers to the medium-variant projected figures based on previous trends, which are usually found between the lower and higher projections.

Several facts from the table deserve emphasis, the most important of which is that the population of the region is expected to more than double between 1994 and 2025, increasing from around 274 million inhabitants to some 557 million people. That represents an average annual growth rate of around 2.3 per cent, which will double any population in less than 30 years. This rate is less than the 3 per cent recorded between 1950 and 1980, but still high when compared to the actual rates in some industrialised countries (between 1 and 1.3 per cent). Whether the rate of

Table 10.1   Middle Eastern populations, 1994 and 2025 (million)[1]

Country	1994	2025[2]
Bahrain	0.5	1.1
Egypt	61.6	100.8
Iran	66.0	152.1
Iraq	19.9	49.1
Jordan	5.2	11.3
Israel	5.5	9.1
Kuwait	1.6	3.8
Lebanon	2.9	4.9
Oman	2.1	4.9
Qatar	0.5	0.8
Saudi Arabia	17.5	42.1
Syria	14.2	37.6
Turkey	60.8	101.4
UAE	1.9	3.0
Yemen	13.9	35.4
Total	274.1	557.4

Notes:
1. *Source*: *World Population Prospects 1994* (New York: UN, 1995).
2. Figures refer to medium variant projections based on previous trends, which
   are usually found between the lower and higher projections.

population growth will be matched by economic development in some
countries in the Middle East is doubtful. What is now sure, however, is
that the demographic explosion in the region is creating some of the most
difficult economic, political and social challenges for the decades ahead.

In fact, unrestrained population growth is already severely straining
public services, housing and transport infrastructure, health and education
services, and financial, food and water resources, causing heavy unemployment (with the exception of the GCC countries), and exacerbating
other development problems in the region. Investable funds are diverted
not merely from capital deepening but from any form of job creation to
social overhead investment (housing, sewage, and water systems). Some
investment may be necessary simply to repair the impact caused by
population growth. Moreover, since funds for investment (in non-oil and
increasingly in oil exporting states) are becoming more and more scarce,
rapid population growth slows the pace of growth and development, and
subsequently increases unemployment. In addition, by increasing the
supply of labour relative to capital, and by raising the ratio of unskilled to

skilled labour, rapid population growth is worsening the distribution of income.

The rapid increase of population contributes to the very rapid growth of cities which are expanding at roughly twice the rate of the overall population in the region. Just over one-fourth (27 per cent) of the population was urban in 1950, but by 1994 an estimated 65 per cent lived in Middle Eastern urban areas as compared to a global average of 45 per cent (see Table 10.2). The cities grew rapidly because of large numbers of migrants from the countryside seeking a better lifestyle, as well as high rates of natural increase. The massive international labour migration to oil-rich Gulf states is also partly responsible for the rapid urbanisation of these countries. Riyadh, Jeddah, and Kuwait City grew spectacularly from 120 000, 30 000 and 70 000 inhabitants respectively in the early 1950s to around 1.8, 1.5 and 1.4 million now.

In Cairo, rapid population growth from 2.2 million in 1945 to around 13 million now along with a housing shortage and other factors has created extremely high population densities. The average for the city is 40 000 persons per km^2 (compared to 7500 in Washington, DC), and

Table 10.2   Urban population in the Middle East, 1950, 1994, and 2025[1]

| Country | Urban population (% of total) | | |
	1950	1994	2025
Bahrain	64	90	96
Egypt	32	45	62
Iran	37	59	77
Iraq	35	74	86
Israel	65	91	94
Jordan	35	71	84
Kuwait	59	97	99
Lebanon	23	87	94
Oman	2	13	33
Qatar	63	91	95
Saudi Arabia	16	80	88
Syria	31	52	70
Turkey	21	67	87
UAE	25	84	91
Yemen	6	33	58
Total	27	65	80

Note:
1. *Source*: *World Urbanisation Prospects 1994* (New York: UN, 1995).

densities exceed 150 000 persons in some old districts. Some people in the city find permanent residence only in graveyards.

In the coming decades, much of the impact of population increase will be manifested through urbanisation. For the year 2025, the UN projects an urbanisation rate of more than 90 per cent in each of Kuwait, Bahrain, Qatar, Lebanon, Israel, and the UAE. More than 80 per cent of the population in Saudi Arabia, Turkey, Iraq, and Jordan will be living in urban areas. In average, around 80 per cent of Middle Eastern population will be urban (see Table 10.2). In less than twenty years from now, the population of cities like Cairo, Tehran and Istanbul could double, hardly a comforting thought to planners struggling with infrastructures that were originally planned and installed for far smaller agglomerations. The population growth of Istanbul is likely to be concentrated in the so-called 'Gecekondu' (literally meaning 'built overnight'), the unplanned slums that encircle the city. Alexandria will top 5 million, and Baghdad will approach 8 million, more if the redevelopment effort concentrates disproportionately on the capital to the detriment of rural areas. Even in smaller Middle Eastern countries, cities will dominate. Amman, today 1.2 million, will grow to more than 1.7 million, while the redeveloped Kuwait will be almost entirely urban.

Rapid population growth and subsequent urban growth strain administrative capacities of governments, divert investment funds, and contribute to a soaring demand for housing, power, food and water in the region, thus adding to the food security problem. That will be aggravated if encroachment on agricultural land is taken into account, especially in countries like Egypt where cultivable land is precious, but where some 600 hectares of this land are used annually for urban purposes.

Rapid urban population growth does foster political, social, and economic problems. Indeed, a critical feature of the demography of Middle Eastern countries, resulting from decades of strong birth rates, is the high number of young people in proportion to total population, with a large share (30–50 per cent) of inhabitants under 15 years old. That is expected to change slightly, however, with a relative ageing of the populations by the year 2025 (see Table 10.3). It is already difficult for outside commentators to read the internal political evolution in the region, to understand and explain away the inconsistencies and apparently paradoxical policy stances. With the burgeoning of youth and the growth of youthful influence in urban areas, it will become more so. Some possible political implications may be foreseen, however, with a very real transformation taking place in political attitudes, responsibilities and power.

Table 10.3   Age structure in the Middle East, 1994 and 2025
(% of total population)[1]

Country	1994	2025	1994	2025
	0–14 years		15–64 years	
Bahrain	35.1	22.5	62.5	69.0
Egypt	39.1	23.9	56.7	66.8
Iran	45.8	37.3	51.0	58.6
Iraq	46.5	32.0	50.8	63.6
Jordan	43.6	27.4	56.7	67.4
Israel	30.9	21.0	62.9	65.6
Kuwait	35.6	21.1	63.0	64.9
Lebanon	34.5	23.4	60.7	69.0
Oman	46.6	37.1	51.1	58.3
Qatar	29.4	23.7	69.4	59.9
Saudi Arabia	43.0	34.8	54.7	59.6
Syria	48.1	35.5	49.3	61.0
Turkey	35.2	23.1	61.8	68.0
UAE	30.8	22.2	67.5	60.7
Yemen	49.3	40.2	49.7	57.5

Note:
1. *Source*: *World Population Prospects 1994* (New York: UN, 1995).

The values of youth constitute an important element in this context. In the small wealthy states of the Gulf, the young are the grandchildren of the traditionally minded generation that saw oil discovered. The values of these young people are shaped by routine acceptance of the wealth that was always seen as a bonus by their grandparents, and by the notion that wealth and success has nothing to do with sweat and toil. The older oil generation could always (and often did) balance the poverty of the past with the bounty of the present. This perspective is generally lacking in a young Gulf citizen.

In the larger poor states, many of the young perceive themselves as part of a line of grinding poverty in a deteriorating physical environment in the middle of growing and pervasive social stresses. They have to get used to declining public services that are resulting in water shortages and increasingly unpleasant cities, among other things, while rural economic progress is constrained by the scarce essential combination of land and water.

With that in mind, it looks reasonable to say that the young age group will contribute significantly to various kinds of radical movements, as it did in the streets of Beirut or within the Islamic militants of Egypt. One would be wrong, however, to attribute common political attitudes to an entire age cohort. Its members are just as likely to be worker migrants to the Gulf states or to be following conventional career paths in the bureaucracy or service sector as they are to be political activists. Yet the opportunities for them to achieve their aspirations will narrow as their numbers increase. They will not probably be passive in the face of such a situation.

Some of the principal consequences of the demographic growth and the youthfulness of Middle Eastern populations consist of implications for the quality of education and effects on labour markets. An immediate challenge to the region's governments will be education provision. Paradoxically, only through education can future population growth be moderated and development be stimulated. Only through education can the youth of the next decades be made aware of their responsibilities and potential within a state and a society. It is true that most countries in the region try very hard to spend money on education. But the rocketing numbers of children cannot be matched even by the burgeoning budgets for education. A country tendering to educate its children will find it more difficult to offer primary education to all of them if their numbers are rapidly growing: rapid population growth swamps even the most determined attempts to diffuse basic education. Egypt, for example, even with the world's most ambitious school construction programme, is unable to keep pace with the relentless education demand of its growing population. University and post-secondary education has to compete for resources with primary and basic studies, leading to a general lower level of education. Moreover, there is an urgent necessity to tailor higher education to the needs of the job market, otherwise more but different problems would be created.

No wonder that while some countries in the region have high rates of adult literacy, there are others with poor literacy performance. It is also noticeable that while primary education in the area is easily available, secondary- and university-level enrolments have been relatively weak (see Table 10.4) This is due to the lack of schools and teachers, but also as a result of a Middle Eastern point of view which is not so enthusiastic for the education of females, who are considered to be created only to be married and to raise children at home.

The problems that a burgeoning number of young people creates are not limited to educational difficulties. The impact on the job market is equally profound. It is probably in unemployment, in unmet aspirations for

Table 10.4   Education in the Middle East, 1995[1]

| Country | Adult illiteracy rate (%) | | | Enrolment (% of population) | | |
	Total	Male	Female	Primary	Secondary	Tertiary
Bahrain	15	10	22	na	na	na
Egypt	49	36	61	100	80	19
Iran	28	22	34	100	57	12
Iraq[2]	17	15	21	96	47	14
Israel[2]	5	4	6	94	85	34
Jordan	13	7	21	100	91	19
Kuwait	21	18	25	93	81	17
Lebanon	8	5	12	99	75	32
Oman	na	na	na	100	57	6
Qatar	21	20	24	na	na	na
Saudi Arabia	37	29	50	78	46	14
Syria[2]	36	22	50	100	57	19
Turkey	18	8	28	100	60	15
UAE	21	21	20	100	69	11
Yemen[2]	61	47	74	76	31	2

Notes:
1. *Sources: UNESCO Statistical Yearbook 1995* (Paris: UNESCO, 1996); *World Development Report 1996* (Washington, DC: World Bank, 1996).
2. Estimates for 1993–4.
na=not available

modern formal work, quickly followed by a desire for any work, that the effects of population growth will be seen. In fact, the new entrants into labour markets will increase with every passing year. According to Courbage and Fargues (1992), 810 000 men (the figures for women are not computed) will annually enter the Egyptian job market in 2025, compared to 520 000 men in 1990. The figures for Syria and Turkey amount to 240 000 and 620 000 men respectively in 2025, compared to 110 000 and 570 000 men respectively in 1990.

The young Middle Easterners are large cohorts of men (and increasing number of women due to their education and emancipation) with high aspirations and sometimes good if not excellent professional credentials. Because they are literate and politically aware, denying them a real material security in form of adequate work and salary is potentially dangerous. Young people are at present being offered make-work jobs or no jobs, salaries that lag behind inflation, and low social status. Indeed, it is particularly difficult to create the entry-level jobs that the very young labour force requires, especially when skilled older workers are so scarce. It is hard to see how and where young people can be productively absorbed into the workforce, especially since people recruited into the civil service and professions twenty to twenty-five years ago are not yet 50 years old and therefore will not retire soon.

In addition, since increasing the amount of capital per worker is typically necessary to raise worker productivity and therefore incomes, rapid population increase slows the growth of *per capita* incomes. Rapid population growth means that money must be spent just to create jobs, rather than to improve those already existing or to create more productive ones.

Thus, the practical consequences resulting from workforce growth would be massive (formal, casual and informal) unemployment, low incomes, poverty, disillusionment, crime (especially in urban areas), and endless extension of ever-lower levels of income-earning opportunities. Some aspects of the issue vary greatly between oil states and non-oil states. The relative wealth of the oil exporting countries, mainly the GCC states, and the theoretical potential to replace non-nationals by nationals mean that they are relatively well placed to cope with the issue of youth unemployment in absolute terms. Their problem, though, will be one of mismatch, with more and more labour market entrants with high but unsuitable qualifications unable to slot into the still immature labour markets.

In the non-oil countries, unemployment will grow, producing a wave of applicants for jobs in the next decades. Public budgets will come under increasing stress, and public-sector employment will only hold close to its present level. Expanded employment in health and education will in large part be offset by declines in other areas. The private sector, while growing in employment terms, will not by any means take up all new labour market entrants. Declines in agricultural employment will ease, though not sufficiently to stop the drift to the cities. Unemployment will appear first in towns, later in the countryside. The problem will be, and in many cases already has been, acutely aggravated by return migration.

Recent history in the Middle East gives an example of the return migration problem. In 1990, following the conflict over Kuwait and its political implications, many non-national employees in some GCC states were forced to return to their home countries. The worst hit by return migration were Jordan, Egypt, Sudan, and Yemen. More than 350 000 Jordanians and Palestinians returned to Jordan, increasing the unemployment rate to 27 per cent and creating great pressure on housing and public services. Meanwhile, the then newly unified Yemen Republic suffered from the return of over 700 000 migrants from Saudi Arabia in the last three months of 1990. Of these, some 350 000 were workers. As a result, unemployment in Yemen shot up to 30 per cent. In that crisis of labour market management, Jordan and Yemen highlighted many aspects of a non-oil Arab future.

To partly contain the adverse impacts of population growth on employment, Middle Eastern regimes have experimented with an array of policies, from the encouragement of migration abroad to the creation of civil service 'non-jobs', a policy causing huge and increasing expenditures and subsequent budget deficits, as in Egypt that tends to absorb university graduates with socialistic ideas into government administration. But until the rate at which jobs can be created comes into equilibrium with the rate at which this generation grows, the young people who are part of the demographic explosion problem will constitute one, if not the most important, source of political instability in the Middle East.

DISPARITY IN POPULATION GROWTH

Population growth is exaggerating, and will further magnify, the different dimensions of the various states in the Middle East. In addition, rapid population growth in the region, by compounding the problems of the people-rich and resource-poor nations, is increasing pressure by the numerous poor on their neighbouring capital-rich, people-sparse conservative petroleum producers in the area. As such, it will probably act as yet one more potential source of instability.

Even with ultra-fast population growth, the small GCC states cannot catch up with the larger countries that surround them. By the year 2025, the six GCC states will have between them a total population of around 56 million people. In contrast, their neighbours – Egypt, Iran, Iraq, Jordan and Yemen – will together have a total population of some 356 million people. This is an inescapable fact which can generate political tension between the GCC states and their neighbours.

Indeed, potential political tension will be almost always present between neighbouring countries that have large population ratios. The 'population ratio' is our indicator for disparity in the size of inhabitants. It is defined as the number of people in one country over that of another, in a given year, actual or future. The population ratios for the years 1950, 1985, and 2025 between neighbouring countries in the Middle East are shown in Table 10.5, revealing interesting upward and downward demographic patterns between different countries.

Table 10.5   Population ratios in the Middle East, 1950, 1985, and 2025[1]

Countries	1950	1985	2025
Egypt–Israel	16.2	11.0	11.8
Egypt–Libya	19.8	12.4	7.2
Egypt–Sudan	2.2	2.1	1.5
Iran–Afghanistan	1.6	3.3	3.2
Iran–Iraq	2.7	3.0	3.1
Iran–Turkey	0.7	0.9	1.5
Iraq–Jordan	4.2	4.7	4.3
Iraq–Kuwait	34.2	9.2	12.9
Iraq–Saudi Arabia	1.6	1.4	1.2
Iraq–Syria	1.5	1.5	1.3
Israel–Jordan	1.0	1.2	0.8
Israel–Lebanon	0.9	1.6	1.9
Oman–UAE	5.9	0.9	1.7
Pakistan–Iran	2.8	2.2	1.8
Saudi Arabia–Bahrain	27.6	27.0	38.3
Saudi Arabia–Jordan	2.6	3.4	3.7
Saudi Arabia–Kuwait	21.1	6.7	11.1
Saudi Arabia–Oman	7.7	9.3	8.6
Saudi Arabia–Qatar	128.0	38.8	52.6
Saudi Arabia–UAE	45.7	8.6	14.1
Saudi Arabia–Yemen	0.7	1.5	1.2
Syria–Israel	2.8	2.5	4.1
Syria–Jordan	2.8	3.1	3.3
Syria–Lebanon	2.4	3.9	7.7
Turkey–Bulgaria	2.9	5.6	10.6
Turkey–Greece	2.8	5.0	9.2
Turkey–Iraq	4.0	3.1	2.1
Turkey–Syria	5.9	4.8	2.7
UAE–Qatar	2.9	4.5	3.7
USSR/FSU–Iran	12.5	5.9	2.4
USSR/FSU–Turkey	8.3	5.6	3.7
Yemen–Oman	10.0	6.2	7.2

Note:
1. *Sources*: Compiled from data in *World Population Prospects* (New York: UN, various issues).

In the year 2025, Iraq would have around thirteen times the population of Kuwait. Striking disparities in population are expected between Saudi Arabia and each of Qatar (53/1), Bahrain (38/1), the UAE (14/1) and Kuwait (11/1). The clear supremacy of Saudi Arabia over the Arabian peninsula is threatened only by the growing population of Yemen (the unified one at least!), its southern neighbour with which many other sources of tension already exist. Nevertheless, the demographic situation of Iran, although not an immediate land neighbour to the GCC states, has been causing most concern in the region.

Another area of concern in the region is the demographic situation between Israel and its neighbours, even in the event of a final settlement of the conflict between them. In 2025, Israel's population will constitute less than 1/11 that of Egypt and 1/4 that of Syria. But the main preoccupation for the Hebrew state remains the Israeli Arabs and the Palestinians. According to UN estimates, the population of Israel will grow from 5.5 million in 1994 to around 9 million in 2025. By then, the ratio will be some 70 per cent for Jews and 30 per cent for Israeli Arabs. Nevertheless, a higher birth rate among the Arabs means that the ratio will change rapidly, especially in the north of the country where, by 2025, Jews will account for less than 35 per cent of the population.

Israel regards the Palestinians, with their high birth rate, as its other main demographic problem. Estimates vary, but most Israelis agree that if Israel had decided to keep holding the West Bank and Gaza Strip, the number of Palestinian Arabs under Israeli rule would have overtake the number of Israeli Jews by early next century. Instead of a Jewish state, Israel would have become a binational state, with a growing Palestinian majority. But even with a self-ruled (or independent) West Bank and Gaza Strip, Israel has now to cope with an expected growth of the Palestinian population.

In mid-1995, around 2.1 million Palestinians were living in the West Bank and Gaza Strip, including East Jerusalem, compared to an estimate of 1.4 million in 1988. They will reach almost 2.5 million in 2000. The establishment of Palestinian autonomy (or a Palestinian state) and the opportunity for Palestinians to exercise their right of return would lead to a considerable increase in the population of the Palestinian territories. It is estimated that nearly 1 million Palestinians living in refugee camps in Lebanon, Syria and Jordan would try to return, Then, the Palestinian population would rise almost immediately to 3.1 million, and by 2000 could reach about 3.8 million. This would give the new territory a density of some 650 persons per km^2, while Gaza's population density could exceed 2900 per km^2. By 2025, the Palestinians in their territories could reach around 6 million.

11 Troubles Caused by Migrated People

While labour migration is the primary type of population movement in the Middle East, the region has been the site of a series of flights within countries, and flows of refugees in response to wars, civil unrest, and political changes.

MIGRATION OF FOREIGN LABOUR

A factor which is regionally based but which poses a threat at the national level is that of expatriate labour migration. Throughout most of the post-1973 period, there have been movements of workers, skilled and unskilled, from oil-poor to oil-rich countries. In fact, the rapid economic growth of the underpopulated Arabian peninsula could not have materialised without foreigners, attracted to the region by the opportunities of earning higher wages.

Labour migration in the Gulf region follows a different pattern from the one familiar in the USA and other industrial countries. Developed countries often attract lower skilled workers from developing countries – Mexicans to the USA, or Algerians to France. In the Gulf, however, migrants are moving from one developing country to another.

Whether the expatriates outnumber the indigenous population, as in the case of the UAE, Qatar, or Kuwait, or whether they form smaller groups, as in the other states, this constantly expanding foreign workforce has proved indispensable for any GCC state embarking on economic development. These expatriates are found in all sectors of the economy and at all levels of skill, at times dominating both owing to their ability or to the lack of inclination or availability of locals to engage in hard labour.

Accurate information as to the size of the expatriate community in each Gulf state is difficult to find, being a politically sensitive issue and a source of embarrassment to some regimes. Government statistics usually try to diminish the size of the immigrant population and to inflate their own. But what is certain is that the dependence of the GCC states on foreigners for labour has no parallel in modern economic history.

In 1990, according to UN estimates, foreign workers comprised over two-thirds of the overall labour force in the GCC. While Saudi Arabia is the biggest magnet for migrant labour, attracting about 55 per cent of the foreign workers in the Gulf, expatriates have the largest impact on the labour forces of the UAE and Qatar. Non-indigenous labours comprised 84 per cent of the labour force in the UAE in 1975; by 1990 their share had grown close to 90 per cent. In Qatar, the foreign share of the labour force grew from 83 per cent to 92 per cent over the same period. Expatriates made up at least 80 per cent of Kuwait's labour force in 1990; since then, the Kuwaiti government has been trying hard to decrease this ratio to as low as possible. In other GCC states, the ratio of non-indigenous labour over nationals amounted in 1990 to 51 per cent in Bahrain and 70 per cent in both Oman and Saudi Arabia. The migration of foreign labour has changed the status of the national population into minority, as in the case of the UAE (where nationals represented only 20 per cent of the total population in 1990), Kuwait and Qatar (both 27 per cent), and Bahrain (47 per cent). The 1990 proportion of the indigenous population over the total was 66 per cent in Saudi Arabia, and 73 per cent in Oman.

According to a study published by the UN Economic and Social Commission for Western Asia (UN ESCWA) in 1993, the numbers of expatriate labour in the GCC region had grown from 1.1 million in 1975 to some 5.7 million in 1992. As the GCC countries strive to attain greater self-sufficiency in agriculture, industry and commerce, the local supply of skilled and unskilled labour will never suffice, and therefore the requirements for expatriate labour will continue. By the year 2000, their number could reach around 9 million.

Generally speaking, and although Asians and Far Easterns have constituted the majority of the non-indigenous labour force in the Gulf since the early 1980s, the group of expatriates that hold highly ranked positions within the public sectors and form the backbone of expanding ministries in the Gulf is of Arab origin. Many sensitive key civil and military positions are filled by Palestinians, Egyptians and Jordanians. This is true mainly in Qatar and the UAE (and Kuwait before the conflict with Iraq). A large part of the Omani civil service is being manned by Yemenis and Zanzibaris. Sudanese are prominent in the UAE's municipal services. Pakistanis (Baluchis) and Yemenis are found in large numbers in non-commissioned levels of Oman's army while many Omanis and Pakistanis serve in the UAE's military forces. Bahraini and Qatari armed forces have many Yemenis. The Palestinians are found in the media and practically control the education system in the Gulf. Many Egyptians, too, are teachers, being traditionally very poor in their performance in trade – a sector that contains many Palestinians, Syrians, Lebanese, and Yemenis and, in the lower Gulf, many Pakistanis and Indians. The other categories of expatriates down the ladder of semi-skilled and unskilled labourers in the public and private sectors are less definable in terms of nationality, but the numbers of Asian and Far Eastern workers mainly from the Philippines, India, Pakistan, Bangladesh, and Sri Lanka are increasing there.

The massive influxes of expatriate workers of all types have had some unusual economic, social and political consequences. As well as adding to the cost of infrastructural and service provision, immigrant communities are transferring a considerable part of the national income of the recipient countries (around US\$ 17 billion from Saudi Arabia in 1995 or some 13 per cent of the GNP at current market prices). They are also seen to pose a threat to national culture and identity. The indigenous population increasingly feel that they are being swamped and their identity diluted. In 1996, a decision to expel illegal expatriate workers in the UAE was mainly motivated by concerns over the dilution of tradition Bedouin cultural values.

A problem faced by all Gulf states consists of the fact that most of the expatriate labourers are male, affecting the social balance within these countries. Some immigrants, once established, introduce their dependants and start behaving like a settled population by having children, demanding housing, education and other services. However, because of restrictions on foreigners owning land and property in most Gulf countries, a fairly strict system of residential segregation between citizens and immigrants has been established with districts for nationals and others for foreigners. Many of the Asian and Far Eastern labourers are living in appalling conditions in an attempt to avoid high rents and evade the police searching for illegal immigrants. But it is not only the conditions under which they live which aggravate them. The accumulated feeling of being regarded as modern slaves is another important element.

Another group is the Iranian immigrants to whom, following the Islamic revolution, the authorities have been devoting far more attention. Many of them are poor, attracted by economic incentives and have left their families in Iran. They are a reservoir of dissent, and in Bahrain and Kuwait they have proved fairly active in response to Shia sentiment.

However, Asian, Far Eastern and Iranian workers are merely interested in bettering their lot, intending to return to their places of origin with their savings, while educated Arab immigrants are perceived by local governments as being interested, in addition to raising their standard of living, in politically participating and in contributing their share to inter-Arab politics. But should conflict erupt between the labour states of origin and their host countries they might have divided loyalties, while they would be regarded as a 'fifth column' by both states. That can be clearly exemplified by the Jordanians and (in particular) Palestinians living in Kuwait during the Iraqi invasion.

Another real danger in depending on outside labour is that the workers themselves, underprivileged and denied rights and benefits enjoyed by the indigenous population, may cease to identify their interests with those of the state employing them and may combine or form associations aimed at obtaining better working conditions and basic rights at the expense of the host country. Short-lived examples of what could occur are the outbursts of anger in the Saudi eastern province in 1953 and 1956, when both locals and expatriates protested against working conditions, bringing the oil industry there to a standstill. This has not happened since then, partly because of the prohibition of trade unions, and indeed almost all kinds of political activity in the Gulf, but also because of the high turnover rates of the immigrant labour forces. However, the fact that they might do so is sufficiently alarming that all host states are actively pursuing policies to diminish their presence and to replace them with nationals.

Nevertheless, the process of replacing expatriates by nationals and the attempts to limit the number of immigrants so as to reverse or at least preserve the ratio of locals to foreigners are both far from being successful. The shortage of suitable, skilled and experienced local administrators (attributed mainly to the relatively late establishment of the education system in the region's countries) and the lack of inclination or availability on the part of the locals to engage in hard labour cripple the rulers' attempts to ease out foreigners. Granting citizenship, or more commonly naturalisation, to a fraction of the early immigrants, as in the case of the UAE, Bahrain, Qatar, and Kuwait, could hardly affect the demographic balance that, with the demand for an even larger workforce, is only further changing it in favour of immigrants.

The only policies which seem to be working are those designed to gradually replace the Arab labour force (especially those who came from highly-politicised countries such as Iraq, Palestine, Yemen) with the more obedient and politically docile Asian and Oriental workers, hoping that this in itself will make the remaining Arab expatriates more amenable. Additional advantages of Asian labour are that it is cheaper – an Asian worker employed in the Saudi private sector was paid one-half as much as his Arab counterpart in 1987, and one-third as much in 1991 – and that workers generally leave their dependants at home so that there is less pressure to provide social and other services for immigrants. The males can therefore be accommodated in rather frugal work camps. However, should the Arab immigrants feel threatened by the waves of Asian and Oriental workers who will lessen the Gulf's dependence on them, they themselves may react aggressively within the host countries.

But the inter-Arab implications of the so-called 'Asian and Oriental connection' could be far-reaching for the Arab sending countries, especially Yemen, Jordan and Egypt – all of whom depend heavily on the Gulf absorbing their surplus manpower, even if this deprives them of many of their best trained personnel and, in turn, hampers their own economic growth. A reduction in opportunities abroad would create unemployment in these states that could in turn cause unrest (see Chapter 10).

No economic aid could substitute for the enormous indirect subsidy paid by the Gulf states to the citizens of the labour sending countries through transferred earnings. At one time in the mid-1980s, remittances of Egyptian expatriates represented more than what the country earned from cotton exports, Suez Canal fees and tourism revenues combined.

INTERNAL FLIGHT

The rapid economic growth in the Gulf following the oil price boom in 1973 and 1979–80 has also had some effects on the movement of citizens inside the states. In addition to importing expatriate labour forces, the original policy in the predominantly rural areas of the Gulf–Iran and Iraq were excluded owing to the sheer size of their population – was to deliberately encourage the migration of the countryside's population, especially Bedouins (amongst whom regimes enjoy immense support), into cities so as to balance the increasing number and weight of immigrants there.

That policy first resulted in the establishment of shanty towns on the outskirts of the cities where land is available and Bedouins could retain their life-style far from urban population. In response to such a common phenomenon, the governments of Saudi Arabia, Kuwait, Qatar, and Bahrain embarked on construction programmes in an attempt to settle the Bedouins by providing them with housing. As far as the Saudis are concerned, such a process has advantages for it helps to dilute the territorial, tribal, and sectarian divisions that have hitherto characterised the kingdom. Thus the government encouraged, for example, the move of the pro-regime Qahtan tribe from the south to other areas where economic development is taking place, and the move of Nejdi Sunnis into the eastern province in order to dilute the political weight of the Shia population.

Another Saudi intention of incorporating the local backward rural economy into the foreign-manned, urban, modern industrial sector was envisaged through the newly-established complexes of Yanbu and Jubail. Bringing industrial development into the countryside would, it was hoped, attract many young villagers and Bedouins without causing a harmful effect on their traditional social fabric. Moreover, the government was confident that the new adjacent cities built with all ultra-modern amenities, schooling and hospitalisation would encourage young members of the nomadic sectors to come and live there, despite the fact that such a way of life was totally alien to them. The traumatic effect of this change and its tempo has left its mark on some of these bewildered and unskilled workers. The high cost of living, limited space and the overcrowded and noisy way of life could not be conducive to mass departures into the city, but it has its temptations with its secularised way of life that is free of the restrictive milieu of the conservative family.

Moreover, the desertion of the rural and tribal structures in the Gulf by some of their younger members, albeit on a small scale, has harmed the economy of the families remaining behind, which have become increasingly dependent on women and children, further crippling the already weakened economic viability of the countryside's traditional social order. The *Cabilah* (the federation of Bedouin tribes), once a unit of immense prestige, has lost much of its unifying force. Similarly, the *Hamulah* (clan) is weakened considerably by the government-encouraged departure of its young members. Even the family unit, once built on firm foundations, is becoming fragmented, especially for families living in places remote from areas of economic development.

The movement of rural people to urban areas has some political implications. This growing drift to towns could eventually result in the emergence of new and inter-related sets of conflicts – within the local population and between the population and the governments concerned – all of which could prove costly to the Gulf regimes. In fact, a new source of mass support for the fundamentalists has been a class of recently urbanised Bedouins whose status of relative deprivation among more affluent urbanites made them eager converts to the activist cause.

Moreover, by virtue of bringing together different sections of the population, urbanisation could lead to further confrontation between religious sects and ethnic minorities on the one hand and the governments on the other. These sections of the population tend to stick together, preserve and even reinforce their social and religious affinities, especially if they are confronted by alienation. A prime example is that of Shia migration from rural areas to the capital of Bahrain where the Shia population is generally economically backward and feels to some degree disadvantaged.

In Iraq, around three-quarters of the population are concentrated in cities. The rapid growth of Mosul in the north and Basra to the south has meant that Baghdad's rate of expansion slightly declined. Nevertheless, the Iraqi government (before 1990!) was alarmed by the rapid growth of the cities' population and the corresponding rural depopulation, for this trend brought into the urban centres many frustrated inhabitants – Kurds into the northern cities and Shias into the southern cities and the capital, most of the latter coming from southern provinces where land tenure conditions are intolerable. The rural depopulation also jeopardised the development of Iraqi agriculture; not even the land reforms that followed the 1958 revolution could stop this trend.

If anything, it was the disparity in wealth distribution that induced the flight from the backward, impoverished countryside to the cities where most economic development was taking place. Becoming daily wage earners in building or service industries appealed to these migrants more than the miserable life of a tenant farmer. But in the cities, construction could not keep pace with residential explosion. With the shortage of housing and the absence of adequate sanitation, squatter settlements constructed by migrants have created tremendous social, economic and political problems for the authorities (see Chapter 10).

FLOWS OF REFUGEES

Conflicts in the Middle East since the Second World War have produced the largest refugee flows than in any other world region. The US Committee for Refugees estimated that around 6 million people – one-third of the world refugee total – were in the Middle East in 1992. The broader region of the Middle East and North Africa, from Afghanistan to Morocco and Turkey to the Horn of Africa, was the source of more than 12 million refugees. These figures do not include the refugees who did not cross national borders. For example, during the eight-year war between Iran and Iraq (1980–8) an estimated 2.5 million Iranians fled to war-free zones to central Iran.

As a result of the Arab–Israeli conflict, many Jews fled or were driven from the Arab states. According to Israeli statistics, around 800 000 Oriental Jews have been resettled in Israel, although their assimilation has created many complex problems. These immigrants are no longer considered as refugees because they have virtually no inclination to return to the land of their birth or ancestry.

Another result of the Arab–Israeli conflict has been the dispersion of the Palestinians, the oldest and most well known refugee group in the region (see Box 11.1). The history of the Palestinians since the Second World War has been a story of continued displacement and dispersion. The first displacement occurred with the establishment of Israel and eruption of the first Arab–Israeli military conflict. By the end of 1948, more than three-quarters of a million Palestinians fled to the West Bank, the Gaza Strip, Jordan, Lebanon, Syria, and other Arab states. A second displacement of about half a million Palestinians occurred after the 1967 Arab–Israeli war when Israel occupied the West Bank and Gaza Strip. The fate of these refugees, estimated by the UN Relief and Works Agency (UNRWA) at over 3 million as of early 1995, is not yet clear, especially as there is no allusion to them in the 1994–5

Box 11.1   The Palestinians

The Palestinians are defined as the people who lived on the territory of Palestine, along with their paternal descendants. Palestine was placed under British control by the League of Nations after the First World War, in an arrangement lasting from 1922 to 1948 when Israel was established. Palestinians speak Arabic and the vast majority practice Islam, although a sizeable minority is Christian or Druze.

With a high rate of natural increase, the Palestinians have grown in number from 1.4 million after the Second World War to roughly 7 million today. About 3 million Palestinians live within the boundaries of historic Palestine, which is now Israel plus the West Bank and Gaza Strip. More than 800 000 of these Palestinians are Israeli citizens. By Israeli law, Palestinians (and their descendants) who were physically present in their usual residences at the time of the first Israeli census in 1949 acquired Israeli citizenship. However, Israeli Arabs cannot qualify for the same government benefits as Jewish citizens, in part because they are excluded from military service.

Over 1.5 million Palestinians reside in nearby Jordan, where they now make up almost half of the population and have full Jordanian citizenship. The neighbouring countries of Syria and Lebanon contain more than 300 000 Palestinians each. More than half a million Palestinians were living elsewhere in the Middle East in 1990, including over 300 000 in Kuwait, although that number is thought to have fallen to around 10 000 following the 1990–1 Gulf war.

Sizeable Palestinian minorities are also domiciled in Europe and the USA. Palestinians who are employed in a variety of countries may or may not be citizens of those states, but they are no longer classified as refugees by UNRWA, which has attempted to maintain a count of the unabsorbed Palestinian refugee community. As of the beginning of 1995, over 3 million Palestinian refugees were registered with UNRWA: 504 000 in West Bank, 645 000 in Gaza Strip, 1 194 000 in Jordan, 338 000 in Lebanon, and 327 000 in Syria.

Israeli–Palestinian peace agreements. Some countries could be ultimately constrained to nationalise those refugees living on their territories. That would create many complex political, social and economic
challenges for host countries, such as Lebanon.

Dispersion of Palestinians also resulted from economic migration.
During the oil boom of the 1970s, many educated Palestinian managers
and professionals found employment in the oil-rich Gulf states. Because
Palestinian leaders sided with Iraq during the 1990–1 Gulf War, Kuwait
permanently expelled almost all the Palestinians who lived and worked
there. Many were born in Kuwait, or had lived there for decades, but
could not become citizens under Kuwaiti law. Many Palestinians subsequently fled Kuwait and other Gulf countries to Jordan; some went to the
West Bank. Some have left the Middle East, relying on existing networks of relatives and friends to help them migrate to the USA, Canada
and Australia.

In fact, the Gulf war and the subsequent civil unrest in Iraq created one
of history's largest, fastest, and most widespread population movements,
involving an estimated 6 million people. Some 2 million Asian and Arab
migrants in Kuwait, Saudi Arabia, and Iraq took refuge in neighbouring
countries until they could return to their home countries. Egyptian workers
were no longer welcomed in Iraq because of the Egyptian support for
Kuwait in the war. As a result, most of the 1.5 million Egyptians working
in Iraq returned home. Likewise, Jordanians and Yemenis were expelled
from Kuwait and Saudi Arabia because their government leaders supported
Iraq.

Following the Gulf war, an estimated 2 million men, women, and
children, mainly Kurds, fled their homes in Iraq in less than six days in
spring 1991 as civil unrest erupted in the north of that country. An estimated 1.5 million took refuge in neighbouring Iran and Turkey, the rest
were stranded in the northern Iraqi regions. Almost all the surviving
Kurdish refugees eventually returned to Iraq, but not necessarily to their
previous homes and towns.

At the height of the Kurdish refugee influx in spring 1991, Iran hosted
more refugees than any other country in the world. In addition to the
estimated 1.4 million Iraqis (including Kurds from the north, and then
some Shias from the south) fleeing the civil unrest following the Gulf war,
half a million Iraqi refugees from the Iran–Iraq war lived in Iran in a
refugee-like setting. Iran also housed around 3 million Afghani refugees
from the Soviet invasion of Afghanistan in 1979 and the subsequent civil
war there. Most Afghani refugees live in towns, where they are economically self-sufficient from low-paying jobs.

Refugees often place a political burden on the host country. The Palestinians, for example, were one principal reason for violent unrest in Jordan in summer 1970, which ended with the repatriation of most of their militias to Lebanon. There, the Palestinians had enjoyed the benefits and privileges accorded to them by the government in Beirut, but had created a state within the Lebanese one. By supporting Lebanese Muslims over Christians, and by fighting the Israelis from Lebanese territories, and then the Syrian forces, the Palestinians were considered as one of the direct and main cause of the Lebanese civil war (1975–90).

Some heavy financial burdens are also created by the presence of refugees on a country's territories. Yemen, for example, had to provide social services and economic aid for Somali and Ethiopian refugees during the early 1990s – the same period when hundreds of thousands of its own people had been expelled from Saudi Arabia in the aftermath of the Gulf war.

Many of the same types of political, social, and economic developments that created the previous refugee flows in the Middle East are still operating today. The manner in which the area's countries deal with these developments will determine whether large-scale refugee movements continue within and among the countries of the region.

12 How Secure are Petroleum Supplies?

While many situations of instability and conflict in the Middle East remain restricted on a limited scale, any internal or regional crisis affecting the security of petroleum supplies from the area to world markets is immediately considered as a threat to international peace. The world, and especially the West, is in fact more interested about a strife in the region if it is associated with either a threat to or an actual disruption of petroleum supplies. This behaviour derives from an implicit conviction that Middle Eastern petroleum is to be 'shared' among its producers and consumers, being vitally and strategically important to the latter's economies.

But while petroleum confers on the Middle East its geopolitical and strategic weight, it is also the region's Achilles' heel: any dispute or conflict there could be tempted to materialise first by striking at the petroleum industry which remains the backbone of many states in the area. Add to that the fact that there are only few industries more vulnerable both on land and at sea than the petroleum industry, and the world has got a major interest in an issue of prime importance: *the security of petroleum supplies from the Middle East.*

VULNERABILITY OF PRODUCTION INSTALLATIONS

The petroleum production installations in the Middle East are highly exposed to internal attack and instability. This was demonstrated during both 1953 and 1956 in the eastern province of Saudi Arabia where both locals and expatriates working in oil fields and terminals protested against working conditions, bringing the petroleum industry there to a standstill, although for only few days. In the late 1970s, and due to the Islamic revolution, the petroleum industry in Iran experienced long periods of cessation. More recently, a strike in March 1995 by around 1200 oil workers in Kuwait had affected, although only partly, the production and export level of the emirate.

The petroleum production installations also remain highly exposed to external attacks, and even small offensives can have major consequences.

The production wells, spread over thousands of square kilometres, would be virtually indefensible in the face of a determined enemy. This was first shown during the Iran–Iraq war (1980–8), when many of the fields near the battle areas and most of the Iranian fields offshore the Gulf were hit.

During the conflict over Kuwait (1990–1), around 800 of the 1000 producing Kuwaiti wells were set on fire, together with refining, storage and loading facilities, destroying the very basis of the petroleum industry of the emirate. In the meantime, the Iraqi fields straddling the border with Kuwait, especially the giant Rumaila field, were badly hit. The destruction of Kuwaiti fields had vast ecological repercussions within the emirate, and some indirect meteorological consequences in many parts of the planet. A subsequent oil spill badly affected the maritime natural life in the Gulf and the desalination plants on its shores, which treat its water to supply a major part of demand. Blowing out the burning Kuwaiti fields took over a year and cost not less than $1 billion. But repairing the real damage occurring to the reservoirs proved to be a more difficult, lengthy and expensive task.

VULNERABILITY OF MARITIME WATERWAYS

The six channels on major shipping lanes in the Middle East – the Suez Canal, the straits of Hormuz, Bab Al Mandeb and Tiran, and the two Turkish straits – and their geographical constraints result in a concentration of petroleum shipping. They have been always faced with the danger of closure or blockade.

Before 1967, attention in Western Europe was sharply focused on the Suez Canal linking the Red Sea and the Mediterranean, and through which a high proportion of Middle Eastern oil was shipped (around 42 million tons in 1995). The Canal, which in the mid-nineteenth century was predicted by Renan from the French Academy to be 'the site of the future heaviest struggles', was governed by the 1888 Constantinople Convention which stated that the waterway would 'always be free and open, in time of war as in time of peace, to every vessel of commerce or of war, without distinction of flag'.

The importance of the Canal to European states became so great that Britain and France decided to fight in July 1956, with the assistance of Israel, to protect their interests there, following nationalisation of the Canal company by the Egyptian President Nasser. Nasser immobilised the Canal by ordering the sinking of a number of vessels in the navigable channel. When the invading forces were pressured by the USA and the

Soviet Union to halt their campaign, the Canal had already been crippled. It took until April 1957 to clear the waterway and to open it again to navigation. Following a further decade of growth in traffic, especially oil cargoes, the Canal was again closed to shipping after the June 1967 invasion of Sinai by Israel during which the waterway had been blocked by sunken vessels. It did not reopen until June 1975.

The second choke point, the most important when considering the maritime petroleum supply from the Middle East, is the Strait of Hormuz, the 'door' of the Gulf linking it to the Gulf of Oman. The free flow of oil through the Strait (averaging around 10 million barrels per day or about 30 per cent of world oil trade in 1995) is regarded as of vital interest to the West. The closure of the Strait never happened, but the threat has been always there.

The Strait of Hormuz has been the subject of more commentary than any other strategic waterway. Indeed, with the Soviet invasion of Afghanistan (1978), the Iranian revolution (1978–9), the Iran–Iraq war (1980–8), and the conflict over Kuwait (1990–1), there were widespread fears that the Strait could be closed to shipping. These anxieties were more acute in the industrialised world that depends upon imported oil passing through Hormuz. The Strait is also vitally important to the Gulf states themselves which depend on oil revenues, and through Hormuz they import large quantities of industrial products and consumer goods including food.

Various efforts have been made to ensure the safety of shipping in the Strait of Hormuz. In 1977, the Iranian Shah secured an agreement with Oman allowing his powerful navy to patrol tanker routes even in Omani water. He argued, however, that freedom of navigation through the Strait was dependent on Iran having control of the tiny Abu Musa and Tunb Islands, to which the UAE also stakes a claim.

After the Iranian revolution, the Omanis appealed for financial and practical help in developing naval forces and bases to resume the task of patrolling the Strait. Hormuz is now regularly patrolled by units of Omani navy, while the USA, Britain, and other powers maintain a naval presence in the area. Meantime, Iran has deployed and readied missiles on the Abu Musa and Tunb Islands, while purchasing two submarines in the early 1990s that could physically choke off the traffic through the Strait.

In order to secure export outlets other than on the Gulf and its 'door', petroleum producers have built many large export pipelines terminating on the coasts of the Red Sea and the Mediterranean[1]. Such pipelines have reduced dependency upon Hormuz chiefly for markets west of the Gulf region. Japan and southeast Asian countries-bound exports, however, are less likely to find alternative routes. Hormuz, therefore, will continue to be the focus of much geopolitical activity.

The Strait of Bab Al Mandeb between the Red Sea and the Gulf of Aden is of great importance to shipping using the Red Sea and the Suez Canal. At the same time it is the only natural outlet to the world's oceans for Jordan, Sudan, and Ethiopia, and is regarded as of great significance by Israel. In the 1970s, the Marxist regime of South Yemen claimed total sovereignty over the Strait – even closing it for few days during the 1973 Arab–Israeli war – but had been then challenged by Saudi Arabia. To the north of the channel, the island of Greater Hanish which controls shipping lanes has been claimed by both Yemen and Eritrea, leading in late 1995 to serious clashes between the forces of the two countries. Britain retained control over the island and neighbouring ones until the early 1970s, then handed them over to the South Yemeni authorities.

Before the 1967–75 closure of the Suez Canal, Bab Al Mandeb was the main sea route for the bulk of oil exported to West European markets. During its closure, the Cape route around Africa came into prominence. Since 1975, the Suez Canal and the Egyptian Sumed pipeline between the Gulf of Suez and the Mediterranean have recaptured some of the oil trade, but several new oil pipelines like the Saudi east-west Petroline by-pass Bab Al Mandeb, and tanker traffic is therefore no longer so significant. The pattern could change markedly, however, if the Suez Canal is further widened to take large supertankers.

The Strait of Tiran between the Red Sea and the Gulf of Aqaba was the focus of many political and military confrontations in both 1956 and 1967 when President Nasser closed the waterway to Israeli shipping, thereby effectively blockading the Israeli port of Eilat. That was followed on both occasions by Israel occupying Sinai's Sharm Al Sheikh, the key to the Strait. Under the Egyptian–Israeli peace treaty of 1979, Israel withdrew from Sharm Al Sheikh after twelve years of occupation. The treaty, meanwhile, spells out the importance of the Strait to maritime nations, assuring its use by Israeli vessels.

Although not crucial for Middle Eastern petroleum supplies like the other transit waterways but for petroleum originating from Black Sea terminals, the strategic significance of the Turkish Straits is quite unequivocal, since they give the Black Sea countries access to the Mediterranean and beyond. Tsarist Russia and its successor, the USSR, had both sought outright control, or at least joint administration, of the waterway. The 1936 Montreux Convention has regulated and limited the passage of warships in and out of the Black Sea, and made Turkey the gatekeeper of the Straits. Merchant ships, however, may use the Straits without restriction. Nevertheless, many of these regulations have been changed with the introduction in July 1994 of stricter shipping separation lanes following a major tanker accident on the Bosporus. Russia opposes the new Turkish regulations, insisting on a new agreement approved by the signatories of the Montreux Convention.

VULNERABILITY OF TANKERS AND TERMINALS

Even when not faced by the closure of one or many of the maritime waterways, the fact remains that tankers are still vulnerable to attack from air, land and sea (including floating mines) and that their safety cannot be fully guaranteed. The shipping routes in the Middle East are vulnerable along their entire length, since even small modern crafts can carry armour-piercing, surface-to-surface missiles fully capable of sinking most tankers or bulk carriers.

Recent history has involved a 'tanker war' that started in 1984 in the Gulf and stopped in 1988 with the cease-fire between Iran and Iraq. During that period, 357 vessels of an aggregate 61.7 million dwt were hit in the Gulf, 308 of them are oil tankers which form the vast bulk of the tonnage figure. There were 205 seamen killed and 53 vessels declared CTLs (Constructive Total Losses).

Meanwhile, Iranian attacks on Kuwaiti tankers in early 1987 pushed the government of the emirate to reflag its tanker fleet seeking more protection, and to ask both the USA and the USSR for assistance. The result was a large allied naval effort in the Gulf throughout the latter part of 1987 and much of 1988.

Back to the early 1980s, the oil analyst Walter Levy was reported to be worried that '60 per cent of Gulf oil was shipped from only three terminals, with eight pumping stations regulating the flow of oil to these ports'. Indeed, such an industry is highly exposed to attack, and even small offensives can have major consequences. This was demonstrated during the Iran–Iraq war when the main Iranian oil terminal in Kharg Island became a major Iraqi target. Significant damage made unusable the exposed and ill-defended outlet and severely hindered traffic at its loading jetty where most of the berths were put out of action. The terminal capacity was not fully restored until the end of 1994. The Iranian terminals of Sirri and Larak were also hit in 1986, but quick repair work had restored export capacity almost immediately.

In the meantime, the Iraqi oil terminals of Fao, Khor Al Amayah and Mina Al Bakr were destroyed during the conflict. Work started in June

1989 on rebuilding Fao terminal, but had to be suspended with the outbreak of the conflict over Kuwait. Similarly, the terminal of Mina Al Bakr saw its capacity rebuilt in mid-1990 to 400 000 barrels per day (b/d) as compared to its design capacity of 1.6 million b/d. Mina Al Bakr was again badly damaged during the Kuwaiti war, and subsequently repaired, although only partly to a handling capacity estimated in early 1996 at around 800 000 b/d.

Moreover, in October 1987, an Iranian land-to-land missile struck Mina Al Ahmadi, Kuwait's main oil export terminal. Although alternative export facilities were quickly improvised, the attack put around one-third of the emirate's daily export totals – about 600 000 b/d – at risk. But the major destruction of Kuwaiti oil terminals occurred during the conflict with Iraq when Mina Al Ahmadi, among others, was seriously damaged by both the Iraqis and the allied forces. Following some reparation work, oil exports resumed in July 1991 from the northern jetty of the terminal.

VULNERABILITY OF PIPELINES

In general, the oil pipelines built in the Middle East have sought the security of supply and export rather than the economic objective of cheaper oil transport. In fact, pipelines have been expensive to build and operate. In the years just after the Second World War, for example, the Arabian American Oil Company (Aramco) had built the Trans-Arabian Pipeline (Tapline) from the Saudi eastern province to Zahrani on the Lebanese coast to avoid the Suez Canal and its transit fees. Yet Aramco had to innovate in the pipeline's construction to keep costs competitive with shipping and had to overcome fierce competition and related political hostility from Britain and its allies in Jordan and Syria. Later, transit fees on Tapline's oil imposed by Syria in particular undermined the line's economic value. Nevertheless, the Tapline, as well as Iraqi lines through Syria and Lebanon, were priceless immediately after the closure of the Suez Canal in 1967. With the introduction of supertankers, shipping regained some of its economic advantage, however.

The eight-year Gulf war was a stimulating factor in both Iran and Iraq for planning and implementing a number of alternative oil export outlets to replace closed pipelines and damaged terminals. That conflict made this diversification attractive to virtually every other Gulf state. Not surprisingly, Iraq whose meagre Gulf coastline was blocked early in the war and its export outlets through the Mediterranean shut down soon after that, most consistently sought the diversification of its export channels through Turkey and Saudi Arabia.

Although Iran's export security problem has never been as serious as that facing Iraq, sporadic Iraqi air strikes on Kharg Island gave Tehran some reasons for planning a number of pipelines aimed principally at by-passing the exposed terminal. However, most of the projects were later on put on hold as an indirect result of the Iraqi strikes on the remote Larak and Sirri terminals in 1986 that raised serious questions in Iran about the usefulness of pipelines and their security.

For Saudi Arabia, its main export pipeline, Petroline from the eastern province to Yanbu on the Red Sea, was basically built to secure outlets other than on the Gulf, and to lessen the kingdom's dependence on the Strait of Hormuz. Yet liftings at the Red Sea must transit the Suez Canal or the Strait of Bab Al Mandeb, or alternatively be piped through Sumed (or Eilat–Ashkelon line?) to the Mediterranean.

The objective of oil supply security sought by Middle Eastern producers has not been met through pipelines. Within a study done by the *Observatoire Méditerranéen de l'Energie*, an assessment of the historical record of the petroleum pipelines in the region until the end of 1995 reveals that of the 260 years representing the cumulative age of the international export pipelines (crossing at least one state boundary), some 134 years of actual pumping, or only 52 per cent, have been recorded. It is also interesting to note that every international export pipeline in the region was shut down at least once. As far as the internal export pipelines are concerned, the ratio of actual pumping has reached 92 per cent. Thus, the overall ratio of actual pumping amounts to some 70 per cent (then an interruption ratio of 30 per cent!) representing 325 years over a cumulative total age of 470 years, or 145 years of interrupted pumping (see Table 12.1).

SUPPLY SECURITY OR POLITICAL STABILITY?

For some analysts in the West, the security of petroleum supplies from the Middle East has tended to have a circumscribed meaning unrelated to its political context. They argue that the two wars involving Iraq in the 1980s and early 1990s show that oil production and export installations are far less vulnerable than is often assumed. According to them the experience of the conflicts suggests that overland oil transportation through pipelines is more resilient to attack than maritime outlets and sea transportation. Then, because of the diversification of the oil transportation system, and with a

Table 12.1 Pipelines' security of supply in the Middle East (end-1995 status)[1]

Pipeline	Date of previous and current shut down	Reason	Actual pumping/ age (year)
International Export Pipelines			
Kirkuk (Iraq)–Haifa (Palestine)	Since 1948	Arab–Israeli conflict	16/63
Kirkuk (Iraq)–Tripoli (Lebanon)	Three days in 1956 June 1972–March 1973 April 1976–December 1981 January and March 1982 Since April 1982	Conflict over Suez Canal Nationalisation of the line by Iraq and Syria Disputes over transit fees Sabotage attacks Iraqi–Syrian antagonism	41/61
Kirkuk (Iraq)–Banias (Syria)	Three days in 1956 June 1972–March 1973 April 1976–February 1979 Since April 1982	Conflict over Suez Canal Nationalisation of the line by Iraq and Syria Disputes over transit fees Iraqi–Syrian antagonism	26/44
Kirkuk (Iraq)–Ceyhan (Turkey) (IT I)	September–November 1980 Since August 1990	Iranian air attacks Conflict over Kuwait and UN embargo against Iraq	13/18
Kirkuk (Iraq)–Ceyhan (Turkey) (IT II)	Since August 1990	Conflict over Kuwait and UN embargo against Iraq	3/8
Iraqi Pipeline across Saudi Arabia (IPSA)	Since August 1990	Conflict over Kuwait and UN embargo against Iraq	5/10
Abqaiq (Saudi Arabia)–Zahrani (Lebanon) (Tapline)	Three days in 1956 Several days in 1969, 1970, 1971, and 1972 May 1970–January 1971 February 1975–September 1990 Since September 1990	Conflict over Suez Canal Sabotage attacks Disputes over transit fees Economic reasons, only some pumping to Lebanon and Jordan for local use. Meanwhile the line was attacked by Israel in 1981 and 1982 Conflict over Kuwait and deterioration in Saudi–Jordanian relations	24/45

Table 12.1 *Continued*

Pipeline	Date of previous and current shut down	Reason	Actual pumping/ age (year)
Rumaila (Iraq)–Shuaiba (Kuwait)	Since August 1990	Conflict over Kuwait	4/9
Bukha (Oman)–Ras Al Khaimah			2/2
Sub-total			134/260
Internal Export Pipelines			
Haditha–Rumaila (Iraq) (Strategic Line)	September 1980–early 1981 Since August 1990	Iranian air attacks Conflict over Kuwait and UN embargo against Iraq	14/20
Iranian Gas Trunkline (IGAT I)	October–November 1978, and December 1978–April 1979 Early 1980–April 1990 Since early 1993	Iranian internal problems following the Islamic revolution Disputes over gas prices with the USSR Disputes over gas prices with the FSU countries	11/24
Other internal export pipelines			166/166
Sub-total			191/210
Grand Total			325/470

Note:
1. *Source: Petroleum Export Routes and the Security Equation in the Middle East* (Sophia Antipolis: Observatoire Méditerranéen de l'Energie, 1995).

few additional pipelines, a stage may be reached where oil exports from the Gulf would be considered as 'very safe'.

In fact, only few pipelines appear to have been shut down as a result of military hostilities. Pipelines in the region running above ground as well as pumping stations were only intermittently hit by direct terrorist attack or air strikes. Both Saudi and Iraqi lines to the Mediterranean have been temporarily cut by terrorist actions and air attack, while only some sections and pumping stations of the Iraqi export system were damaged as a result of the military conflict over Kuwait.

However, this analysis seems not to take into consideration the main reasons behind the shut down of many export pipelines in the Middle East, which remain the political conflicts within producing countries or transit states, and the interstate disputes. In fact, most of the pipelines crossing state boundaries have fallen victim to the region's political rivalries and conflicts. The pipelines built to carry oil from Iraq to the Mediterranean coasts help to demonstrate the point. The line built before the Second World War to Haifa was closed permanently in 1948 as a result of the first Arab–Israeli conflict, while lines to Tripoli and Banias repeatedly fell (and are still) victim to Iraqi–Syrian antagonism. Recently, since 1990, the pipelines through Saudi Arabia and Turkey have also been shut down in the political aftermath of the conflict over Kuwait.

To sum up, decades of pipeline construction have diversified Middle Eastern oil export routes and significantly reduced their vulnerability, a trend that will be reinforced by the execution of some of the planned pipelines. But the threats of political disruption in producing or in transit countries and of interstate conflicts and/or subsequent military hostilities, fuelled further by many elements of instability in the region, are strongly present, at a time when long-range missiles are being developed and acquired by countries in the area, shaking the military balance and leading to a rethinking of security in global terms.

Nevertheless, considering that producing countries in the Middle East are living on their hydrocarbon resources and consequently having to sell them, and that transit fees constitute an important share of the transit countries' revenues, the risk of permanent or sustained interruption of petroleum supplies from the region is considered as slight. That is what we call 'the mutual dependency stabilising factor'. But the possibility of short-term (weeks, months, or even years) dislocation or interruption of petroleum supplies because of governments in the region losing control over one or more of the endogenous pressures along the area is considered to be high. Arab oil embargoes applied in the aftermath of the 1967 and 1973 conflicts with Israel, and the international sanctions against Iraq since August 1990 have further demonstrated the point.

All this leads us to reply to the question suggested by the title of the present chapter by confirming that there is no security for petroleum supply from the Middle East without real stability in the region. Unfortunately, the turbulent history of the area does not augur well for stability: if it is not one country it is another, and if it is not one issue it is another. That induces us to conclude that one of the greatest threat to petroleum market stability in the years ahead remains the potential for conflicts and disputes in the Middle East.

Conclusion

There is no doubt that a *final* solution (if there is one) for the Arab–Israeli conflict, which has dominated much of the general discussion about Middle Eastern developments over the past fifty years will shift the perception of political risk of the area, but will not be able to eliminate all of the factors of conflict and instability militating in favour of the region's continuous political volatility. By elucidating the main elements of instability and conflict, we hope the present book has drawn sufficient attention to these important issues which may not be so eye-catching or newsworthy.

Although many hope to see the region experiencing the same peaceful atmosphere prevailing in Western Europe since the end of the Second World War after long centuries of wars, conflicts, and disputes, and despite growing good prospects for peace between Arabs and Israel, many underlying causes of Middle East instability and conflict appear to be strengthening. This reflects a new political environment in which major threats have been replaced by less-than-vital concerns. The reduction of major threats, like the Israeli one, has diminished the need for regional cohesion and national unity, and has led to states and communities feeling able to pursue past claims.

The surfacing of many underlying causes of instability and conflict in the Middle East is symptomatic of far deeper political differences in a region that is not monolithic, and where many divisive elements exist – witness the tribal and dynastic differences which are at times accentuated by resource considerations and historical or cultural animosities.

It is extremely difficult, and may even be pointless, to try to devise a scale that will quantify how potent are the various sources of conflict and instability in each of the region's states. With the different issues interwoven and mutually reinforcing, any attempts to point to the saliency of certain factors in an attempt to create a hierarchy of threats could be misleading. Ultimately, no conflict factor is inherently more important than another.

Rather than identifiable threats to peace, these factors of conflict and instability are grounds for uncertainty about the future. They may remain dormant or deferred, yet always bearing the potential to re-emerge as catalysts of conflicts under the appropriate conditions. Instability and unrest could erupt any time and anywhere in the region regardless of what has happened in the past, leading to 'a chain of conflict reaction'. Such a chain of reaction, launched and fuelled by many subjective and concrete elements, is unpredictable by nature.

Likewise, listing the region's states according to their potential strengths or weaknesses so as to forecast the likelihood of survival of the regimes could prove to be a futile exercise. Besides, periods of peacefulness in some states should not be seen as stability nor as a reflection of their governments' capacity to withstand internal challenges. Furthermore, it would be undesirable to fall into the temptation of extrapolating capacity and strength from a given regime's past performance and present situation.

It is nevertheless worth looking at existing patterns and trends in all states of the region, because they are intimately linked. A chain reaction in the area due to interstate conflict or internal instability might indeed be triggered off by a change in one country, broadening the scope of friction and implicating other states within the region. How and to which extent, the chain reaction will be triggered off remains an open question.

The threats are real, and their unpredictable and varied nature renders the problems of countering them even more difficult. They need to be dealt with in a comprehensive manner but, truth to tell, there are no easy solutions.

A whole set of new relationships have perhaps to be found along truly democratic lines between the governed and those who govern them. States have to treat internal problems and pressures as challenges to be embraced rather than dangers to be suppressed. They have now the incentive to restructure not only their economies but also many aspects of their political systems. Likewise, new relationships must be forged among the states of the region so as to eliminate all possibilities of damaging conflict. Regional co-operation by itself is unlikely to substitute for regime competence should these regimes need to face domestic challenges, while the absence of co-operation will make it more difficult to confront internal dangers.

Nevertheless, regional co-operation is unlikely to endure, with some of the governments attempting to manipulate each other's internal problems to acquire leverage over their neighbours, and to promote their own regional interests. The participating states may be able to subsume their differences in a common endeavour, but they also may not. Thus, the viability of regional security as an approach to contain conflicts is at best doubtful, the main factor hindering such a development remaining the contending perceptions of security and definitions of threat amongst the local actors. It is the contending patterns of interests reflected in these divergent security perspectives which militate in favour of the region's continuing volatility.

The outbreak of conflict and instability is not solely linked to internal and regional dynamics, however. It is also a function of the relationship between local actors and external great powers in an area of considerable competition. Maybe it is time for the great powers to be fair, even-handed and respectful of the sensitivities of all the people in the area. After the disintegration of the USSR and the change in the Russian focus to the former Soviet republics while reducing commitments in the Middle East, the present challenge for the USA and the West is in defining security where stability is precarious, and in formulating policies that will enhance development and welfare in the region. But, as a prerequisite, they have to perceive the delicate balance between people, politics and resources that forms an intricate mosaic among the countries of the region. Each country brings distinctive patterns and traditions to the area, and will seek unique solutions to its own set of problems and challenges.

Although limited, Western power is not inconsequential. At least it should demonstrate more sensitivity to regional politics and local priorities and avoid exacerbating existing instabilities, by unbridled commercialism or by encouraging a military arms race. That may not bias events directly but it will influence, through the perceptions of local states, their choices as they weigh the balance of risks involved in potential policies.

Unfortunately, it seems that present practices do consist of implicitly encouraging Middle Eastern countries, especially those in the Gulf, to purchase weapons in large quantities in the name of self-defence. These practices by Western arms producers will almost certainly exacerbate the financial difficulties faced by these countries. What is more, these practices are ultimately self-defeating because the extra expenditure adds to the social and political pressures bubbling away under the surface. A short-sighted interest in short-term gains could thus threaten to jeopardise the West's long-term economic interests.

The magnitude of great power interests in the region and the absence of a viable regional framework for security co-operation ensure the continuation of a high level of active involvement on their part. In an area of chronic domestic instability, in which the so-called process of conflict resolution has more often been a function of manipulation rather than management, the problem of conflict escalation remains acute.

Seen from another angle, it would be quite illusory to continue talking of the 'stability' of the Middle East while disregarding the legitimate national aspirations and economic development imperatives of its countries. Thus, market prices that reflect the real economic value of these countries' resources, lower budget deficits, more investment, greater shared prosperity, relevant budgets and development plans and less military spending, but also more democracy and regional co-operation, and less (or at least fair and respectful) foreign intervention, all form a 'virtuous circle'.

Only if the Middle East manages to enter this virtuous circle and let energy and peace work for each other will the region emerge into a new era. At that time, and let us hope to reach it one day, the area will be able to unleash the huge economic potential it has and only then will the world be able to rely on the region's greatest asset after its people, its petroleum.

Appendix: Petroleum in the Middle East

CRUDE OIL IN THE MIDDLE EAST

As holder of the world's most abundant proved reserves of crude oil (about 65 per cent of the total in 1995), the basic foundation of modern economy, or around 664 000 million barrels,[1] as well as the world's highest reserve-to-production ratio (87 years, see Table A.1), a measure often used as an indication of supply capability, the paramount importance of the Middle East within the international system is self-evident.

Table A.1   Crude oil reserves and production in the Middle East, 1995[1]

Country	Proven reserves (million barrels)[2]	Share of world total (%)	Production (000 b/d)	Share of world total (%)	Reserves-to-production (years)
Bahrain	210	<0.1	105	0.2	5.6
Egypt	3879	0.4	920	1.4	11.8
Iran	88 200	8.7	3705	5.6	65.9
Iraq	100 000	9.8	545	0.8	>100
Israel	4	<0.1	<1	<0.1	–
Jordan	<1	<0.1	<1	<0.1	–
Kuwait	96 500	9.5	2105	3.2	>100
Lebanon	–	–	–	–	–
Oman	5138	0.5	870	1.3	16.2
Qatar	3700	0.4	460	0.7	23.1
Saudi Arabia	261 203	25.7	8885	13.1	83.8
Syria	2500	0.2	610	1.0	11.2
Turkey	488	<0.1	68	0.1	19.6
UAE	98 100	9.7	2485	3.5	>100
Yemen	4000	0.4	335	0.5	32.9
Total	663 922	65.3	21 133	31.3	87.3

Notes:
1. *Source*: *BP Statistical Review of World Energy 1996* (London: British Petroleum, 1996).
2. Reserves figures as of 1 January 1996.

According to Ivanhoe and Leckie (1993), the world's two megagiant oil fields, 27 of the 40 supergiant oil fields, and four of the 15 supergiant natural gas fields,[2] as well as 120 and 15 of the giant oil and gas fields respectively are located in the Middle East. Saudi Arabia's Ghawar field, the world's largest, alone has twice as much oil as the entire proved reserves of the USA. The average median size of an oil field in the region is around 100 million barrels, or 20 times as large as in Latin America, and 1000 times as large as in Eastern Europe. In the Gulf, the median size of an oil field is some 370 million barrels, compared to a US average of about 100 000 barrels and a world (outside the USA) mean of around 3 million barrels. Moreover, geology and undivided ownership permit extraordinarily high production rates for individual wells. As a way of comparison, an oil well in Saudi Arabia produced an average of 5580 barrels per day (b/d) in 1994, while in the USA it yielded a mean of only 11.4 b/d.

Most of the vast fields in the Middle East are concentrated within the so-called Arabian–Iranian oil province, an area measuring some 1200 by 800 km around the head of the Gulf. Consequently, Saudi Arabia, Iraq, Iran, Kuwait, and the UAE between them have roughly 97 per cent of the region's proved reserves, while many countries in the region have little or no oil.

The concept of 'proved reserves' is defined as oil reserves that may be estimated with reasonable certainty to be recoverable from known (in some systems of classification also drilled) reservoirs, using available technology and under existing economic conditions. Then, in theory, higher real oil prices should mean larger oil reserves because higher prices should induce further exploration and discovery of new fields; stimulate improvements in the technology of recovery from existing fields; and for existing wells, with existing technology, higher prices should make some additional oil recoverable.

The Institut Français du Pétrole (IFP) believes that a systematic review of the real potential of all the structures of the Middle East could spring many surprises, especially since the presence of giant and supergiant reserves made it unnecessary in the past to mobilise sophisticated and technically advanced approaches. The proved reserves in the region would be much higher when new and improved technologies are applied.

Besides, no serious exhaustive investigation has yet been attempted to identify the satellite accumulations of the main fields discovered in the Middle East. In the North Sea, for example, this type of approach has helped to double the producible reserves and to revive activity. Without drawing a parallel with this region, it is reasonable to assume that this approach should also benefit the Middle East.

It has also been noticed that the huge increases in the Middle East over the last twenty years have been almost completely the result of development work, not of exploration. Indeed, exploration has become insignificant in the area. Out of some 1926 active exploration rigs in June 1996 in the world (outside the former centrally planned economies or CPEs), only about 138 were doing work in the region, a disproportionately small figure (7.2 per cent of the total) in relation to the area's existing reserve stock and production level, or discovery prospects.

In addition to the concept of proved reserves, the 'ultimate resources' are becoming more and more important. They are defined as the resources of hydrocarbons believed to exist or to be eventually discovered. This may be regarded as a purely geological concept that is not concerned with technological or economic constraints or with a time scale.

There is only one source estimating the world's petroleum resources, namely the US Geological Survey (USGS) that publishes its figures once every three years. The latest resource figures were released in 1993 when the USGS estimated the ultimate oil resources of the region at 904.7 billion barrels (mode), representing 39 per cent of the world total. More importantly, the USGS estimated the undiscovered oil resources[3] of the region at 114.7 billion barrels (mode), representing some 24 per cent of the world total. Saudi Arabia alone still contains some 51 billion barrels of undiscovered oil, followed by Iraq (35 billion barrels) and Iran (19 billion barrels, see Table A.2).

Because so much Middle Eastern oil lies in a few giant shallow and high pressured fields within a small area and close to marine terminals, and due to the availability of oil infrastructure in almost every producing (or potentially producing)

Table A.2   Crude oil resources in the Middle East, 1 January 1993 (billion barrels)[1]

Country	Undiscovered resources[2] 95%	Mode	5%	Mean	Ultimate oil resources
Bahrain	0	0	0	0	1.0
Egypt	0.7	1.5	8.9	3.4	13.5
Iran	11.0	19.0	35.0	22.0	128.9
Iraq	15.0	35.0	80.0	44.7	147.8
Israel	na	na	na	na	na
Jordan	na	na	na	na	na
Kuwait	1.5	3.0	9.0	4.4	122.6
Lebanon	na	na	na	na	na
Oman	0.4	1.0	4.0	1.8	12.3
Qatar	0	0	0	0	8.7
Saudi Arabia	31.7	51.0	107.0	62.5	384.5
Syria	0	0	0	0	5.7
Turkey	na	na	na	na	na
UAE	2.4	4.2	10.9	5.7	79.7
Yemen	na	na	na	na	na
Total	62.7	114.7	254.8	144.5	904.7

Notes:
1. *Source*: *World Petroleum Resources* (USGS, 1994).
2. The USGS figures are recorded as low, most likely, and high estimates which are intended to reflect a 90 per cent range of probability (95 to 5 per cent) that the occurrence of oil will lie between the two stated values. The most likely occurrence is referred to as the mode. If the consistency between the USGS assessors and average values produces a consensus, the estimates are then fitted to a log-normal distribution to calculate the mean and other fractiles.
na Not available.

area in the region, exploration and production costs have been exceptionally low. The 'expansion investment intensity' (EII), defined as the amount of US dollars needed to add one peak daily barrel of production capacity is estimated at between $4700 and $5900 (1992 $) in the Middle East on average. Middle Eastern EII is still the lowest in the world, where it is estimated at between $5500 and $10 000 (1992 $) per peak daily barrel in Venezuela, at around $10 000 in Brazil, $15 000 in Algeria, up to $20 000 in the North Sea, and at between $30 000 and $40 000 in Canada.

Middle Eastern oil production amounted to around 31 per cent of the world's total in 1995. Although this was less than the 40 per cent registered in 1979, the ratio is expected to increase with every passing year due to an anticipated decline in production outside the region, especially in the USA, Russia, and many non-Middle East OPEC countries, while several of the producing states in the area have adopted plans to expand their output capacity. Because local oil consumption is relatively small in the Middle East, being roughly equivalent to that of France while the population of the latter constitutes one-fifth of that of the region, there are vast surpluses available for export. In 1995, around 50 per cent of the world's oil trade originated from the Middle East which is expected to retain the role of major source of incremental supplies that has had since the 1940s.

Most Middle Eastern oil is shipped to the consuming markets of Western Europe, Japan, and North America by tanker. Accordingly, an elaborate network of pipelines has been built to link oil fields with marine export terminals and loading platforms (see Table A.3). Of particular interest are the strategic pipelines (see Table A.4) that greatly shorten tanker voyages and, in certain cases, by-pass shipping routes which are perceived to be vulnerable to political interference. One of the most important export oil pipelines was the Trans-Arabian Pipeline (Tapline) from the eastern province of Saudi Arabia to the Lebanese coast through Jordan and Syria. Of much greater importance now is Saudi's Petroline that connects the eastern oil fields of the kingdom to Yanbu on the Red Sea by-passing the Strait of Hormuz, and which can be used in conjunction with Egypt's Sumed pipeline between the Gulf of Suez and the Mediterranean. Sumed, and to some extent Israel's Eilat–Ashkelon pipeline (Tipline), have a function which is directly complementary to that of the Suez Canal.

Of all oil producing countries in the region, Iraq is most dependent on international pipelines for exporting its crude. Until 1982, almost all of its oil had been pumped from Kirkuk to the Mediterranean terminals of Tripoli in Lebanon and Banias in Syria. In the late 1970s and early 1980s, Iraqi crude had increasingly flowed through the Iraq–Turkey (IT) pipeline to Ceyhan on the Mediterranean. An advanced scheme implemented in the 1980s was the Iraqi pipeline across Saudi Arabia (IPSA), which is linked up with and then runs parallel to Petroline to Yanbu.

Many projects for oil export pipelines have been recently proposed in the Middle East. Iraq is planning an oil line to Aqaba in Jordan, and another to Batman in Turkey. Iran is considering a pipeline to Jask on the Gulf of Oman, a second from Turkmenistan and a third to Iskenderun on the Turkish Mediterranean coast. Israel has proposed an extension of the Tapline to Haifa, while a scheme to link the Petroline with Sumed has been considered. Before the conflict over Kuwait, the emirate was studying an oil pipeline parallel to Petroline to Yanbu. Meanwhile, the Gulf Co-operation Council (GCC) was planning a loop to collect the oil from its states to a terminal on the Gulf of Oman.

Table A.3   Oil loading terminals in the Middle East, 1996

Country and location	Largest tanker (dwt)
Bahrain	
Sitra Island (Gulf)	71 500
Egypt	
Ain Sukhna (Gulf of Suez)	500 000
Sidi Kerir (Mediterranean)	285 000
Marsa Al Hamra (Mediterranean)	na
Ras Shukheir (Gulf of Suez)	200 000
Wadi Feiran (Gulf of Suez)	150 000
Iran	
Bandar Abbas (Gulf)	na
Cyrus (Gulf)	70 000
Ganaveh (Gulf)	na
Kharg Island (Gulf)	500 000
Larak Island (Gulf)	na
Lavan Island (Gulf)	200 000
Ras Bahregan (Gulf)	250 000
Sirri (Gulf)	330 000
Iraq	
Fao (Gulf)	na
Khor Al Amayah (Gulf)	330 000
Mina Al Bakr (Gulf)	350 000
Israel	
Ashkelon (Mediterranean)	250 000
Jordan	
Aqaba (Gulf of Aqaba)	300 000
Kuwait and the Neutral Zone	
Mina Abdallah (Gulf)	150 000
Mina Al Ahmadi (Gulf)	320 000
Mina Saud (Gulf)	300 000
Ras Al Khafji (Gulf)	320 000
Lebanon	
Tripoli (Mediterranean)	250 000
Zahrani (Mediterranean)	150 000
Oman	
Mina Al Fahal (Gulf of Oman)	550 000
Qatar	
Halul Island (Gulf)	550 000
Umm Said (Gulf)	320 000

Table A.3   *Continued*

Country and location	Largest tanker (dwt)
Saudi Arabia	
Juaymah (Gulf)	55 000
Jubail (Gulf)	500 000
Ras Tannura (Gulf)	400 000
Yanbu (Red Sea)	500 000
Al Moajjez (Red Sea)	400 000
Zuluf (Gulf)	300 000
Rabigh (Gulf)	312 000
Syria	
Banias (Mediterranean)	210 000
Tartous (Mediterranean)	100 000
Turkey	
Ceyhan (Mediterranean)	300 000
UAE	
Abu Dhabi	
Abu Al Bukhoosh (Gulf)	300 000
Das Island (Gulf)	410 000
Jebel Dhanna (Gulf)	280 000
Mubarras (Gulf)	250 000
Ruwais (Gulf)	100 000
Zirku Island (Gulf)	320 000
Dubai	
Fateh (Gulf)	300 000
Jebel Ali (Gulf)	400 000
Sharjah	
Hamriyah (Gulf)	80 000
Mubarek (Gulf)	350 000
Yemen	
Ras Isa (Red Sea)	400 000
Rudhum (Gulf of Aden)	70 000
Ash Shihr (Gulf of Aden)	300 000

NATURAL GAS IN THE MIDDLE EAST

The Middle East includes large actual and potential natural gas producers that can significantly alter the international supply picture. A helping factor is the quite huge gas resource base in the area in relation to its current and expected level of demand, although natural gas as such has for long been rarely looked for in most

Table A.4   Export oil pipelines in the Middle East, 1996

Route	Year of commission	Length (km)	Diameter (in)	Capacity (b/d)
Kirkuk (Iraq)–Haifa (Palestine)	1934	1000	12	100 000
Kirkuk (Iraq)–Tripoli (Lebanon)	1934	855	12/16/30	480 000
Kirkuk (Iraq)–Banias (Syria)	1952	890	12/16/30	700 000
Kirkuk (Iraq)–Ceyhan (Turkey) (IT I)	1977	980	46	1 000 000
Kirkuk (Iraq)–Ceyhan (Turkey) (IT II)	1987	980	46	650 000
Iraqi Pipeline across Saudi Arabia (IPSA)	1987	1380	48/56	1 700 000
Haditha–Rumaila (Iraq) (Strategic Line)	1975	655	18/42	980 000
Abqaiq (Saudi Arabia)–Zahrani (Lebanon) (Tapline)	1950	1213	30/36	470 000
Abqaiq–Yanbu (Saudi Arabia) (Petroline)	1980	1250	48/56	4 800 000
Suez–Mediterranean Line (Egypt) (Sumed)	1977	320	42	2 400 000
Meleiha–El-Hamra (Egypt)	1986	170	16	90 000
Shabwa–Bir Ali (Yemen)	1991	204	20	135 000
Marib–Ras Isa (Yemen)	1987	438	24/36	200 000
Karatchok–Tartous (Syria)	1968	663	18/20/28	250 000
Yibal–Mina Al Fahal (Oman)	1973	300	30/36	650 000
Marmul–Qarn Alam (Oman)	1980	445	18	70 000
Masilah/Bariyah–Mukalla (Yemen)	1993	160	24	490 000
Eilat–Ashkelon (Israel) (Tipline)	1964	275	42	700 000

Appendix

of the countries in the region. This has been reflected by the fact that most of the gas discovered in the region is in the associated form (found in conjunction with crude oil, either in solution or as an overlying gas cap).

At the beginning of 1996, natural gas reserves in the Middle East accounted for about 30.5 per cent of the world total, or around 45 900 billion cubic metres[4] (cu m). That figure gives the region the second rank after the former Soviet Union (FSU) whose gas reserves were estimated at around 58 500 billion cu m. The 1996 Middle Eastern gas reserves alone are sufficient, even if no further discoveries are to be made, to satisfy current world-wide consumption for more than twenty years. The gas reserves of six countries, namely Iran, Qatar, the UAE, Saudi Arabia, Iraq, and Kuwait (in decreasing size of reserves) represent around 96 per cent of the region's total. The remaining percentage is distributed among the other nine states, many of which have quite small reserves but often large in relation to their internal market potential (see Table A.5).

The US Geological Survey (USGS) in 1993 estimated the ultimate natural gas resources of the Middle East at 73 100 billion cu m, representing 22 per cent of the world total, while the undiscovered gas resources of the region were estimated at around 23 903 billion cu m (mode), or 18 per cent of the world total. Iran alone still contains some 10 460 billion cu m of undiscovered gas, followed by Saudi

Table A.5   Natural gas reserves and production in the Middle East, 1995[1]

Country	Reserves (billion cu m)[2]	Share of world total (%)	Gross production (billion cu m)	Share of world total (%)	Marketed production (billion cu m)	Share of world total (%)	Reserves-to-production (year)[3]
Bahrain	147	0.10	9.61	0.35	6.49	0.29	22
Egypt	645	0.43	15.93	0.58	12.43	0.56	43
Iran	20 963	13.95	75.54	2.75	35.10	1.59	422
Iraq	3360	2.24	3.38	0.12	3.15	0.14	994
Israel	1	<0.1	0.02	<0.1	0.02	<0.1	50
Jordan	28	<0.1	0.30	<0.1	0.30	<0.1	93
Kuwait	1494	0.99	7.56	0.27	5.97	0.27	198
Lebanon	–	–	–	–	–	–	–
Oman	283	0.19	7.79	0.28	4.84	0.22	51
Qatar	7070	4.71	18.80	0.68	13.60	0.62	445
Saudi Arabia	5341	3.55	73.97	2.69	40.34	1.83	80
Syria	236	0.16	5.87	0.21	4.79	0.22	44
Turkey	26	<0.1	0.20	<0.1	0.20	<0.1	130
UAE	5831	3.88	39.31	1.43	30.13	1.37	186
Yemen	481	0.32	13.35	0.49	0.00	0	1603
Total	45 906	30.55	271.63	9.88	157.36	7.13	221

Notes:

1. *Source: Natural Gas in the World 1996* (Rueil Malmaison: Cedigaz, 1996).
2. Reserves figures as of 1 January 1996.
3. Production equals gross production minus reinjection.

Arabia with about 8400 billion cu m, and the UAE (1385 billion cu m, see Table A.6).

In general, considering the enormous potential of the Middle East, little has been done so far to exploit its natural gas reserves. The 1995 gas reserves-to-production ratio was relatively very high, covering 221 years compared to only 62 years world-wide. Since most of the natural gas in the region is in associated form, gas production had always fluctuated with the level of crude oil output. In 1995, the area's gross and marketed output represented some 9.9 per cent and around 7.1 per cent of the world's total respectively (see Table A.5).

The bulk of marketed gas production is consumed locally. While the domestic consumption of the region does not match its resources, only exports to the major consuming zones will allow the full utilisation of its reserves. In 1995, the Middle

Table A.6   Natural gas resources in the Middle East, 1 January 1993
(billion cubic metres)[1]

Country	Undiscovered resources[2] 95%	Mode	5%	Mean	Ultimate natural gas resources
Bahrain	0	0	0	0	350
Egypt	278	490	1402	705	1100
Iran	6399	10 459	23 238	13 170	35 370
Iraq	1805	2833	5666	3397	5050
Israel	na	na	na	na	na
Jordan	na	na	na	na	na
Kuwait	99	159	331	193	2060
Lebanon	na	na	na	na	na
Oman	105	170	385	215	640
Qatar	0	0	0	0	7170
Saudi Arabia	5355	8407	16800	10 078	13 920
Syria	0	0	0	0	160
Turkey	na	na	na	na	na
UAE	883	1385	2772	1659	7280
Yemen	na	na	na	na	na
Total	14 924	23 903	50 594	29 417	73 100

Notes:
1. *Source*: *World Petroleum Resources* (USGS, 1994).
2. The USGS figures are recorded as low, most likely, and high estimates which are intended to reflect a 90 per cent range of probability (95 to 5 per cent) that the occurrence of natural gas will lie between the two stated values. The most likely occurrence is referred to as the mode. If the consistency between the USGS assessors and average values produces a consensus, the estimates are then fitted to a log-normal distribution to calculate the mean and other fractiles.

na=not available

East had a very marginal share (1.8 per cent) in the international gas trade, but in the near future it will come to play an important role on the world gas market. Currently, only two gas export lines are operating (even though partly) in the region, namely the 1070 km, 40/42 in, 16.3 billion cu m/year Iranian Gas Trunkline (IGAT) linking since 1970 with the states of the FSU, and the recently-built 35 km, 16 in gasline from offshore Oman to Ras Al Khaimah. Another gas line (170 km, 40 in, 4.1 billion cu m/year), built in 1986 between Iraq and Kuwait, was put out of order in 1990.

An expected intensive natural gas trade both regionally and inter-regionally will lead in the near future to the construction of liquefaction plants (see Table A.7) and large gas export pipelines. While IGAT II is still under construction, several gasline projects have been planned in the Middle East. The GCC has been studying a regional loop, and Qatar has proposed a network with the Eastern Mediterranean countries, and has lately considered a gasline to Western Europe through Israel and Egypt, or via Turkey. Qatar has been planning a gasline to Pakistan and India, like Oman and Iran; the latter has also examined lines to the Gulf Arab countries, Armenia, Turkey, and Western Europe. Syria has planned gaslines to Lebanon, Turkey and Jordan, while schemes are on the table to export Egyptian gas to Israel, Jordan, and Lebanon up to Turkey. An ambitious project consists of a huge loop collecting gas reserves from the region, and then connecting them to export pipelines to North Africa and Western Europe, and to liquefaction plants channelling liquefied natural gas (LNG) to the Far East and Japan.

Table A.7 Natural gas liquefaction plants in the Middle East (end-1995 status)

Country–Location–Project	Year of commission	Capacity (million tons LNG/year)
Existing		
Abu Dhabi–Das Island–Adgas	1971	5
Under construction or planned		
Qatar–Umm Said–Qatargas	1997	6
Qatar–Ras Laffan–Rasgas	1999–2001	5–10
Qatar–Ras Laffan–Eurogas	??	6
Qatar–??–Elf/Sumitomo	??	4
Qatar–??–Enron	1999?	5
Iran–Bandar Abbas/Qeshm	??	??
Oman–Bimma–Oman LNG	1999?	5
Yemen–Hodeidah/Aden–Total	2001?	5

Notes

Introduction

1.　The UAE includes the seven emirates of Abu Dhabi, Ajman, Dubai, Fujairah, Ras Al Khaimah, Sharjah, and Umm Al Qaiwain.
2.　The Appendix (p. 191) offers a more detailed analysis of petroleum in the Middle East.

1　Autocratic Regimes and Struggles for Power

1.　Some prefer to use terms like 'traditionalists' (defined by F. Burgat, 1988, as those who seek to attain a conservative utopia), or 'Islamists' (who, also according to Burgat, are traditionalists with an integrated political project).
2.　Some put the figure at 29, others at 31, 39 or even 44.

12　How Secure are Petroleum Supplies?

1.　More details are to be found in the Appendix, p. 191.

Appendix: Petroleum in the Middle East

1.　According to *BP Statistical Review of World Energy*, 1996.
2.　A 'megagiant' field refers to that of more than 50 billion barrels of oil, or 14.17 trillion cubic metres (cu m) of estimated ultimate recoverable reserves. A 'supergiant' field refers to that with estimated ultimate recoverable reserves of between 5 and 50 billion barrels of oil, or between 1.42 and 14.17 trillion cu m; a 'giant' field refers to that with estimated ultimate recoverable reserves of between 0.5 billion and 5 billion barrels of oil, or between 0.142 and 1.42 trillion cu m.
3.　The USGS figures are recorded as low, most likely, and high estimates which are intended to reflect a 90 per cent range of probability (95 to 5 per cent) that the occurrence of oil/gas will lie between the two stated values. The most likely occurrence is referred to as the mode. If the consistency between the USGS assessors and average values produces a consensus, the estimates are then fitted to a log-normal distribution to calculate the mean and other fractiles.
4.　According to Cedigaz.

Select Bibliography

Books and Articles

Aarts, P. (1995) 'Saudi Arabia: From Fiscal Crisis to Political Crisis?', *JIME (Japan Institute for the Middle East) Review*, 29 (Summer).

Abdel Meguid, W. (1992) 'Regional Relations in the Middle East: A View for the 1990s', *JIME Review*, 16 (Spring).

Abi-Aad, N. (1994) *Oil Production Capacity in the Gulf, Expansion Programmes and Financial Challenges* (Grenoble, IEPE).

Abou Taleb, H. (1991) 'The Iraqi Invasion and Political Reform in the Gulf', *JIME Review*, 14 (Autumn).

Abu Jaber, K. S. (1993) 'The Middle East Political Perspective', *The 7th APS Annual Conference* (Larnaca).

Abukhalil, A. (1994) 'The Incoherence of Islamic Fundamentalism: Arab Islamic Thought at the End of the 20th Century', *Middle East Journal*, 48 (4) (Autumn).

Ahrari, M. E. *et al.* (eds) (1989) *The Gulf and International Security* (London: Macmillan).

Al Moosa A. R. *et al.* (1985) *Immigrant Labour in Kuwait* (London: Croom Helm).

Amin, S. H. (1981) *International and Legal Problems of the Gulf* (London: Menas Press).

Amirsadeghi, H. (ed.) (1981) *The Security of the Persian Gulf* (London: Croom Helm).

Amjad, R. (ed.) (1989) *To the Gulf and Back: Studies on the Economic Impact of Asian Labour Migration* (New Delhi: International Labour Organisation).

Arberry, A. J. (ed.) (1969) *Religion in the Middle East* (Cambridge: Cambridge University Press).

Beaumont, P. *et al.* (1976) *The Middle East: A Geographic Study* (Chichester: Wiley).

Beschorner, N. (1989) *Water and Instability in the Middle East* (London: IISS).

Beydoun, Z. (1988) *The Middle East: Regional Geology and Petroleum Resources* (Beaconsfield: Scientific Press).

Birks, J. S. *et al.* (1980) *Arab Manpower: The Crisis of Development* (London: Croom Helm).

Bowen-Jones, H. *et al.* (eds) (1981) *Change and Development in the Middle East* (London: Methuen).

Bulloch, J. *et al.* (1993) *Water Wars: Coming Conflicts in the Middle East* (London: Gollanz).

Burgat, F. (1988) *L'Islamisme au Maghreb* (Paris: Karthala).

Cambridge Energy Research Associates (CERA) (1992) 'Iran Resurgent?', private report (Cambridge).

Carke, J. I. *et al.* (eds.) (1972) *Populations of the Middle East and North Africa* (London: University of London Press).

Carré, O. (1993) *Le Nationalism Arabe* (Paris: Fayard).

Chubin, S. (1992a) Iran's Security and Defence Policies', *Middle East Monitor* (May).

Chubin, S. (1992b) 'Iraq: Domestic Politics, Foreign Policy', *Middle East Monitor* (December).

Chubin, S. (1993) 'The Persian Gulf: After Desert Storm and Before the New World Order', *Middle East Monitor* (March).

Chubin, S. (eds.) (1982) *Security in the Persian Gulf* (London: IISS).

Conant and Associates (1987) *US Strategic Goals in the Middle East and the Gulf* (Washington, DC).

Conant, M. A. (1994) 'The Geopolitics of Oil', *Geopolitics of Energy*, 16 (7) (1 July).

Conant, M. A. (1994) 'A Perspective on Riyadh', *Geopolitics of Energy*, 16 (8) (1 August).

Cordesman, A. H. (1984) *The Gulf and the Search for Strategic Stability* (Boulder, Col.: Westview Press).

Cordesman, A. H. (1987) *The Iran–Iraq War and Western Security 1984–87* (London: Jane's).

Cottrell, A. J. (ed.) (1980), *The Persian Gulf States* (Baltimore and London: Johns Hopkins University Press).

Courbage, Y. (1994) 'Peninsule Arabique: les Surprises de la Demographie', *Monde Arabe Maghreb Machrek*, 144 (April–June).

Courbages, Y. and Fargues P. (1992) *L'Avenir Demographique de la Rive Sud de la Méditerranée* (Sophia Antipolis: Plan Bleu).

Dessouki, A. H. (1992) 'The Foreign Policies of Middle Eastern Countries: Change and Continuity', *JIME Review*, 16 (Spring).

Drysdale, A. *et al.* (1985) *The Middle East and North Africa: a Political Geography* (New York and Oxford: Oxford University Press).

Economic Intelligence Unit (EIU) (1984) The *Gulf War* (London).

Economic Intelligence Unit (EIU) (1991) *Post-War Gulf* (London).

El-Hakim, A. A. (1979) *The Middle Eastern States and the Law of the Sea* (Manchester: Manchester University Press).

Fandy, M. (1994) 'Egypt's Islamic Group: Regional Revenge?', *Middle East Journal*, 48 (4) (Autumn).

Farid, A. M. (ed.) (1984) *The Red Sea: Prospects for Stability* (London: Croom Helm).

Foucher, M. (1988) *Fronts et Frontières* (Paris: Fayard).

Gart, M. J. (1993) 'Middle East Policy in the Clinton Era', *Geopolitics of Energy*, 15 (8) (1 August).

Gavlak, D. (1992/93) 'The Kuwaiti 1992 Election: "Rainbow Coalition After a Desert Storm"', *JIME Review*, 19 (Winter).

Gischler, C. (1979) *Water Resources in the Arab Middle East and North Africa* (London: Menas Press).

Gordon, M. (ed.), (1981) *Conflict in the Persian Gulf* (London: Macmillan).

Grenon, M. *et al.* (1989) *The Blue Plan: Future for the Mediterranean Basin* (Oxford: Oxford University Press).

Gurr, T. D. *et al.* (1994) *Ethnic Conflict in World Politics* (Boulder; Col.: Westview Press).

Gursdon, C. (1993) 'Iran and the West: Who's Threatening Who?', *JIME Review*, 21 (Summer).

Henderson, S. (1994) *After King Fahd: Succession in Saudi Arabia* (Washington DC: Washington Institute for Near East Policy).

Henderson, S. (1996) *The Middle East in the Year 2000, New Opportunities, New Dangers* (London: *Financial Times* Energy Publishing).

Herrmann, R. (1994) 'Russian Policy in the Middle East: Strategic Change and Tactical Contradictions', *Middle East Journal*, 48 (3)(Summer).

Howaidi, F. (1993) 'Historical Background of Islamic Movements', *JIME Review*, 23 (Winter).

Hrair Demekjian, R. (1994) 'The Rise of Political Islamism in Saudi Arabia', *Middle East Journal*, 48. (4)(Autumn).

Ivanhoe, L. F. and Leckie, G. (1993) 'Global Oil, Gas Fields, Sizes Tallied, Analysed', *Oil and Gas Journal* (15 February).

Joffe, G. (1992) 'Conflict in the Middle East and North Africa in the Light of the New World Order', *JIME Review*, 16 (Spring).

Kadioglu, A. (1994) 'Women's Subordination in Turkey: Is Islam Really the Villain?', *Middle East Journal*, 48 (4) (Autumn).

Kemp, G. (1991) 'The Middle East Arms Race: Can It Be Controlled?', *Middle East Journal*, 45 (3) (Summer).

Kerr, M. *et al.* (eds) (1982) *Rich and Poor States in the Middle East* (Boulder, Col: Westview Press).

Kerr, M. *et al.* (eds) (1990) *The Political Economy of the Middle East* (Boulder, Col.: Westview Press).

Kleinwort Benson (1993) *Outlook for Oil Prices in the 1990s* (London).

Lamb, D. (1987) *The Arabs: Journeys beyond the Mirage* (New York: Random House).

Lloyds (1988) *Conflict in the Gulf: Economic and Maritime Implications of the Iran–Iraq War* (London).

Looney, R. (1993) 'The Budgetary Impact of Defence Expenditures in the Middle East', *The Middle East Business and Economic Review* (July).

Luciani, G. (ed.) (1984) *The Mediterranean Region* (London: Crom Helm).

Luciani, G. (ed.) (1987) *The Rentier State* (London: Crom Helm).

Mabro, R. (1991) 'The Political Instability of the Middle East and its Impact on Oil Production and Trade', *SNS Energy Day* Stockholm (October 1991).

Maull, H *et al.* (eds) (1989) *The Gulf War: Regional and International Dimensions* (London: Pintero Publishers).

Moberly, J. (1992) 'The Gulf War in Retrospect and Post-War Security', *Energy Policy* (November).

OAPEC Secretariat (1985) *OAPEC in Brief* (Kuwait).

Observatoire Méditerranéen de l'Energie (1995) *Petroleum Supply Routes and the Security Equation in the Middle East* (Sophia Antipolis).

Observatiore Méditerranéen de l'Energie (1996) *Natural Gas in the Middle East:: Actual Status and Future Prospects* (Sophia Autipolis).

Odell, P. (1983) *Oil and World Power*, 7th edn (Harmondsworth: Penguin Books).

Omran, A. R. (1992) *Family Planning in the Legacy of Islam* (London and New York: Routledge).

Omran, A. and Roudi, F. (1993) 'The Middle East Population Puzzle', *UN Population Bulletin*, 48 (1) (July).

OPEC Secretariat (1993) *OPEC at a Glance* (Vienna).

Prescott, J. R. V. (1985) *The Maritime Political Boundaries of the World* (London: Methuen).

Rengger, N. J. (1990) *Treaties and Alliances of the World*, 5th edn (London: Longman).

Robins, P. (1995) 'Political Islam in Turkey: the Rise of the Welfare Party', *JIME Review*, 28 (Spring).

Safran, N. (1988) *The Ceaseless Quest for Security* (London: Cornell University Press).

Salamé, G. (ed.) (1994) *Democracy Without Democrats? The Renewal of Politics in the Muslim World* (London: I.B. Tauris).

Salameh, E. (1989) 'Water and Other Resources in the Middle East and their Developmental and Strategic Importance up to 2002', *The 3rd APS Annual Conference* (Nicosia).

Salameh, E. (1991) 'Politics of Middle East and African Water Resources', *The 5th APS Annual Conference* (Nicosia).

Sayari, S. (1992) 'Turkey: The Changing European Security Environment and the Gulf Crisis', *Middle East Journal*, 46 (1) (Winter).

Schofield, R. (ed.) (1994) *Territorial Foundations of the Gulf States* (London: UCL Press).

Serageldin, I. *et al.* (1983) *Manpower and International Labour Migration in the Middle East and North Africa* (Oxford: Oxford University Press).

Shammas, P. (1993) 'Border Disputes in the Greater Middle East', *The 7th APS Annual Conference* (Nicosia).

Tawil, H. (1992) 'Political Change in the Arab World: Contemporary Political Islam', *JIME Review*, 16 (Spring).

Taylor, T. (1992) 'Arms Control and the Middle East', *JIME Review*, 16 (Spring).

UN Economic and Social Commission for Western Asia (UNESCWA) (1993) *Arab Labour Migration* (Amman).

US Geological Survey (USGS, Masters *et al.*) (1994) *World Petroleum Resources*.

Valdani, A. J. (1993/4) 'Unstable Borders in the Persian Gulf', *The Iranian Journal of International Affairs*, V (3/4) (Fall/Winter).

Ziring, L. (1984) *The Middle East Political Dictionary* (Santa Barbara and Oxford: Clio Press).

Zisser, E. (1995) 'Toward the Post-Asad Era in Syria', *JIME Review*, 28 (Spring).

Reference Documents

Atlas du Monde Arabe: Géopolitique et Sociétés (Paris: Bordas, 1990).

Atlas Géopolitique du Moyen-Orient et du Monde Arabe (Paris: Complexe, 1993).

Atlas of the Middle East (Washington, DC: CIA, 1993).

Atlas of World Population History (Harmondsworth: Penguin Books, 1978).

BP Statistical Review of World Energy (London: British Petroleum, annual)

Cambridge Atlas of the Middle East and North Africa (Cambridge: Cambridge University Press, 1987).

Environmental Data Report (Nairobi: United Nations Environmental Programme, annual).

Middle East Review (London: ABC World of Information, Saffron Walden, annual).

Natural Gas in the World (Rueil Malmaison: Cedigaz, annual).

OPEC Annual Statistical Bulletin (Vienna, annual).

Political Risk Yearbook (Syracuse University: Political Risk Services, annual).

Ports of the World (London: Benn Publications, annual).

The Middle East and North Africa Yearbook (London: Europa Publications, annual).

The Military Balance (London: IISS, annual).

The World Fact Book (Washington, DC: CIA, annual).

United Nations Demographic Yearbook (New York: UN, annual).

United Nations World Population Prospects (New York: UN, annual).

United Nations World Urbanisation Prospects (New York: UN, annual).

World Development Report (Washington, DC: World Bank, annual).

World Petroleum Trends (Geneva: Petroconsultants, annual).

World Resources (New York: World Resources Institute, annual).

Index

Note: **bold** = main; *italic* = tables and illustrations.